TOWARD A CYBERLEGAL CULTURE

Mirela Roznovschi

Transnational Publishers, Inc.
Ardsley, New York

Published and distributed by *Transnational Publishers, Inc.*
Ardsley Park
Science and Technology Center
410 Saw Mill River Road
Ardsley, NY 10502

Phone: 914-693-5100
Fax: 914-693-4430
E-mail: info@transnationalpubs.com
Web: www.transnationalpubs.com

Library of Congress Cataloging-in-Publication Data

Roznovschi, Mirela.
Toward a cyberlegal culture / Mirela Roznovschi.
p.cm.
ISBN 1-57105-168-6
1. Legal research—Computer network resources. 2. Information storage and retrieval systems—Law. 3. Internet searching. I. Title.

K87 .R69 2000
343.09'944—dc21 2001027882

Manufactured in the United States of America

To my mother, Hrisula

Contents

Acknowledgments

First, I would like to thank Heike Fenton, the President of Transnational Publishers, for giving me the chance to transform an idea into a book.

Thanks to Professor M. Kathleen Price, my mentor, for encouraging my professional growth. Without her, I could not have succeeded.

I owe a debt of thanks to the New York University Law Library faculty, and especially to Radu Popa, Jeanne Rehberg, Leslie Rich and Liz Evans, my colleagues and partners in projects developed over the years, for their friendship and assistance.

Thanks to Terence Hegarty for his pertinent suggestions regarding the manuscript and for his editorial work.

Thanks to writer Aurora Cornu, who responded to a conversation about the future of legal research with strong encouragement to write this book. This conversation happened in Saint-Malo in Brittany, a magical place close to the tomb of René de Chateaubriand, to the island where Victor Hugo spent his exile, and to the home of Jules Verne. Saint-Malo is also in the vicinity of Brocéliande, the mythological forest of the wizard Merlin and the fairy Vivian, where the knight Yvain discovered the miraculous fountain of Berénton.

Introduction

In theory, we live in the golden age of access to information, including legal information. At the beginning of the twenty-first century, governments, high courts and tribunals, international organizations, non-governmental organizations, legal institutes, universities, and private publishers from all over the world are distributing—often for free—high quality primary and secondary legal materials through multilingual interfaces. Concern with accuracy and reliability is paramount. More and more, the electronic version tends to be the perfect image of the printed document. The electronic official seal or the electronic signature of courts, governments, or private databases—displayed as a sign of authenticity on every page of each electronic document—represent evidence that the digital product obtained through an Internet connection or a CD-ROM is the same document printed by the legal body, agency, organization, or publishing house in reporters, codes, loose-leaf services or other media.

The overwhelmingly positive involvement of legal institutions, organizations, and governments in this new reality strongly suggests that the future of legal research lies primarily in the electronic domain.

However, with my first words above—"in theory"—I hinted at the crucially important fact that, by any global standard, easy access to and utilization of the new information sources remains a distinct privilege. The reasons for this are extremely complex. Psychology, politics, technological development, economics, and cultural values all play a part, interfering with the universal human propensity for law and the inevitable need everywhere for reliable legal resources.

Nonetheless, what I will call the *Cyberlegal Culture* has clearly entered a stage of stability, credibility, and confidence, and is poised for a vast and pervasive growth throughout the legal community worldwide. The need to elucidate it, evaluate it, learn to use it, and decipher its future is peremptory. That is why I decided to write this book.

Let me describe what I mean by the cyberlegal culture.

Legal databases have gained the respect of legal professionals through revolutionary technicalities and legal publishing expertise.

Servers, software, powerful computers, data encryption, preservation of digital information, copyright issues, watch groups (i.e., legal "listservs" or online discussion groups), and legal associations cooperate on an international scale. Law schools, and especially academic law libraries, have played a major role in creating, developing, and instructing a new dimension of international, comparative, and foreign law research. The online universe has become an instrument in legal teaching and legal research. Building on the online availability of legal documents, law professors and law librarians have shaped a new research methodology with new criteria, needs, and expectations. An extremely powerful impetus is generated by the continuous feedback inherent in the direct connection, more timely than ever in history, between legal professionals and legal bodies. Individuals and institutions communicate with one another without traditional intermediaries. This "live" interaction is one of the most crucial events of our profession, a revolutionary reality that has changed all prior patterns.

Recently, at the 2000 Annual Meeting Program of the Section on International Law of the American Association of Law Schools (http://www.uky.edu/Law/aals-int/y2k.htm), a panel on the Internet and public international law discussed the effect of the information revolution on public international law. Speakers addressed the fact that the Internet has changed the nature of international relations among professionals, companies, and governments. Futurist scenarios, such as a breakdown of the system of territorial allocation of government jurisdiction and the hypothetical appearance of Internet-based micro-nations, were taken into consideration.

A new pattern of legal documentation and legal research has been created all over the world. The internationalization of legal research operates across and beyond borders. Virtual reference transactions implicating many parties are a reality of our lives.

The cyberlegal culture exists in the virtual legal world. Its availability is instantaneous. It is now the territory of legal specialists all over the world, a virtual "place" having legal patterns, traits, and products specific to all jurisdictions and developed through the electronic milieu of the Internet and the World Wide Web (WWW).[1] Cyberlegal culture represents the international and foreign law disciplines' intellectual activity on the "Web". New behaviors and communication patterns generated by the online medium, by institutions with a virtual presence, by new forms of electronic publishing and strategies for accessing online legal documents, and by new models of teaching substantive law and education over the Internet express the essence of the cyberlegal culture.

As I write these lines, I experience two contradictory sensations. The first is that, while electronic legal research is enormously developed in the USA, Canada, Australia, and New Zealand, in the rest of the world (even in Western Europe) there are merely singular competencies or small elite groups. The other thought is that legal information professionals like myself must offer assistance and guidance to the legal community at large from our expertise in accessing legal information and acquiring new research skills. We must also critically assess our own strengths and weaknesses as we strive to communicate what we have learned about this new and ever-changing field of knowledge.

The obstacles we must overcome as teachers, trainers, and mentors are many and challenging. They range from technical complications, arising from obsolete standards and protocols, to simple economics that make Internet access, in most of the world, a luxury. Because of these two factors alone, even such superb resources as the European Union databases are frequently inaccessible because of overcrowded access lines. Language differences also present problems; web-based re-

[1] WWW: A system of Internet servers that support specially formatted documents. The documents are formatted in a language called HTML (Hyper Text Markup Language) that supports links to other documents, as well as graphics, audio, and video files. See more at http://webopedia.internet.com/TERM/W/World_Wide_Web.html.

sources in Japan (for instance), a globally significant and technologically advanced jurisdiction, provide no translated materials to speak of. In Russia and former Soviet Union countries generally, proxy servers used to filter data are rejected by many sophisticated databases (such as Lexis), so that the scope of available online information is severely limited. In China, outright censorship of the Internet prevails. Everywhere, moreover, the very idea of teaching online legal research is as yet virtually unknown outside of a few major (or adventurous) institutions.

At this stage, what is most needed is a review of the reliable international and foreign law databases, as well as a guide to strategies used to benefit from these resources. I might add the evaluation criteria for selecting databases, as well as the legal research teaching models for different jurisdictions and different groups, on different levels of comprehension. In this book I will illustrate such a review with my own observations based on exposure to many jurisdictions of the world through my work with the New York University School of Law Global Program, New York University Law School's courses on international and comparative law, and New York University Law Library international projects with USAID and the STARR Foundation (the Legal Information Transfer Network with partners in Australia, South Africa, Belgium, China, Armenia, and England). Further, I will add insights based on my teaching and lectures in Armenia, Hungary, Russia, and Brazil, my participation in the drafting of the ITN project training template, and my online experience with Tsingua University Law School (China), as well as my work with legal information specialists from many countries of the world as LLRX.com contributing editor for foreign and international law.

I should point out that I will use "Internet" and "WWW" interchangeably. Though "Internet" has a broader sense, and "WWW" evokes the right context in which to speak about databases, both terms are often used to designate the same reality. Internet means email, servers, file transfer protocols (FTP), etc., while WWW is restricted to the hypertext medium. Here, however, I will use both terms, because the common language of information specialists does. I will also use "legal specialist", "legal information specialist", "legal information professional", and "law librarian" to name the same person. The law librarian of today is an individual with knowledge of law librarianship, information science, and computer science to a degree that is deepening every day.

He or she must be familiar with online catalogs and servers; know how to build home pages and databases and write documents in different formats (html, pdf, etc); manage and/or participate in listservs (online discussion groups); and evaluate databases and search engines for acquisition and respectively implementation.

However, important actors in the cyberlegal culture (international organizations, foreign governments, legal information specialists, etc.) have altered their involvement in response to new patterns, dynamics, and values. They have adapted to the cyberlegal world. This is a resonance issue, with implications on a broader scale than librarianship.

I would like also to add that this book is not intended to give exhaustive coverage to all matters discussed. No one book can replace the many sources mentioned in the text or replace the teacher/instructor.

I hope this book will be of value as a teaching tool, as an orientation tool, and as an inspiration for the legal specialist engaged in the discovery of the world electronic environment.

If the Phoenicians invented the alphabet and brought humanity to the stage of writing; if Gutenberg wrote through a printer and made the printed book the vehicle of civilization, the Information Age has transported us to another sphere, complementary to reality and to the universe of the printed word. This new three-dimensionality allows us to experience a level of complexity and richness of concept never experienced before by humanity. Trying to compare how we live today with whatever humanity has traversed in history, I consider that we experience or live in a kind of Homeric oral world, but at a different level along the spiral of civilization. At the end of the twentieth century, humanity invented a new way of being and expressing itself that, among many other innovations, has radically transformed the legal field. We are engaged in exploring this extraordinary universe as if it were a new continent of our planet. And we are pioneers.

Chapter 1

Electronic Reference and the Internationalization of Legal Research

What does a legal information specialist do in the cyberlegal culture?

The legal information specialist of the information technology (IT) era is a professional linked to online catalogs and peers from all over the world. He or she has access to a multitude of databases with different content and coverage, is an active contributor to online publications, contributes to listserv discussions, and, in many cases, acts as webmaster of a home page or other electronic products.

In order to operate, a legal information specialist has continuously to improve managerial skills using a new, still-developing set of reference strategies. The crucial factor is the decision-making process involved in selecting from the maze of available legal resources in order to prioritize urgencies. Decisions may be immediate or long-term. The latter must help professionals perform in the near future according to job environment needs and the library's primary goals (i.e., an academic specialist must support the curriculum; a law firm specialist must support the law firm's research requirements).

Managerial skills include improving personal research skills; imparting skills to others through teaching modules; evaluating and acquiring databases either as updating tools or as new sources of legal documents; gathering information under patron and peer pressure; and evaluating and selecting information to be displayed in institutions' home pages. The legal information specialist interacts both with the daily work environment and with the cyberlegal culture as a whole. The amount of daily interaction with the cyberlegal culture depends on the kind of choices that must be made.

For instance, there is a difference between selecting sources for a bibliography and finding a primary source, or between a question requiring an immediate answer and a long-term project.

If the task cannot be accomplished with available resources, the legal specialist may seek help through the cyberlegal culture.

In doing so, however, he/she enters a path of commitments where cooperation and sharing are key words.

It is not unusual for a conflict to arise between the workplace and the outside world, so that thinking strategically becomes a part of the legal specialist's job.

Priorities are more crucial than ever. In many ways, the strategy of decision-making called *game theory* is appropriate. How else can we learn strategy and think strategically as well? To illustrate, I will draw on my experience.

I work in a high-tech academic environment where internal email links me to all my colleagues, faculty, students, and administration. Research questions from faculty and students come mostly by email. Reference questions often need work beyond the shifts at the reference desk.

I am the webmaster and editor of the *Guide to Foreign and International Legal Databases* (http://www.law.nyu.edu/library/foreign_intl/index.html), and my email address is on every page of the Guide. I receive email from all over the world containing thanks, observations, suggestions, queries. I have also an email alias on the library's home page (http://www.law.nyu.edu/library/). One of my functions is to answer any email coming from outside the US, while my team colleague responds to domestic email. Visiting professors, PhD candidates, and others from all over the world send messages which I must answer.

As an active user of many databases I have a personal connection with almost every database webmaster. That person will always give me a quick answer if something is wrong with the database or if the needed sources cannot be found there. Sometimes, they need my help too.

As I monitor and recommend the acquisition of foreign and international databases for my workplace, I am constantly in touch with foreign vendors and private providers from India, France, Russia, and Argentina, to mention a few of the countries I contact daily. I am also responsible for the database collection and selection of foreign databases of the Information Transfer Network (http://www.law.nyu.edu/library/itn/) project. I instruct foreign interns as well.

As an author of articles published on the Internet, my email address is displayed on files found on many different servers. Whenever a link is not correct, or a new database appears, I receive messages. I must fix the link or add new entries after a careful evaluation.

As contributing editor of the online publication LLRX.com (http://www.llrx.com)—the acronym stands for Law Library Resource Xchange—I have built a network of contributors in many countries of the world. I am connected to them for research purposes also.

Visiting professors, global faculty, and former NYU JDs, LLMs, and MCJs often contact me after returning to their countries. Once in a while, when my time allows, I answer questions from INT-LAW, EUROLEX, FCIL, EURUNION (The European Union's depository library mailing list), and other listservs of which I am a member. I read posted messages daily and have created through the lists something which I can name friendship based on mutual assistance.

As I teach abroad, it is my duty to answer former students' email asking for guidance. In order to be in touch with my peers abroad, I must always adjust my time to theirs. If I am waiting for an answer from a legal institution in Europe, I check my email at 6 AM. If I want to send back a message and expect a response the same day, this is the only way to do it. Regarding New Zealand and Australia, the best time to communicate with my peers from those countries is late in the evening. Latin American time is more or less the same as North American.

For further illustration, I would like to describe a regular day in my working life. I have chosen for this purpose, Monday, September 18, 2000.

I checked my messages at 6 AM to see if I had news from Russia. In three weeks' time I will go to Moscow to teach in a joint program put together by the Constitutional and Legal Policy Institute (COLPI) in Budapest and the Library of Foreign Literature (Moscow).

At 9AM I found in my office a diskette with a guide to USA legal research, a contribution written for LLRX.com. Going through the guide, I discovered an inconsistency related to the html[2] editing, so I sent an email to the LLRX.com Editor-in-Chief in Washington asking for a solution. The answer came right away, allowing me to pass it along.

From 10 to11AM I was on duty at the reference desk. I decided to see what I could do for a student from Dickinson School of Law, an associate editor of the *Dickinson Journal of Environmental Law.*

He needed to locate Russian legislation in English related to endangered species and especially to the Siberian Tiger. His email had been on my computer since Thursday. I hadn't had time to do anything with it. Yesterday morning, however, I started working on that query.

I looked in the *BNA International Environment Reporter, Russia and the Republics: Legal Materials* by Vratislav Pechota, Kluwer's *International Encyclopaedia of Laws—Environmental Law,* and Butterworth's *International Environment Law and Regulations.* I found a 1991 environment law enforced in Russia in 1992, but I could not find it in English. I decided to go online for databases of Russian laws. In the database of the Slavic Research Center of Hokkaido University (http://www.slavweb.com/index-e.html) there was something related to the subject. Next, using a metasearch engine[3] I discovered articles on this topic and even a scientist who knew Russian and had commented on the law. The only source in English was the fee-based World News Connection. Here I decided to stop. I sent a message with all these data, apologizing for not having more time.

[2] Hypertext Markup Language (HTML) is the language programmers use to mark up texts that are intended to be presented through a Web browser.

[3] A search engine is a computer program which automatically searches the Internet for keywords and returns a list of databases which contain those

Later on, I met a professor from Italy who had been a visiting professor with the NYU Law School the previous year and had returned for a conference. She talked about her teaching in Paris and Moscow, giving me some hints about Russian students. Meantime, another visiting professor from Italy needed some training to enable her to find legal literature for her course. We set up a session for the following day.

On my return from lunch I found an email from the coordinator of the LLMs International Tax Program, a course for which I provide training and a home page (http://www.law.nyu.edu/library/foreign_intl/taxint.html). It was a list of foreign students, listed by jurisdictions. The email also told me that the program uploaded[4] a file of tax links (http://www.law.nyu.edu/gtp/gtplinks.html) that needed my help. Looking at it, I made a few observations, asked to be linked to it, received the answer, and asked for the name of the person loading that file to the server in order to start the cooperation.

Both an email and a message on the answering machine from a colleague from a Canadian academic law library asked questions regarding a French database, Jurifrance (http://www.jurifrance.com/). My colleague had received a different offer from the one I had described to her when we talked about this database. I looked through her email and I realized that the French vendor wanted to get from her as much money as possible, disregarding the fact that the subscription was for an academic institution. I pulled out the Jurifrance file from the file cabinet and called my colleague in Toronto. While talking, I sent her the name and email of my vendor indicating the amount of money we pay for the database.

Back at the reference desk, I did some editing to a file from the *Guide to Foreign and International Legal Databases* using FrontPage. I also added a new United Nations database,

keywords. A metasearch engine is a search engine which searches other search engines. The list of URLs returned to you is composed of the top hits of many search engines for the keywords you entered. The URL (Uniform Resource Locator) describes the address and method of reaching a file on the Internet.

[4] "Upload" and "download" refer to the acts of transferring a copy of a file onto a server or from a server to a computer via the File Transfer Protocol (FTP). See more definitions of Internet terms and computer terms at http://www.clienthelpdesk.com/dictionary/internet_terms.html.

recommended by one of my colleagues, to the United Nations file, and evaluated a European database on privacy and decided to include it in the *Guide*'s Human Rights file, and transferred these edited files to the server.

Later in the day I looked through my daily correspondence; forwarded to my colleague in charge of the server and the library's home page a message about the latest IBM computer, considered the fastest on earth; and wrote a letter for a PhD from Spain who had finished his project in the library (the letter was an acknowledgment for his superiors at the Carlos III University of Madrid that he did research in the library during his stay with us). An email from the *Canadian Journal of Family Law* in Vancouver signed by a senior editor appeared on my screen. They had received a manuscript referring to various European cases and legislation with no legal citation providing assistance beyond England and France. I sent a reply.

Internationalization in our field means an increasing load of international and foreign law research questions in our dealings with peers from all over the world. The internationalization of legal research has become a reality that is doubtless recognized by all my readers. We actually live in all time zones of the world. Or, to be more accurate, our time is Internet time. And our place is the place of the Internet where *ubiquity*—the privilege of being in many places simultaneously—has now become a privilege of mortals after being the privilege only of gods. Ubiquity has become *la raison d'être* of the cyberlegal culture constituency.

The cyberlegal culture is a new but burgeoning tradition that was created by the behavior of legal specialists from all over the world when they entered the realm of communication, researching, and teaching in the high-tech information (information technology or IT) environment, facilitated by the Internet and the World Wide Web.

Cyber comes from the Greek root *kubernan* which means *steersman*, related to the art of navigation on free oceans.

Cyberlegal culture is not a space of freedom beyond states' borders or a supranational form of legal jurisdiction. It is rather a way of exchanging ideas, and contributing to the development of legal research and legal teaching through scholarship in the virtual reality environment. In the Gutenberg era the dissemination of information was centrifugal.

A publisher, for example, sends out copies of the same product which are acquired by many different consumers.

In the cyberculture era, and subsequently in the cyberlegal culture milieu, the dissemination of information is centripetal. A publisher releases or deposits information in its own server, and consumers from all over the world come to access it through the means of the Internet environment. What has changed is the consumer orientation (from centrifugal to centripetal), and the format of publishing (from print to electronic). It is a change that will take time to be fully acknowledged and considered. Printed versus online is after all simply a manner of information dissemination.

Each cyberlegal culture hierarchy is self-created by its members, and may originate in any country. Hierarchies are based on merit and competence. Their language is often a mixture of English, French, German, Spanish, Italian, and other languages. INT-LAW (http://listhost.ciesin.org/), based in the USA, and EUROLEX (http://www.listserv.gmd.de/archives/euro-lex.html), based in Europe, have played historical roles in this respect. Individual personalities perform the indispensable roles of moderators and of influential channels, gathering electronic resources (from news to case law and primary statutory materials) and redistributing them to the members. A significant amount of cyberlegal information is channeled to them personally. There are *virtual personae* playing these roles in the US, Europe, Australia, New Zealand, China, Japan, and throughout the world .

There are also specialists in various legal fields and institutions, such as the United Nations, the European Union, the World Trade Organization (WTO), human rights, and almost all other fields of public and private international law, comparative law and foreign law. Actually, every legal field and jurisdiction is represented in the cyberlegal culture by its leading specialists. These individuals have created a professional network over and above the legal structure of the nations; as members of a legal community, they rely on new rules and different behaviors. They are active writers in their fields. They are watching, referring to, authoring, and developing the cyberlegal culture environment. Their scholarship gives a new meaning to legal teaching and legal research, complementary to and coexisting with traditional methods. They are the pioneers of a revolutionary trend, expanding online knowledge and research skills. The legal traditions of the world, foreign jurisdictions, and international law are brought together on to a new level of coexistence. Linked together, they achieve a beauty of legal thinking that combines its past, present, and future endeavors.

However, not all jurisdictions are linked to the cyberlegal culture. Linking all the world's legal centers, bringing them together by a joint effort, building new skills and networking law libraries all over the world—this is a major and worthwhile task. Building electronic legal centers or libraries must be accomplished by countries individually, after which competencies must be created that are to use these resources. Only then can the skills necessary to enter the cyberlegal culture be developed. My involvement in teaching legal specialists from other countries has helped me to understand how the approach should be made and how this job should be accomplished. The strategic insight on this matter presented in this book will perhaps speed up the process of uniting many jurisdictions worldwide in the cyberlegal culture.

Tales of Strategy for Surviving in the Cyberlegal Culture

Managerial skills in the World Wide Web environment are critical for linkage. Being linked modifies life's routine. Dixit and Nalebuff's book on thinking strategically[5] showed how much we owe to strategy in everyday life and business where competition and performance are crucial. This is especially true in the WWW environment where we also experience *ubiquity*—being in many different places simultaneously—and *atemporality*, being in an abstract time that overrides all global time zones.

Define your work "jurisdiction"

There is a point at which you must define the "jurisdiction" of your work, as in the following example.

[5] Dixit, K. Avinash and Barry J. Nalebuff, *Thinking Strategically: The Competitive Edge in Business, Politics, and Everyday Life.* New York: W.W.Norton & Company, 1991.

A visiting professor was writing a book on human rights during his visit at our library. He needed assistance locating legal documents from United Nations and foreign jurisdictions. I gave him all needed assistance. After he went back to his country he realized that his research was not finished yet and that he needed more help. As a reference librarian I had finished my job in assisting him, but at the personal level I considered it my duty to help him finish his project. I should add that he was instrumental in establishing contacts with his country's partners for the ITN/STARR (http://www.law.nyu.edu/library/itn/) project for the library.

I continued to give him assistance by email. One late afternoon I received about ten requests for legal documents. A young lady, introducing herself as the professor's former research assistant, came to me saying that the need was urgent. I went to a database containing the desired documents and realized that in order to send them I had to download and unzip each file, one by one, and then send them individually by email. The former research assistant confessed she was not ready to perform all these operations. After a few hours' work I realized I was overextending myself. My task that evening was to help my students in doing their research projects.

Realize that each action incurs a series of reactions

The fifteen-hour training in cyberlegal research for NYU School of Law LLMs enrolled in the International Tax Program was a pilot project set up in the 1996/1997 academic year. A group of advanced degree students and one professor went through a syllabus designed to cover issues from html editing and building a home page to international and foreign law research on the WWW databases. It was an extraordinarily fulfilling experience with great feedback. As a result, the International Tax Program decided to provide training for students in WWW specialized databases every year. The director of the library determined that such training at the beginning of each academic year was needed for all JD, MCJ and LLM students in order to give them the skills to navigate through online catalogs, online legal journals, and international and foreign databases. Some professors required specialized training in order to bring their classes into the cyberlegal culture. Many professors also needed training and assistance with their own online skills and computers. The work load on every librarian increased, as well as the complexity of work. We had to decide where the library's responsibilities stopped and where the computer center's began—a line that is still undecided, but is now nevertheless enforced to the degree possible.

Anticipate "hidden costs" in subscription decisions

How do you know when to replace printed services for online ones? Look carefully before you leap. Try and compare. It may cost you more than you think. Many European and Chinese databases have a way of charging for viewing and downloading that is not practicable for academic purposes. They might be reasonable for some special projects, or for the work of some specialized lawyers, but not for academic use. Although I was happy when my library subscribed to *Jurifrance*—for it is a comprehensive database for French primary and secondary legal sources, an excellent updating tool, and also a great way to fill gaps in the library's French collection—eventually we had to restrict access and use it only as a last resort. The database charges per amount of information, so prices are high even though the academic subscription might appear reasonable.

Learn from your imitators

This is important especially for WWW webmasters,[6] to whom my story might be of some help.

I observed that the links I had made for the *Guide to Foreign and International Legal Databases* (http://www.law.nyu.edu/library/foreign_intl/index.html) were copied by other databases, clearly appropriating my work. At first I felt frustrated, but I decided to pay no attention. The *Guide* was designed to support the NYU School of Law curriculum and needs. A strong international curriculum and the Global Law School needed my work. In any event, my followers were only copying my links; they stayed away from copying my annotations, knowing that such a thing was recognizable.

[6] The webmaster is an individual who manages a web site. The webmaster might be responsible for properly managing the server hardware and software, designing the site, creating and updating web pages, replying to user feedback, and monitoring traffic through the site.

However, I could not help noticing that my followers were improving the look and design of their home pages while I was occupied almost exclusively with content. Their interfaces were more appealing. They had time to employ new features because I had done a lot of the groundwork for them.

These observations induced me to completely transform the *Guide,* employing a new design with features which were both more attractive and impossible to copy. Now, by applying the bibliographic principle of "see also", a person while using the *Guide* can simultaneously access any other file. This improvement gives not only the layout but also the substance of the electronic and international library superior *syndetic* structure. The user is allowed a "global" approach from any point on the sphere. A feature of the FrontPage editor helped me to apply this type of indexing. A search engine was implemented. Due in great measure to this improvement, the *Guide* has become very popular and many libraries in the USA and around the world employ it for teaching and for legal research.

Integrate complementary collections

A colleague from an academic library asked me to give his students a tour of our foreign collection. He sent me in advance a list of the students, the jurisdictions they were interested in, and a few topics for research projects. One of these required the 1993 Israel Basic Law on Human Dignity and Liberty in English. When I went to the collection to locate the desired law, I discovered that the English service of Israeli laws was far behind while only the collection in Hebrew was updated. I looked in the Israeli English journals and the *Israel Yearbook on Human Rights,* but without success. When I asked my colleague in charge of the collection for help, he verified that the only version of that law in the library was in Hebrew. At this point I went online to the Israeli Parliament—the Knesset database (http://www.knesset.gov.il/index.html). Fortunately, it contained the Basic Laws and the full-text English version of the needed law.

Use teamwork

An email received from Estonia requested a copy of a law. The German Government was negotiating a bilateral treaty with the Estonian government. An official from the German Embassy in Estonia needed an English translation of a German act required by the Estonian Government in order to continue the dialogue. Through Julius (http://julius.law.nyu.edu/), the library's online catalog, he knew that we had the law in English, and he wanted a copy of it.

I went to the head of the library's Interlibrary Loan Services and discussed the situation. He decided that we could send the document by Fedex to Estonia as a form of courtesy to a foreign embassy in a foreign country. However, when a French agency needed the French bankruptcy law in English a few months latter, I decided to scan the document, convert it to rtf and pdf[7] and send it by email.

Better teach than provide

It is often wise for librarians to teach users some cyberlegal managerial techniques so they, the librarians, are not inundated with routine work. Here is an example of what I mean.

I work closely with a professor who is an active writer and researcher. His need for legal international materials and secondary sources is so great that working for him alone is sometimes a full time job. Although I work for him with pleasure, one day I reached a point where I realized I had to teach him to do his own routine work, so I would have more time for my projects and be more available to other faculty in need of legal research. I calculated that the professor's needs were seventy percent routine, so that if I succeeded in training him, I would only have to give him the thirty percent left. Moreover, he was an active traveler, asking for assistance in places all over the world, so he needed a measure of independence.

I began his training with relatively simple things such as sending attachment files by email, installing Acrobat Reader on

[7] Rich Text Format (RTF) provides a format for text and graphics interchange that can be used with different operating systems. RTF files are actually ASCII files with commands that indicate formatting information such as fonts and margins. ASCII (American Standard Code for Information Interchange) is a code for representing English characters as numbers, with each letter assigned a number from 0 to 127. Computers use ASCII codes to transfer data from one computer to another. Portable Document Format (PDF) is created by Adobe Acrobat, a software program that converts any document into a file that you can view and read, as long as you have the free Adobe Acrobat Reader on your computer.

his computer, and setting up a bookmark file on his browser with databases related to his research. After that, it was not hard to teach him how to use those databases. The next step was teaching him how to use search and metasearch engines, and finally, how to download files from the databases in various formats. His satisfaction was tremendous. He proved to me that this was an important part of doing my job in the electronic reference environment. So I set up training sessions for other professors as well as for research assistants.

Be aware of security protocols and devices

Be aware of what database you buy or subscribe to and how it is used. You might be confronted with needless and painful situations.

Recently, we decided to buy a CD-ROM with Indian case-law, JUDIS. It was inexpensive, and it was supplemented by an online database (http://www.judis.nic.in/). The entire protocol of acquiring the CD-ROM from the provider in Delhi took overall about six months.

The envelope with the CD-ROM finally arrived, with some instructions and a device. The device was a lock which had to be installed in the back of the computer in order to see the contents of the CD-ROM. So only the person with the lock was able to use the CD-ROM. But this was not all. A few weeks later, I replaced my computer with a faster one, in which it was impossible to reinstall the Indian CD-ROM, as an exe file allowed only one installation. I asked the computer center for help. After a few days of work they figured out a way to beat the system. But the CD-ROM was still limited to use in my computer. And there it remains. If a student, research assistant or a professor needs Indian cases, I must surrender my computer for the duration or do the work myself. Moreover, the CD-ROM does not permit any kind of "save as", and printing a case is painful when (as is frequently true) it has more than 100 pages. I did find a way of copying and pasting text, but it is time-consuming. Thinking of ways to escape this Trojan horse consumes a disproportionate amount of my time and resources.

Try not to assume that one source is better than another

I was asked to locate a bilateral treaty between Poland and Germany, in German. The given information was very vague, only a few words about the title but no year. I tried all conventional sources with no success. A colleague suggested a search in German, using an Internet search engine. I found the treaty in a free German database, an archiving database for foreign policy acts. I looked in the Bundesgesetzblatt, Teil II and verified the information. It was right.

Now, the reverse situation. A colleague from another law school asked for a German act in English, mentioning the year 2000 as the year of the published and of the enacted law. I looked through all German statutory laws for 2000 in the library's collection, in the vernacular and English translation, and searched through the World News Connection (http://wnc.fedworld.gov/) limiting the given data. The law was not there. A search through Lexis/Nexis (http://www.lexis.com) led to the discovery that the law had been published one year earlier. I was wrong in beginning my search with a sophisticated database, limiting my search by year because I trusted the accuracy of given data.

Work on many projects simultaneously

Working with many projects at the same time is becoming more and more common. From the tales I have described it is clear that the one-by-one approach is often time-consuming and self-defeating. Working to solve many problems at the same time with a list of priorities is the key to success in the cyberlegal culture. Organization and a simultaneous approach to all levels of attribution offer the only ways to a successful performance. Reference, teaching, learning, writing, communicating with one's peers, and involvement in job-related and profession-related projects are the usual skills and attributions of the cyberlegal specialist. But there will soon be more.

The Legal Information Specialist's Role in Designing the Interfaces of Legal Databases

This task requires not only substantive law research skills, but also knowledge of the information technology environment. Record retrieval systems, indexing, search forms, site maps, navigational tools, document formats, and access are negotiated with database providers during free trial sessions or product presentations. Databases must be designed to meet reference requirements and legal research criteria. Cyberlegal community pressure is essential for the proper development of legal databases on the World Wide Web.

The United Nations Treaty Collection (http://un treaty.un.org/) was use-free for more than one year. During that time, the search form and the document format both improved as the text format migrated from html to tif.[8] The server and the URL were both changed, so the database is no longer merely a directory on the very busy United Nations (http://www.un.org) server. The Treaty Collection Database is now more reliable and has become a great updating tool and primary source all over the world. Unfortunately, the cost makes it unapproachable for third world countries which cannot afford the subscription. One of its extraordinary accomplishments is the imaged version of the United Nations Treaty Series set, despite the painful slowness of going from page to page in order to see the treaty. In this case, reliability was considered more important than fast access to the entire document.

The fee-based United Nations Optical Disk System (ODS) (http://www.ods.un.org/) uses an extremely complicated search form with the capability of searching the full text of any document and many types of publications as well as legal documents issued by different UN bodies. Texts are offered in pdf. Files on ODS may also be in WordPerfect 5.1 DOS, 6.1 WIN, WORD 6 or Great Wall for Chinese. When it first appeared, ODS was difficult if not impossible to use. The search engine is still out of order once in a while. For best results it is wise to first use indexes such as Readex (http://infoweb1.newsbank.com/), UNBISnet (http://unbisnet.un.org/) or Unique (http://www.un.org/Depts/dhl/unique/index.html) to get the citation to the document, and then retrieve it in full text from ODS. This database is an indispensable source of reliable United Nations documents, slowly replacing the microfiche system. Some time in the (I hope) near future, it will be comprehensive. I believe that the ODS search engine will continue to improve as it did

[8] Tagged Image File (TIF) is a file format for storing and transferring graphic images. It is often used to exchange such files between dissimilar computers. It is also used by scanners to convert pictures (such as the image of a document) into computer files.

during 1998–2000. Database staff have shown receptiveness to criticism and adjusted accordingly.

The development of the Global Legal Information Network (http://lcweb2.loc.gov/law/GLINv1/GLIN.html) was more dramatic. GLIN is a meta-database with six interfaces. Documents of 50 countries are available in the vernacular. The search form has improved over the years, but, despite criticism, it still presents basic problems. The only way of searching GLIN is by means of a controlled vocabulary search. To search the database, training is needed in order to understand the procedure. A thesaurus is provided to help users find the appropriate search terms. Unfortunately, the thesaurus is poor, so the retrieved records are always more than expected.

The Canadian database law.pro (http://www.carswell.com/ecarswell/law.pro/index.html) asked for feedback from the beginning of 1999. Training sessions gathered legal specialists and database vendors together. The improvement process took more than a year. The main concern was the retrieval system, especially the search engine, although the document format, the pagination, and other factors were considered.

Quicklaw (http://www.quicklaw.com/) changed very slowly to hypertext. During 1999/2000 vendors were receptive to access concerns, search difficulties and records retrieval, in part because of competition with Carswell. Quicklaw was extremely rigid. We used it for the wealth of caselaw (especially labor law and taxation) and legal literature. Today's Quicklaw America (http://www.quicklawAmerica.com) is more flexible and is as manageable as any good database using the html format.

Oceana's Treaties and International Agreements Online (former TIARA) (http://www.oceanalaw.com/) was hard to use at the beginning of its trial period, in 1998. There were missing countries; I could not find a USA treaty of 1783; the search engine for the Index of Treaties did not retrieve the same results as the search engine for the full-text US Treaties; the descending order and the ascending order were mixed up; Oceana's accession number and the treaty date were hardly distinguishable. However, by May 1999 it had shown a tremendous improvement. As of the year 2000 the database is credible.

European and Chinese databases are reluctant to change their charging systems, making their use unfeasible for wide-ranging users like libraries. These databases are addressed to sole practitioners, and not to the academic world. Charging by the amount of viewed and downloaded information (bytes) means that a bill will be issued every time the database is accessed. Such vendors should implement simpler charging systems that are more manageable and feasible. Indian databases, offering a combination of CD-ROM and online subscriptions, have to be urged to move entirely to the Internet.

Russian and Chinese databases provide data mostly only in the vernacular. They offer no indexes or any other disclosure about the content, no information on pricing, and no access in any other language. Cyrillic and Chinese scripts are not a barrier as long as the browser can be set up for these alphabets. Even so, searching remains a problem. In order to write in the search box form, special software is often needed.

Latin American databases are not flexible. Search forms are not clear. With a few exceptions, there is no care for accuracy, reliability or currency of legal documents. Servers are extremely slow and hard to access. PDF and TIF formats are not available. Statutory material and jurisprudence are there, but coverage, content completeness, source and updating information is rarely provided.

My own experience provides an example of cooperation between a legal information specialist and an important North American legal publisher. The publisher wanted to know if law libraries would use and buy a database on a specific subject. I told him that a database on that subject would not be of any interest because good products already exist in that area. However, I was able to convince him that something else—an online index to bilateral treaties of countries of the world linked to full-text documents—would be of great value to the legal community. I hope that database will be on the market soon, filling a gap that is more and more serious.

Chapter 2

Legal Research on the Frontier of Innovation

In the past legal research was mostly routine. Few legal specialists engaged in substantive law research were in touch with imagination and creativity. But this has changed. Imagination and creativity are today at the heart of this profession. The engine of transformation is the hypertext's "linked reality", the mode of thought of the virtual reality environment.

In the cyberlegal culture generated by information technology and the World Wide Web phenomenon, a different kind of legal information specialist has emerged. He or she is charged with more skill and greater capability in substantive legal research and the location of reliable information sources. This information specialist has proved that legal research is not restricted to finding primary and secondary authoritative legal materials, but is also of great value in retrieving information concerning the legal subject, in any format, through a combination of all available resources.

Research skills have expanded to a virtuosity close to art. Though online legal research is taught in library schools and law schools, a good legal research professional goes beyond his or her training and always shows curiosity, imagination, talent, a personal approach to the electronic world. This means exploring, discovering, and building ways of understanding the WWW "disorganization". This legal information specialist is not the "bookmark" librarian, or the "keeper of the library's bookmarks" or "links" as he or she is sometimes described. He/she is an information specialist in charge of knowledge management and information age resources management. Searching the World Wide Web does not mean merely "clicking" on links, but knowing ways of finding, evaluating, using, teaching, and managing substantive legal resources in the cyberlegal culture.

Because authors often fail to understand the dynamic and the logic of the World Wide Web and its metamorphic nature, books about online legal research and legal databases are often out of date from the day of printing. The Web is a medium in a permanent state of transformation. In writing on this subject, it is important to replicate as far as possible the structure, the approach, the hypertextual link, and even the publishing environment that characterizes online research. Not description, but the logic of changes and networking sources should be the priority. The WWW version must necessarily be the counterpart of the printed book. Not only is this book available in an online version, but it is also supported by two online guides that will be updated regularly to reflect the dynamic of change: *The Guide to Foreign and International Legal Databases* (http://www.law.nyu.edu/library/foreign_intl), and *The Guide to European Legal Databases* (http://www.llrx.com/features/europenew.htm).

A friend suggested that I print the *Guide to Foreign and International Legal Databases* and publish it as a book. My friend wanted a hard copy of it. It was not easy to explain why such an enterprise would make little sense. Analogies are often the best avenues to understanding, so I compared a WWW index and portal[9] with a live leaf from a tree. Although we can take a picture of that leaf and capture a moment of that live tissue, we kill it by placing it under the microscope. To truly comprehend it, we must understand the cells' *raison d'être* as well as their continuous transformation. Hypertext products are similar to live creatures in this way. Any explanation of their value must refer to such elements as their inner logic, their substance, their role in the WWW universe, ways to access them, and strategies to find them even if their URLs are changed.

This last factor has given rise to anomalies in the cyberlegal culture. Very few legal databases have preserved their initial URL from the day of their inception. Migrations from servers and directories to better servers, domain names and directories are commonplace. General search engines and metasearch engines

[9] A portal is a Web site or service that offers a broad range of resources and services on many subjects (a "horizontal portal") or on a specific subject (a "vertical portal," or "vortal").

are often slow to recognize these changes and retrieved records may display out-of-date URLs. The International Court of Justice URL has changed three times in the past three years, as has its Cornell mirror site. A simple strategy in a case like this is to go to the organization hosting the mirror database (i.e., Cornell Law School) and find out the new directory of the mirror site. Another technique is to go to the root of the database organization (i.e., the United Nations). Another strategy is to apply your knowledge of the hierarchy of the legal organization or its legal bodies and to figure out the corresponding new paths in the server's directories—a method that works well in the case of the continuous reorganization of the European Union databases.

Several examples of outdated materials that are still available show how much things have changed in the cyberlegal culture. *Law on the Net: Easy Access to Over 2000 Law-Related Sites* by James Evans and edited by Albin Renauer[10] purports to present an inventory and a description of legal databases on a global scale: domestic, foreign, and international. The book has not been revised since 1997. Aside from short descriptions of a few databases and their names, it is of little value today. Almost all URLs, as well as content and coverage, have changed. Regarding foreign jurisdictions the situation is even worse. *Codes de France* by Jerome Rabenou, an index of French materials declared obsolete by the author long ago, is still listed as authoritative. A reliable index of German law databases is nonexistent. Global Legal Information Network (GLIN)—which is marketed as a free database, although only the index is free, not the content—offers no indication whatsoever of reliability.

Legal Research: FUN-damentals and Principles by Myra A. Harris[11] discusses only Lexis and Westlaw as sources for US electronic legal research. Amy E. Sloan in *Basic Legal Research: Tools and Strategies*[12] courageously lists a few databases besides Lexis and Westlaw: the fee-based LOIS (http://www. pita.com/)

[10] Evans, James, *Law on the Net: Easy Access to Over 2000 Law-Related Sites*, Second Edition. Berkeley, CA: Nolo Press, 1997.

[11] Harris, Myra A., *Legal Research: FUN-damentals and Principles*. Upper Saddle River, NJ: Prentice Hall Paralegal Series, 2000.

[12] Sloan, Amy E., *Basic Legal Research: Tools and Strategies*. New York: Aspen Law and Business, 2000.

and VERSUSLAW (http://www.versuslaw.com/), which contain US statutes and cases, and also two databases operated by the US government, Thomas and the Government Printing Office. Thomas (http://thomas.loc.gov/) contains the full texts of federal legislation, *The Congressional Record*, committee reports, congressional documents and debates, the hearings schedule, updates on bill status, congressional directories, notes on the legislative process, and historical documents. Harris strongly recommends GPO Access (http://www.gpo.gov/gpoaccess). GPO Access via Federal Depository Library Gateways (http://www.access.gpo.gov/su_docs/acesaaces 004.html) is also strongly recommended as well as "Legal Research Sites" and "Internet Search Engines". She offers no commentary on the reliability of using the last two categories of database for legal research.

A more valuable book, showing how fast things are moving towards hypertext, is *Law on the Internet* by Cate Banks and Heather Douglas,[13] a directory of Australian legal databases with an online counterpart in the publisher's database (http://www.fedpress.aust.com). With extreme care, the authors have emphasized Australian government legal databases, and thus their usefulness is easy to evaluate. However, in reviewing fee-based databases such as *Butterworths Online* (http://www.butterworths.com.au), the authors fail to mention that this is a commercial service, forget to compare it with free Australian databases, and never explain the advantages of subscribing to it. More typical publications include Robert Watt's book,[14] which mentions databases without specifying anything about their value, and Cohen and Olson's volume,[15] which remains in the "public domain" in the sense that only databases with an aura of reliability (such as United Nations and WTO databases) are mentioned, with no indication that anything else exists.[16]

[13] Banks, Cate and Heather Douglas, *Law on the Internet.* Leichhardt, NSW: The Federation Press, 2000.

[14] Watt, Robert, *Concise Legal Research.* Sydney: The Federation Press, 1997.

[15] Cohen, L. Morris and Kent C. Olson, *Legal Research in a Nutshell.* Saint Paul, MN: West, 2000.

[16] URLs of databases of international organizations composed of the abbreviation of their names, such as United Nations (http://www.un.org) and World Trade Organization (http://www.wto.org) will not always be mentioned in this text as they are very easy to identify.

The Legal List: Research on the Internet by Diana Botluk[17] is one of the best books explaining the new electronic environment. The author formulates search strategies and advice on starting points. Explanations are merged with lists of databases. The trouble is that the evaluation and description of database content is largely absent for the sake of having them all listed. It is a book focused on the US legal system. Botluk's book will soon be obsolete because of the dramatically changing structure of the WWW.

The Guide to International Legal Research[18] shows the willingness to integrate the WWW databases, and Lexis and Westlaw with printed primary and secondary sources. As of February 2001, the book is obsolete concerning electronic documents. It is merely necessary to point out that European Union materials have disappeared from Lexis, as have many other databases in the World Wide Web; URLs have changed; there is no indication of database reliability, etc. The *2000 Cumulative Supplement* is even more frustrating. Entries are changed, deleted, or added, often referring to out-of-date databases, while relating to the main volume. There is no improvement in the general structure of the database presentation. The same database (such as GLIN) may be obsessively mentioned for almost every listed country.

As if reading the above considerations, Ken Kozlowski published in March 2001 *The Internet Guide for the Legal Researcher*, Third Edition, both in print and online at the Infosources Publishing (http://www.infosourcespub.com/). Subscribers receive a free password to the web site which is updated every 60-90 days. *The Lawyer's Guide to the Internet* by Kathy Biehl and Tara Calishain was also published both in print and online at the Fortuna Works (http://www.fortunaworks.com) database. Subscribers to the online version receive email alerts when new updates to the book are available.

In recognition of the trends of the future, governments all over the world have built electronic collections as parallel

[17] Botluk, Diana, *The Legal List: Research on the Internet.* Saint Paul, MN: West, 2000.

[18] *The Guide to International Legal Research*, Third Edition. The George Washington University Journal of International Law and Economics. Charlottesville, VA: Lexis Law Publishing, 1998.

sources or alternatives to traditional printed collections and fee-based databases. The distinction among them is one of degree of comprehensiveness. Without question, the diversity of online legal resources is a great accomplishment of our time. It is important to remember that access-free and fee-based databases having more or less the same content do not generally exclude each other. Fee-based databases offer editorial enhancements (editorial notes, historical notes, classification notes, amendment notes, etc.), the most current consolidation of law, supplementary legal literature, customer service support, simpler user interfaces, and other value-added features. Methods of online legal research become a matter of choice depending not only on search skills but also on financial resources, and of course on knowledge of the cyberlegal culture resources.

In the US, access-free legal portals and vortals have created alternatives to Westlaw and Lexis, from code to caselaw, at federal and state level. Generally speaking, the *caveat* of free-of-charge databases, in comparison with fee-based databases, refers to their less extensive coverage and fewer value-added features. For example, as of February 2001, the last version of the United States Code in GPO databases is as follows: Titles 1 through 34 current through 1/23/00; Titles 35 through 50 current through 1/5/99—while Lexis, Westlaw, and LOIS have up-to-date codifications. In order to update the online version found at the United States House of Representatives Law Revision Counsel (http://uscode.house.gov/usc.htm), the researcher must go to the United States Code Classification Tables (http://uscode.house.gov/uscct.htm) providing the list of amended sections since 1998. These amendments are sorted in Public Law order and in U.S. Code order. The researcher must go over the tables to find out if a code section has been amended. If this is the case, the public law number and section are provided. Then the researcher must go to Thomas (http://thomas.loc.gov) or to some other GPO gateway to gain access to public laws. None of these maneuvers are necessary in Lexis and Westlaw, which provide much easier access to updated law. However, current legal documents are very well covered by GPO databases (http://www.access.gpo.gov/), where the researcher can also find out more about this issue as well as about the commitment to include the old backlog of government documents.

In Australia, Argentina, Brazil, Belgium, Canada, Israel, India, Italy, Mexico, Sweden, France, South Africa, the United Kingdom, Switzerland, Norway, The Netherlands, Lithuania, and other countries, legal databases in the vernacular, published and maintained by governments and legal institutes, provide free and reliable statutory material and jurisprudence (cases). When updating is not an issue, as in many civil law jurisdictions, these legal databases are very valuable collections of primary legal materials.

International organizations publish their documents in a more timely manner than any other fee-based databases. For European Union documentation, CELEX (http://europa.eu.int/celex/) generally provides more current information than, for example, WESTLAW. The World Trade Organization presents the same advantage, as do NAFTA (the North American Free Trade Agreement, http://www.nafta-sec-alena.org/english/index.htm), the Organization of American States (http://www.oas.org/), the European Court of Human Rights (http://www.echr.coe.int/hudoc/), and other supranational entities.

Free or fee-based subject-oriented databases (environment, human rights, treaties, international trade, international criminal law, etc.) arrived on the scene as precious primary legal resources, supplementing topical loose-leafs and microfiche collections. Working with complementary libraries (print, electronic, microfiche) is one of the research challenges of our time. A database may be used as a main resource or an updating tool, depending on the legal specialist's needs and talent to provide the right source at the right moment. Speed has increased in our profession. It is the speed of virtual reality. Coping with it demands changes in our mental speed and intellectual biology.

Modern libraries and organizations have acknowledged the need to maintain and manage information as an organizational asset. Information resources management (IRM) is an expanding field which recognizes information as a key resource (see IRM Model Curriculum at http://www.irma-international.org). Information management principles, data resource and administration, concepts and practices of information resources management, management procedures to collect, analyze and disseminate information throughout the organization—all these are today on the legal specialist's agenda. The literature on this topic is growing. Many articles appear in Legal Information Service (*Law Technology Journal*), an online publication based in the UK (http://www.law.warwick.ac.uk/ltj). The European Association for Grey Literature Exploitation (http://www.kb.nl/infolev/eagle/mission.htm) is a cooperative network which also provides access to literature on this topic. A portion of this database, the Personal Management Library (http://www.pm-library.com/main.htm), provides abstracts and articles from leading management journals. The Personal Management Library is a comprehensive database of more that one hundred thousand management articles and abstracts.

Notably, the powerful presence of the cyberlegal culture has accentuated the trend of *disintermediation*, which requires individuals to develop technology-related skills in order to perform their own electronic legal research.[19] This phenomenon has also created a trend of legal research *disintervention*, defined as a "false freedom" set up for users who, through training, gain "some control over the information universe."[20] *Disintermediation* and *disintervention* in the WWW "disorganization" have significantly shifted the librarian's task to more customized teaching and also to sophisticated legal research services for patrons with different levels of knowledge. Broad research can be carried out by trained lawyers and students, thereby allowing the legal specialist more time for professional and personal growth.

It was in the United States, Canada, the United Kingdom, and somewhat later Australia and New Zealand—all common law countries—that the information revolution first linked legal information specialists together. Beginning with the year 2000, I have noticed a similar trend in the Scandinavian countries and in some ways also at the European Union level, although not yet at the various EU countries' level. Legal specialists (in this case, law professors and lawyers more than librarians) have begun to

[19] Halvorson, T.R., *Law of the Super Searchers: The Online Secrets of Top Legal Researchers.* Edited by Reva Basch. Medford, NJ: CyberAge Books, 2000, p. xii. Available WWW: The Foreword discusses the AALL definition of disintermediation: discrimination necessary to identify reliable sources; information literacy; prioritization of sources; flexibility; and consumer advocacy.

[20] *Ibid.*, p. 113.

work systematically with complementary libraries (paper, online, microfiche), becoming active in the development of the online resources era. It is as though legal research has exploded and transformed itself into an enormous network. Almost overnight, online legal databases have become popular. Online annotated guides to domestic, international and foreign law databases, legal portals, and legal gateways are emerging everywhere. The next step is to evaluate and recommend by subject accurate and reliable law resources.

Throughout the last years of the twentieth century, we learned new skills, not only through our personal experience, but also from discussions posted in listservs, and from books, WWW guides, and articles distributed through home pages all over the world. If librarianship means sharing knowledge, never did librarianship do more than it does today in the burgeoning cyberlegal culture phenomenon. Foreign, comparative, and international law research has escalated all over the world. As the US expands its active role in the international arena, so does legal research. I have observed this in domestic listservs such as LawLib, and at AALL programs; for instance, at the 2000 American Association of Law Libraries Annual Convention in Philadelphia, a group of librarians from the Supreme Court asserted that they needed greater skills in international and foreign law research. The Workshop on Treaty Research, and programs such as Teaching Foreign-Trained Students and Law Librarians and French Legal Research, were unexpectedly crowded. The truth is that today's law libraries have to deal almost on a daily basis with specific questions of foreign law, the status of multilateral treaties, and similar issues. The law librarian has become an active learner, continuously developing expertise in the domestic laws of other jurisdictions.

In Europe, Asia, and Latin America, the law librarian is more of a clerical employee than the legal professional he or she is in the US. In the US, librarians do what law professors do elsewhere. In civil law countries where *stare decisis* doesn't apply (even though we see a form of it in some high court or administrative tribunals), legal research is mainly the lawyers' or the law professors' task. Interpretation of the law, not the line of similar cases, is the high priority. So the need for legal literature—*la doctrine, komentar,* etc., a primary source in civil law jurisdictions—is more critical. From the civil law countries' point of view, Westlaw and Lexis are valuable not for the amount of common law jurisdictions' statutory materials and caselaw, but for their collection of foreign laws and online law reviews and journals.

During the past few years, the activity of the European Union and the Council of Europe brought up the implementation on national levels of European Union legislation and EU and ECHR jurisprudence. The intense growth in the activity of international human rights organizations and the expanded importance of the European Court of Human Rights have perforce made the civil law librarian more of a legal professional. Another fact contributing to this is the increase in international tribunals and their case law, related especially to international human rights issues and humanitarian law.

The European Union and the process of European integration have also brought high-ranking officials of Central and Eastern European governments to the legal research scene. In the former Soviet countries (Armenia, Estonia, Latvia, Lithuania, Russia, and so on), the need for drafting new laws and the desire to open national legal systems to the world have spawned legal centers and law libraries and a corresponding need for well-trained law librarians. In many ways the United Nations, the World Trade Organization, the European Union and the Council of Europe have speeded up this process.

The international criminal tribunals of the nineties have also convinced many legal specialists from all over the world to pay attention to the most recent judgements and actions related to a case, and to learn more not only about other jurisdictions and legal systems but also about the structure of international courts, a hybrid between common and civil law systems. International business transactions and contracts, international taxation, trade courts, international trade organizations, and electronic commerce all require transjurisdictional legal research. This is complicated by the fact that Internet law (or the very new Cyber law domain) and the law of electronic commerce are growing. The Internet Corporation for Assigned Names and Numbers (ICANN, http://www.icann.org) and the World Intellectual Property Organization (WIPO, http://www.wipo.org) have been instrumental in this area, regulating the growing amount of databases on the World Wide Web. As more and more international documents are available only on the Web, international legal research has moved dramatically to hypertext.

There is always a need to find or locate the legal document, piece of law, case, directive, or administrative rule from a foreign jurisdiction. Domestic case law and new legislation continually increase foreign and international correlations. Business and cross-border issues demand model codes and up-to-date legal information both in the vernacular and in English translation. Imagination and creativity, as well as good knowledge of legal systems and tools for researching foreign jurisdictions, are increasingly necessary to perform as a legal information professional anywhere in the world.

Despite the fact that substantive law research still needs collections of books and reputable printed law services, vast printed resources are no longer essential. International and foreign law research may now be performed in the law libraries of countries without rich holdings of foreign and international collections, loose-leaf services, and treatises. I have seen this at work in libraries with a very basic collection, almost without books compared to our libraries. The fact is that it is possible today to perform international and foreign law research relying on online sources in combination with regional legal collections and commentaries.

Substantive international law research is possible as long as international organizations publish online *travaux préparatoires* of treaties, proceed with the conversion of earlier documentation into electronic format, and provide online commentaries on specific aspects of treaty implementation at domestic level. With a subscription to CELEX (for European Union law), access to Lexis or Westlaw legal literature (especially if these two databases offer customized interfaces according to customers' needs, i.e., legal literature only), and selective domestic/regional legal databases, journals, and official gazettes, an European library's international legal resources are virtually unlimited.

The library of the French *Conseil Constitutionnel* (http://www.conseil-constitutionnel.fr) is an example. Aside from domestic statutory materials, legal journals and well-known treatises and commentaries, this library's collection is very small: selected European and North African official gazettes, reporters, supreme court caselaw if it exists, constitutional caselaw of various countries, and not very many foreign legal journals. European Union publications are also represented. Legal information specialists rely primarily on CELEX, SCAD, and foreign legal databases as well as on legal collections of other government agencies.

At the library of the Central European University in Budapest in October 1999, I saw a unique collection of international, comparative and foreign law. BNA's International Environment Reporter, the Constitutional set by Blaustein and Flanz, Reynolds and Flores' *Foreign Law: Current Sources of Codes and Basic Legislation in Jurisdictions of the World*, BNA's International Trade Reporter, *Tax Laws and Commercial Laws of the World* , the International Copyright Laws, *The Encyclopedia of Comparative Law*, and even the USCAN. However, the library director was very concerned, because the collection's upkeep depended on Soros Foundation money. The USA loose-leaf services were very much behind. The director was considering shifting to online resources.

The Yerevan School of Law Library had a collection of one thousand books in March 1999. Many printed sources, such as the UN Multilateral Treaties deposited with the General Secretary, had been received as gifts, and were out of date. The law professors relied on online sources and foreign libraries. The Parliament representative in charge of the implementation of the European Convention on Human Rights in Armenia was ecstatic when his training gave him access to Lexis European Union legal materials and legal literature on that subject. It is not unusual for Armenian PhDs to go to Moscow to prepare their dissertations or books. This is not uncommon in Europe: if an article or a book must be written, the professor, the graduate student, or the PhD candidate will go to the nearest or most convenient university with a good collection on the particular subject. This phenomenon is visible today in the US academic law libraries, where the traffic of European PhD candidates, law professors, and students is on the increase. US collections lead the world in recent books of legal literature, impossible to be bought at current prices by European libraries. *Oppenheim's International Law* or Lauterpacht's *International Law Reports* are dreams of many libraries in the world almost impossible to fulfill.

Legal centers and libraries in Moscow—and more so throughout most of the former Soviet Union countries—have few books in foreign languages. Foreign and international legal information is usually available only in Russian translation. Baltic academic libraries, however, collect legal research books in all languages; some Baltic libraries are discarding Russian textbooks and treatises published after 1990 because their point of view still relies on Soviet propaganda.

In an inventory of the collection and research strength of the Legal Center at the Library of Foreign Literature in Moscow in October 2000, I found around 5,000 books and about 60 legal journals. The collection included basic books on international and foreign law research such as Ian Brownlie's *Principles of Public International Law*, Marry Ann Glendon's *Comparative Legal Traditions*, books on constitutional law, treatises on contracts, etc., and subscriptions to all Russian online and CD-ROM legal databases. The Legal Center was founded with Soros Foundation money, in addition to funds provided by the Russian DUMA and Russian government agencies. Online resources seemed vital for both domestic and international and foreign law research. The center was considering a subscription to Lexis or Westlaw.

If a library does not have valuable printed research tools such as Bowman and Harris' *Multilateral Treaties: Index and Current Status*, *Modern Legal Systems Cyclopedia*, *World Treaty Index*, the Multilateral Treaties Deposited with the UN General Secretary, Arturo Flores and Thomas Reynolds' *Foreign Law: Current Sources of Codes and Basic Legislation in Jurisdictions of the World*, *The International Encyclopedia of Comparative Law* and other similar major services, then acquiring online indexes and full-text databases is the only way to access important law resources. Many libraries do not have Lexis or Westlaw subscriptions. Apart from the US, Canada, Australia, the UK, Belgium, and the Netherlands, such a subscription is a luxury. Costs are too high. In such a case, online indexes and databases at a much lower price and online services delivering documents on demand, as well as free databases, guides, library catalogs, dictionaries, and yearbooks, are essential for any law library or legal information center if they are to provide access to primary and secondary sources in international and foreign law. With access to online catalogs and WWW legal portals, legal information specialists can have all the libraries of the world at their fingertips, as well as the world's full-text databases. The needed document (if it exists in electronic format!) is there. The only question is: which path must one follow to find it?

Legal research as defined by *Black's Law Dictionary*, Seventh Edition, is "the finding and assembling of authorities that bear on a question of law; the field of study concerned with the effective marshaling of authorities that bear on a question of law." But this definition has different meanings, depending on the jurisdiction or the legal system in discussion. In the US, legal research "involves a search for materials that provide the best possible indication of how the judge would deal with the issue being researched."[21] This is not true for every jurisdiction in the world. Also, we do not see the same type of authority (primary and secondary) in all jurisdictions. Moreover, there is the question of what is considered mandatory and persuasive authority. There is little or almost no need outside the common law jurisdictions for case law or for learning how a statute or regulation had been interpreted by courts. Finding out whether a court opinion still stands or has been overruled by a higher court is not a priority and seldom even necessary.

Legal knowledge of the topic or jurisdiction under discussion is required in more dramatic terms in the cyberlegal culture whenever one has to decide which path to search as well as which database to choose. For example, it is important to know while searching for Canadian bankruptcy law that in the Canadian legal system the right legal concept is "insolvency law". Another example: it is important to know whether a multilateral treaty deals with public or private international law. Trying to find a private law multilateral treaty in the UN Treaty Collection (http://untreaty.un.org/) will not yield any results; the right database is The Hague Conference on Private International Law (http://www.hcch.net). A search for a bilateral tax treaty in English between two foreign non-English-speaking countries, or a regional tax treaty from Scandinavia for example, should lead the researcher to the Worldwide Tax Treaties of the fee-based TaxBase (http://taxbase.tax.org) ; to the Tax Library in Westlaw; or to the fee-based Economist Intelligence Unit—EIU (http://www.eiu.com), a leading pro-

[21] James Evans, *Law on the Net*, *supra* n.2, p. 5.

vider of economic, political and business intelligence on 195 countries, containing commercial laws and business regulations of 60 countries worldwide and providing guidance on critical issues such as obtaining proper permits and registrations, protecting intellectual property in the Internet age, and complying with local tax laws, e-commerce rules, etc. If it is about taxation in Canada, the fee-based QuicklawAmerica (http:/www. quicklawamerica.com) could be the best source. Looking for foreign banking laws in English will lead to Global Banking Law Database (http://www.gbld.org/). GBLD consists of a collection of commercial banking, central bank, and deposit insurance laws of jurisdictions that are representative of the regions of the world as well as international financial centers.

Researching the implementation of a multilateral treaty in a domestic jurisdiction or a foreign case is a very difficult matter. It may require finding a law in the vernacular, searching International Legal Materials, and/or going to Lexis and to INT-LAW Legal News to search *International Law Update*, a newsletter of Georgetown University, in order to trace the document. For example, attempting to find in English the facts related to the extradition of a German citizen to the US for insider trading, and what the German High Court ruled, I was able to retrieve from International Law Update the text of the opinion and the citation to the Supreme Court of Germany case.

Locating a case from a foreign supreme court or constitutional court should follow the same strategy as in the last example. If there is an online constitutional court, The CourtNet (http://www.sigov.si/us/courtnet.html) or the International Court Network (http://www.uni-wuerzburg.de/law/courts.html) will list it. But many courts, such as the Latin American countries' supreme courts, are not indexed anywhere or have no online presence. ASILEX (http://www.asil.org/asilex.htm) or International Law In Brief (http://www.asil.org/ilibindx.htm), might help the researcher to trace a publication containing the desired case. If not, a call to INT-LAW (International Law) and EURO-LEX (All European Legal Information EXchange List) listservs may be the last resort.

The Online Concept

There is a resistance to the use of online documents in any format from HTML to RTF and PDF, despite the fact that many legal databases offer the perfect image of the officially printed documents and/or expressly state their authenticity. Although the official seal or electronic signature of the legal institutions is there, as well as the pagination of the authoritative series and journal issue, the reluctance to rely on database documents is very strong. Guidelines for the citation of electronic documents—individual works, US government documents, legal sources, and international and foreign government documents—exist in both print[22] and electronic format (http://www.law.nyu.edu/library/foreign_intl/citing.html), but many professors, publishers, authors, and even legal bodies fail to cite electronic sources. Apart from citations to Lexis, Westlaw, and Butterworth's in the common law jurisdictions and Celex in Europe, acceptance of electronic records is still restricted to a few enlightened publishers and organizations.

The problem may lie with the term "online", viewed as antithetical to the reliable printed source. To some minds, it brands a document as "unreliable". Recently, in order to bolster users' confidence, legal databases have emphasized their disclaimers, explanations, and their comparisons with printed sources. Perhaps more of them should offer greater guarantees regarding reliability of content, and disclose their archiving procedures and sources of documents.

I am an advocate of locating legal documents (primary sources) online because, in a global context, it is cheaper, faster, and more convenient to gain access to them by this means. In the United States we are blessed with great publishers, books, loose-leaf services. But few libraries in the world can afford to buy our printed services and foreign collections of laws. Even if a library in Europe decides to buy the *United States Code Annotated*, updating is slow and the cost is high in comparison

[22] See, e.g., Xia Li and Nancy B. Crane, *Electronic Styles: A Handbook for Citing Electronic Information*, Third Edition. Medford, N.J.: Information Today, 2000; Garner, Diane L., and Diane H. Smith, *The Complete Guide to Citing Government Information Resources: A Manual for Writers and Librarians*, Revised Edition. Bethesda, MD: Congressional Information Service, 1993.

with other library needs. The same is true of the *International Environmental Law Reporter* and the *United Nations Treaty Series.* For many libraries, the USA GOP free-of-charge databases, the ENTRY/CIESIN Environmental Library, or a subscription to the online United Nations Treaty Collection are more practical than printed services. The same is generally true for, e.g., a collection of French law: it is more convenient to pay a flat subscription to Jurifrance (http://www.jurifrance.com/) than to subscribe to the Dalloz-Sirey services. Of course, all of these choices are related to a library's needs, such as the amount of usage of the specific information and the number of users.

Even in the United States, however, it is obvious that not every law firm or academic library dealing with international and foreign law issues can afford to have all foreign and international materials. Outsourcing helps, but in the day-to-day routine it is unwise to rely on outside information providers. Online law databases are a better solution. In order to use them, however, the information specialists have, first and foremost, to know that they exist. Next, they must know how to buy (many databases sell affordable modules for customized needs) and how to access them.

Online Access Politics

As academic, private libraries, and legal centers abandon their lists of online fee-based journals and databases and move records to online catalogs with hot links to the Internet, the need arises to make IP addresses or passwords conditions of access, so an outsider cannot see or use the documents. However, IP access as well as multi-user passwords are not always available. Refusal to give one-user-single-access passwords to online databases to individuals limits the independence of the user.

The question is: how strictly must we limit patrons' use of these databases, when fee-based databases free the user not only of passwords, but of many other requirements in order to access them? The possibility of changing the configuration of the browser through a proxy server gives users access to databases from remote locations. However, one cannot always change the browser configuration to a proxy if the computer operates already in a very access-restrictive proxy server.

One-user-single-access passwords can also be saved on PCs. A "cookie" can provide access to a database without typing the password in the login box. This makes it technically possible to give users access without having to give them the password. The librarian does not need to spend time conducting searches for patrons. All of these issues depend on the kind of access provided when a database was acquired, and the type of licensing agreements related to any database under discussion. What gradually emerges from the feedback of the patrons is the requirement to give them the privileges of the virtual world: access from any place, at any time, without password restrictions.

Online Legal Research

In the new electronic environment, librarians looking for primary and secondary sources in international and foreign law should have an idea of the kinds of information available online. More important, however, they must know how to use legal research tools in the Internet context in order to locate substantive law efficiently. They must also consider the reference question in its legal and cultural context, as legal terms may have different meanings in different jurisdictions.

Most legal databases are in the vernacular, so it is not unusual to add some knowledge of foreign languages to awareness of the nuances of different legal systems and cultures. Legal researchers must know where and how to go online (depending on the reference question), decide what type of law or legal document they are looking for, and choose the most appropriate search tool. Moreover, to determine the path to follow in the context of a reference question, the searcher needs to understand the jurisdictional research territory and its relation to the special syntax and concepts. Ultimately, the goal is to develop a personal research style which reflects the researcher's expertise, practice and area of interest, and that is flexible enough to develop a strategy for any research question in a timely manner.

In Brasilia (Brazil), in May 2001, during my lecture organized by the Secretariat of Information and Legal Documentation of the Federal Senate (Interlegis), my belief in the crucial role of online skills in legal research was once again substantiated. Workers at a government legal research center, for example, with a password to the UN Optical Disc System (ODS, http://www.ods.un.org), were frustrated because they could not locate the UN Security Council Resolutions they were looking for. They did not know that they were available for free at the United Nations main portal. In Brasilia, as in many other national government centers throughout the world, law librarians are still struggling with the methodology of online research; they are only beginning to understand the enormous range and reliability of the sources available to them through the information technology infrastructure at their disposal.

Online legal research in foreign and international law depends on the legal specialist's knowledge of the legal systems of the world, settings (academic, legal practice, etc.), the needs of the job, and the ability to build the searching pattern. Computer skills and legal research knowledge must be refined according to many factors, ranging from the legal domain of specialization to the continuous learning fueled by scholarship and intellectual curiosity. Familiarity with the WWW structure of databases and the information technology environment become essential. However, knowledge of the techniques of substantive law research is the only meaningful way to evaluate a database's content and performance. No matter where you are in the world, a core collection of legal research books for international and foreign law is required. [23]

[23] I will list a few published in English in the U.S. and U.K.:

Guide to International Legal Research, 2d ed. Charlottesville, VA: LEXIS Law Publishing, 1998. Compiled by the editors and staff of the George Washington Journal of International Law and Economics. Previous edition published: Salem, NH.: Butterworth Legal Publishers, c. 1993.
Barton, John, et. al., *Law in Radically Different Cultures.* Saint Paul, MN: West Publishing Co., 1983.
Bowman, M. J., and D.J. Harris, *Multilateral Treaties: Index and Current Status.* London: Butterworths, 1984. Kept up to date by supplements through 1995.
Brownlie, Ian, *Principles of Public International Law.* Oxford: Clarendon Press; New York: Oxford University Press, 1998.
Cohen, Morris, Robert Berring and Kent Olson, *How to Find the Law,* 9th ed. Saint Paul, MN: West, 1989.
Danner, Richard A., and Marie-Louise Bernal, I*ntroduction to Foreign Legal Systems. New York: Oceana Publications, c. 1994.*
David, Rene, et.al., *International Encyclopedia of Comparative Law.* Tübingen: Mohr ; New York: Oceana, 1971–.

The region of the world in which the legal specialist lives is also important. In North America, for example, the North American Free Trade Agreement is an important legal topic related to business, environment, labor, health, etc., while in Russia NAFTA is an exotic issue. None of my twenty students (law librarians, JDs, law professors) from Central and Eastern Europe and former Soviet Union countries ever came across a NAFTA question while in Brazil this is an important issue as well as the US legal system.

Evaluate your resources: what kind of document is needed?

What resources do you have in your work place? What is available in your nearby libraries? In your country? Do you need the citation to an official gazette? The full text of a document? In what language?

If you don't have the necessary books and legal services, consult the available databases.

David, René and John Brierley, *Major Legal Systems in the World Today: An Introduction to the Comparative Study of Law,* 3rd ed. London: Steven & Sons, 1985.
Fox, James R., *Dictionary of International and Comparative Law.* Dobbs Ferry, NY: Oceana Publications, 1997.
Glendon, Mary Ann, *Comparative Legal Traditions in a Nutshell.* Saint Paul, MN: West Group, 1999; and Comparative Legal Traditions. Saint Paul, MN: West Publishing, 1994.
Germain, Claire, *Germain's Transnational Law Research: A Guide for Attorneys.* Ardsley, NY: Transnational Juris Publications, Inc., c. 1991–.
Jacobstein, Mersky, & Dunn, *Legal Research Illustrated,* 5th ed. Westbury, NY: Foundation Press, 1990.
Kavass, Igor, *World Dictionary of Legal Abbreviations.* Buffalo, NY: W.S. Hein, 1991-.
Merryman, Henry, *The Civil Law Tradition: An Introduction to the Legal Systems of Western Europe and Latin America.* Stanford,CA : Stanford University Press, c. 1985.
Oppenheim, L., *Oppenheim's International Law,* 9th ed. Harlow, Essex, England: Longman, 1992–.
Reynolds, Thomas, and Arturo Flores, *Foreign Law: Current Sources of Codes and Basic Legislation in Jurisdictions of the World.* Loose-leaf. Littleton, CO: F.B. Rothman, 1989–.
Redden, Kenneth R., and William Brock, *Modern Legal Systems Cyclopedia.* Buffalo, NY: W.S. Hein, 1984.
Rohn, Peter H., *World Treaty Index.* Santa Barbara, CA: ABC-Clio Information Services, c. 1983.

To find a citation to an official gazette, GLIN (The Global Legal Information Network, http://lcweb2.loc.gov/law/GLINv1/GLIN.html) is an excellent source if the specific country you are researching is a GLIN participant. NATLAW (The National Law Center for Inter-American Free Trade: The Inter-American Database for Latin American Countries, http://www.natlaw.com/index.htm) provides free indexes and fee-based full texts of Latin American documents. Many foreign fee-based legal databases also provide free indexes.

If there is a need for a United Nations resolution, the clear source is the United Nations (http://www.un.org/) database. If United Nations voting records are required, consult UNBISnet (http://unbisnet.un.org/). If there is a need for an European Court of Human Rights case, HUDOC (http://www.echr.coe.int/hudoc/) is the best source, although not all cases are online. HUDOC Manual (http://www.echr.coe.int/HudocManual Eng.pdf) lists all HUDOC documents (cases, Commission decisions, Committee of Ministers resolutions). The database is gradually introducing the backlog of earlier cases to the system. If there is a need for a French bilateral treaty, the right database is Base Pacte (http://www.doc.diplomatie.gouv.fr/pacte/) offering all

---

Shaffer, Ellen, *Dictionary of Foreign Law Collections in Selected Law Libraries.* Littleton, CO: F.R.Rothman & Co., 1991. AALL Publication Series No. 41.

Zweigert, Konrad, *Introduction to Comparative Law.* Oxford: Clarendon Press, 1998.

See also guides to foreign jurisdictions such as:

Guide to Foreign Legal Materials: French, by Charles Szladits and Claire Germain. New York: Oceana Publications, 1985.

Sourcebook on French Law, by David Pollard. London: Cavendish Pub., c. 1998.

"English and Commonwealth Legal Materials," *in How to Find the Law*, 9th ed., by Morris L. Cohen, Robert Berring, and Kent Olson. Saint Paul, MN: West Publishing Co., 1989.

Charles Szladits' Guide to Foreign Legal Materials: German, by Timothy Kearley. Dobbs Ferry, NY: Published for the Parker School of Foreign and Comparative Law, Columbia University in the City of New York, by Oceana Publications, Inc., c. 1990.

French bilateral and multilateral treaties in French. Here is the first page of Base Pacte's listing of bilateral treaties between France and Mexico:

LES ARCHIVES DIPLOMATIQUES

AIDE

BASE PACTE

RETOUR AU SOMMAIRE

LEXIQUE AUTRES SITES NOUS ÉCRIRE

TRAITES BILATERAUX

Nombre de documents trouvés : **33**

	Date signature de la France	Date signature du pays étranger	Pays ou organisation internationale	Titre
1	10.04.1899	10.04.1899	**Mexique**	Propriété industrielle.
2	10.04.1899	10.04.1899	**Mexique**	Propriété industrielle.
3	10.05.1905	10.05.1905	**Mexique**	Mandats de poste.
4	03.06.1908	03.06.1908	**Mexique**	Validité des mariages des ressortissants respectifs célébrés par les agents diplomatiques et consulaires

Constitutions are free of charge in the Wuerzburg database, but they must be verified. A mistake related to Eritrea was recently brought to my attention. The new Constitution was not yet in force in 1999, although Wuerzburg (http://www.uni-wuerzburg.de/law/index.html) presented it as such. The rule of thumb is that any country's government legal database should contain the Constitution in the vernacular, and the date of enactment should be on it. The draft should be listed also.

Many official gazettes are free of charge, such as the Belgian Official Journal (*Moniteur Belge*) (http://194.7.188.126/html_fr/f1-bsf.htm), the French *Journal Officiel* (http://www.journal-officiel.gouv.fr), Spain's *Boletin Oficial del Estado* (http://www.boenet.com), the German *Bundesgesetzblatt* Teil I (http://www.bundesanzeiger.de/bgbl1.htm), Italy's *Gazzetta Ufficiale* (http://www.connect.it/gazzetta), Switzerland's *Feuille fédérale* (from 1999, Fascicule No 24, June 22, 1999) (http://www.ad min.ch/ch/f/ff/index.html), etc.

Codes and statutes are published online worldwide. If laws outside the English-speaking area (or any native language area) are needed, searches should if possible be performed in the vernacular, as translations are not always available. Swiss laws (http://www.admin.ch/ch/f/rs/rs.html) are in French, Italian, and German, but not in English. Some Russian laws are translated into English but not all of them (http://www.slavweb.com/index-e.html). The fee-based Russian databases Kodeks and Garant offer English translations, but only very selectively. Some penal codes are translated into English at the Buffalo Criminal Law Center (http://wings.buffalo.edu/law/bclc/resource.htm). The PENELOPE project offers a specialized resource tool designed to assist the understanding of how an environmental law is developed and applied in Europe (http://www.penelope.gr/penelope/about.htm), with national environmental laws in French and English translations. For civil codes there are good links at *Projecte Norma Civil* (http://civil.udg.es/normacivil/ and http://civil.udg.es/epclp/), at New York University (http://www.law.nyu.edu/library/foreign_intl/civiljuris.html), and elsewhere.

Courts' jurisprudence is increasingly available online. The Australasian Legal Information Institute (AUSTLII) (http://www.austlii.edu.au/) is more reliable for old and current Australian jurisprudence than it is for legislation. Sítios jurídicos brasileiros (http://www.solar.com.br/~amatra/linkjur.html) offers full-text cases from all Brazilian federal and regional courts. Hong Kong Judgments of the Court of Final Appeal are available in full text at http://www.info.gov.hk/jud/sitemap/index.htm. Legifrance (http://www.legifrance.gouv.fr/html/frame_jurisprudence.htm) contains recent jurisprudence from the French civil, constitutional, administrative, and supreme courts. All US courts, from the US Supreme Court (http://fedbbs.access.gpo.gov/court03.html) to district courts and courts of appeals (http://vls.law.vill.edu/Locator/fedcourt.html), are online, as are all international courts and international tribunals.

Legal journals from many jurisdictions, covering different topics of international and comparative law, are also online. See RAVE for articles and decisions in Public International Law and European Law (http://www.jura.uni-duesseldorf.de/rave/e/englhome.htm). Other online sources for journals include the

French E-Juris, a legal magazine and awareness service (http://www.ejuris.org/), European Journal of International Law (http://www.ejil.org/), Derecho (http://www.derecho.org/), V-Lex (http://Vlex.com), and many others. See the later section of this chapter called "Online Legal Journals".

Leading newspapers and news agencies of various countries of the world publish enacted laws and recent cases from their countries' high courts. See *The Times* for the UK (http://www.thetimes.co.uk/), *The New York Times* (http://www.nyt.com/) for the USA, *Le Monde* (http://tout.lemonde.fr/) for France, etc. World News Connection (http://wnc. fedworld. gov; about $2,700 per year per one password), a full-text database covering news from the entire world, reports immediately if any new law has been enacted in any jurisdiction of the world. If the official newspaper of that particular country published it, an unofficial English translation of that law is provided. BBC Monitoring (http://www.monitor.bbc.co.uk/intro.htm) assembles radio, television and news agency reports (http://news.bbc.co.uk/) from over 1000 sources in over 140 countries, providing fast, reliable coverage of political and economic news. Bulletins are monitored live, and then translated into English and edited by BBC World Service journalists. Another extraordinary news service is CNN (http://www.cnn.com).

What is the subject area?

Subject databases are a valuable resource. They are the online counterpart of the topical loose leafs and case reporters that cover developments in specific areas of law and practice. The World Trade Organization, the World Bank, the U. N. Convention on Contracts for the International Sale of Goods (CISG) (http://www.jura.uni-freiburg.de/ipr1/cisg/title.htm), and the International Centre for Settlement of Investment Disputes (ICSID) (http://www.worldbank.org/icsid/cases/cases.htm) are current sources for international trade primary legal materials. For copyright laws of the countries of the world in English, French and Spanish, the best online sources are the World Intellectual Property Organization (http://clea.wipo.int/) and UNESCO (http://www.unesco.org/culture/copy/index.html) databases. Domestic health laws and labor laws may be found in the World Health Organization (http://www.who.org) and International Labor Organization (http://www.ilo/org)

databases. Multilateral environmental treaties may be found at CIESIN/ENTRI-Environment Information Resources (http://sedac.ciesin.org/entri); national environmental legislation of European countries is available at the European Environmental Law Home page (http://www.asser.nl/EEL/index6.htm). Primary legal materials on refugees (Executive Committee documents, Statute of the Office of the United Nations High Commissioner for Refugees, Speeches of the High Commissioner, etc.) are published by UNHCR REFWORLD (http://www.unhcr.ch/refworld/). The Food and Agriculture Organization (FAO) (http://www.fao.org) provides relevant statistics for all countries of the world. The fee-based International Bureau of Fiscal Documentation (IBFD)(http://www.ibfd.nl/MAINPg_Framest.htm) database is essential for international and domestic tax research; it contains tax laws, treaties, security treaties (obtained by email), and legal literature. The Organization for Economic Cooperation and Development (http://www.sourceoecd.org) is a major source for full-text articles on taxation, statistics, and economic trends. USA Supreme Court and Constitutional issues are discussed and linked to full-text primary materials at the FindLaw Constitutional Law Center (http://supreme.lp.findlaw.com).

Online Sources for Tracing Laws in Different Jurisdictions and Different Subjects

Guides, pathfinders, Internet indexes

There is a wealth of guides to international and foreign law that can help the legal information specialist. As no library in the world holds all the necessary guides—not to mention full-text primary sources and research tools—online guides are preferable in such situations. They are especially useful in that they discuss both printed and online legal materials, giving the legal researcher the vital jurisdictional framework and linkage to the best online sources.

The Law on the Internet Booklist (International) (http://www.abanet.org/lpm/magazine/booklist.html) from the American Bar Association recommends guides to legal resources on the Internet published in different countries (Italy, the UK, the Netherlands, Germany, etc.). Similar information is available in the guides on foreign and international law published by LLRX.com (http://www.llrx.com/resources4.htm); The Jean Monnet (http://www.law.harvard.edu/programs/JeanMonnet) Working Papers (http://www.jeanmonnetprogram. org/papers/index.html); JURIST (http://jurist.law.pitt.edu); the American Society of International Law Guide to Electronic Resources (http://www.asil.org/info.htm); the Guide to Overseas Laws and Statutes in the National Library of Australia (http://www.nla.gov.au/guides/law), and the Virtual Chase (http://www.vir tualchase.com). Information in the field is also published by periodicals such as *Europe, Database, Searcher, Law Library Journal, the American Society of International Law Newsletter* (http://asil.org/news.htm), the *AALL FCIL News-letter* (http://www.aallnet.org/sis/fcilsis/fcilsis.html), and many others.

The Library of Congress GLIN Home Page (http://lcweb2.loc.gov/law/GLINv1/GLIN.html) contains reliable guides to foreign jurisdiction databases.

WashLaw Web Links (http://www.washlaw.edu/forint/forintmain.html) is a service of the Washburn University School of Law Library. The goal "is to provide links to primary foreign and international legal resources, research aids, and sites useful in conducting research in these areas of the law." The ForInt-Law site can be searched using the search engine; sites linked from this page are arranged alphabetically by subject, author (i.e., the person, government body, organization or institution responsible for the site or for the information contained in the site), country, and title.

The New York University Guide to Foreign and International Legal Databases (http://www.law.nyu.edu/library/foreign_intl/index.html) is described by SOSIG (http://www.sosig.ac.uk/law) as follows : "Hosted by the website of the New York University Law Library, these pages form an annotated listing of a wide range of resources on, and links to, foreign and international law. The resources mentioned in the guide include databases, electronic journals, journal articles, resource guides, and sets of legislation. (...)"

The database of the Bodleian Law Library of the University of Oxford (http://www.bodley.ox.ac.uk/guides/law) incorporates guides to web resources, major subject areas, special collections, a European documentation center, electronic resources, mobile computing, training, and a weekly new books list.

The Meta-Index for Legal Research (http://indexmaster.com) is the best way to find legal treatises. The fee-based database holds an exhaustive collection of indices and tables of contents from thousands of legal treatises. IndexMaster allows the user to view the actual indices and tables of contents.

The Chicago Kent Lawlinks Index (http://www.kentlaw.edu/clc/lrs/lawlinks) and the Index of Law Related Meta Indexes (http://www.kentlaw.edu/clc/lrs/lawlinks/meta.shtml) supply links to legal research guides, full-text databases, and other meta indexes.

The World List: Non-US Law Related Resources for the Internet Users (http://www.law.osaka-u.ac.jp/legal-info/worldlist/worldlst.htm) by Makoto Ibusuki is a useful guide relating to the law and government of over 60 countries.

The World Law Index DIAL (http://www.austlii.edu.au/links/World/) (Development of the Internet for Asian Law) at AUSTLII (http://www.austlii.edu.au) is a project funded by the Asian Development Bank. It offers links to foreign country databases, governments, etc.

ELSweb (http://www2.unimaas.nl/~elsweb/) is a project of the European Law School at Maastricht University in the Netherlands. It consists of an annotated index of legal resources for every European Union country, as does the Guide to European Legal Databases (http://www.llrx.com/features/europenew.htm).

Legal portals and vortals

A portal is a highly selective gateway to information, working as a catalog does for a library. Like a library catalog, a portal is not absolutely comprehensive, nor can it be. A portal comprises acquisition criteria and evaluation standards. Many portals attempt to catalog WWW databases. A *vertical* portal, or "vortal", includes specialty search engines and topical search engines, allowing the user to search within a specific topic. Vortals are dedicated to special fields of interest, with tailored interfaces reflecting a rich assortment of choices and customization in content and layout. Instead of presenting information horizontally, vortals work vertically within a specific field.

Hieros Gamos (http://hg.org/hierosgamos.html) was one of the first legal gateways on the Internet. From the beginning, its object was to be the comprehensive starting point for all law and law-related information. It was the first to offer multiple free listings, email notices, and audio seminars. Its search engine covers about 11,000 law and government databases.

Indiana University School of Law—Bloomington WWW Virtual Library—Law (http://www.law.indiana.edu/v-lib/) was chosen by CERN, originators of the World Wide Web Consortium, to be the Virtual Library host for the subject of law. The World Wide Web Virtual Library is a collection of subject-related databases maintained by institutions throughout the world, each administering a different subject. The material is categorized by organization type (e.g., US Government servers) and by legal topic (e.g., contracts). There is also a list of search tools and other comprehensive sites for law.

FindLAW (http://www.findlaw.com/index.html) is a classic example of a vertical portal (vortal) with more than one search engine. It catalogs resources relating to the law and legal issues. The search engine LawCrawler searches vertically within the legal field. It is focused on law and government, and supplies access to a comprehensive and fast-growing online library of legal resources for use by legal professionals, students, consumers and small businesses. It provides access to full-text databases (USA cases, codes, foreign and international).

SOSIG Law Gateway. The Legal Gateway of the UK (http://www.sosig.ac.uk/law) provides guidance and access to global legal information resources on the Internet. The portal aims to identify and evaluate legal databases offering primary and secondary materials and other items of legal interest. Descriptive records and links are created for legal service sites and specific documents. SOSIG offers separate databases for General Law; United Kingdom Law; Scotland; England and Wales; European Union Law; Other Jurisdictions; International Law, and other categories. SOSIG catalogs databases, and is one of the most sophisticated and complex legal portals in the world. An email with suggestions sent to the webmaster received a response in less than 24 hours.

Institute of Advanced Legal Studies eagle-i service electronic access to global legal information (http://ials.sas.ac.uk/eagle-i.htm) provides links to independently maintained sites throughout the Internet. The categories include databases by country, by international organizations, and by subject; electronic journals and law reports; law dictionaries and directories; news, broadcasting and publishing resources; worldwide academic institutions; and worldwide library catalogs.

Internet Scout Project (http://scout.cs.wisc.edu/index.html) and the Scout Report (http://scout.cs.wisc.edu/report/sr/current/index.html) offer both a news service and a filter to the leading Internet resources based in the USA. ISP cooperates with SOSIG in common projects related to cataloging WWW resources and evaluation.

LLRX.com (http://www.llrx.com) is a unique, free portal dedicated to providing legal professionals with the most up-to-date information on a wide range of Internet legal research and technology-related issues.

Law.Com (http://www.law.com), the former LawJournal Extra and CounselConnect, is a fee-based comprehensive legal vortal containing news, analysis, commentaries, and links to courts, cases, and statutes, mainly for common law jurisdictions.

V-Lex (http://vlex.com), formerly Derecho, is a legal vortal for the Spanish and Portuguese-speaking world. It provides access to legislative news, links to databases (http://vlex.com/es/bbdd/), codes, legislation, official gazettes, legal journals, and administrative legal materials for Spain, Argentina, Brazil, Chile, Costa Rica, Cuba, Ecuador, Mexico, Peru, Puerto Rico, and Venezuela .

For more legal portals and vortals see Foreign Databases—Collections at New York University Law Library (http://www.law.nyu.edu/library/foreign_intl/foreign.html).

Online encyclopedias

Martindale-Hubbel Lawyers Locator (http://www.marhub.com) and Britannica (http://www.eb.com) or (http://www. brit annica.com) can be searched regarding any question of legal assistance and law. Searching Britannica for "England legal system" I retrieved excellent commentaries on "Common Law—Comparisons of English, American, and Commonwealth Law."

JURIST—the Legal Education Network (http://www.jurist.law.pitt.edu/) has some features resembling an encyclopedia. Searching JURIST from the main menu search box, you retrieve all entries in the database containing, for example, "Spain". If you go to "Researching—World Law", a file similar to an encyclopedia entry (http://jurist.law.pitt.edu/world/spain.htm) will be displayed.

The Internet Library for Librarians (http://www.itcompany.com/inforetriever/ency.htm#GENERAL) contains links to many available online encyclopedias.

International digests

WHO International Digest of Heath Legislation (http://www-nt.who.int/idhl/) contains a selection of national and international health legislation. Texts are summarized in English or mentioned by title. Where possible, links are provided to full texts of legislation. Official publications and other documents forwarded by Member States constitute the principal sources of the Digest.

International Labor Organization (http://www.ilo.org/public/english/index.htm): NATLEX (http://natlex.ilo.org/) is the ILO's database of national laws on labor, social security, and related human rights issues. Abstracts and full text are both provided in English. When the full text is not available, citations to official gazettes are provided.

UNESCO's national legislation database in English on Copyright and Neighboring Rights (http://www.unesco.org/culture/copy/index.html) gives free access to national legislation regularly communicated to UNESCO by Member States.

ASILEX (http://www.asil.org/asilex.htm) is a searchable database of ASIL publications, including the *American Journal of International Law* and *International Legal Materials* from 1990 onwards. It is a very useful tool for finding clues (bibliographic records) on international and foreign issues. A weekly digest is mailed to subscribers (see *International Law In Brief* archived at http://www.asil.org/ilibindx.htm).

Many databases email weekly digests to subscribers. Among them are the International Court of Justice and PICT—The Project on International Courts and Tribunals (http://www.pict-pcti.org/home.html). PICT archives its digest under NEWS (http://www.pict-pcti.org/news/news.html).

Some national domestic databases provide the same service. An example is the electronic weekly newsletter of the Romanian legal database DSCNet (www.dsclex.ro) named DscLex Promote (in both Romanian and English).

Yearbooks

Not too many yearbooks are free, but you may find some of them (or at least their tables of contents) online. These include Harvard Jean Monnet Table of Contents Service of the *Yearbook of European Law* (http://www.law.harvard.edu/programs/JeanMonnet/TOC/art438.html) and the New Zealand Official Yearbook on the Web 1999 (http://www.stats.govt.nz/domino/external/pasfull/pasfull.nsf/web/Yearbook+New+Zealand+Official+Yearbook+On+The+Web+1999?open).

News sources

Dialog@carl (http://dialog.carl.org) is a fee-based database offering access to nearly 300 commercial databases. The files come from content providers and cover nearly every subject area. Almost 60% of the database is in full text . Dialog@carl offers three subscription options that allow a library to select the database that best suits its patrons' information needs: the Basic Collection, containing approximately 300 multidisciplinary databases, including the News Collection; the News Collection consisting of nearly 115 newspaper/newswire databases; and the Target Collection, a subset of 27 databases from the Basic Collection.

The Universal Database of Russian Newspapers (UDB-COM) (http://news.eastview.com) is a fee-based database providing direct access to the full-text files of over 30 of the most influential Russian newspapers. Within hours of their availability in Russian cities, articles are accessible online for browsing, searching and analyzing. Over 450,000 articles are available to date.

Global Newsbank (http://www.newsbank.com) covers news from 1985 to the present. Fee-based, it contains information from newspapers, newswires, business journals and periodicals, as well as historical and scholarly documents. Information is delivered to schools and libraries via the Internet, on CD-ROM, and microfiche.

The LEXIS News database is among the best sources in finding news about legal developments around the world. All important domestic newspapers, in the vernacular, are there. In February 2001, Lexis/Nexis launched the Major World Newspapers (Library / File: NEWS; MWN), a collection of 50 full-text key national newspapers from around the world, generally regarded by the reading public as those giving the most comprehensive and reliable coverage of any topic, whether local, national, or international. However, most domestic newspapers may be found on the Internet free of charge. Every country has a main newspaper comparable to *The New York Times* or *The Washington Post* discussing or publishing important laws or landmark cases. CNN (http://www.cnn.com), and all news agencies on the Internet (such as ABCNews.com and Bloom berg.com) keep the legal information specialist informed with legal news coming from foreign governments, international organizations, domestic courts, and other sources.

World News Connection (http://wnc.fedworld.gov/) is a fee-based database providing news and full-text articles in unofficial English translations from all regions of the world.

Listservs

I recommend the discussion lists hosted by CIESIN/SEDAC (http://listhost.ciesin.org), Euro-Lex (http://www.listserv.gmd.de/archives/euro-lex.html), and Law Lists Info (http://www.lib.uchicago.edu/~llou/lawlists/info.html). These sites help legal professionals from all over the world choose the best listservs to subscribe to. Listservs' archives and discussions lists are among the most constructive practices in the cyberlegal culture. JURIST—The Legal Information Network (http://www.jurist.law.pitt.edu/index.htm) is also a sort of listserv, with its news service and collection of guides. BigEar: Current Legal Resources on the Net (http://barratry.law.cornell.edu/notify/buzz.html) "listens" to a variety of law-related mailing lists and newsgroups. BigEar listens to LAWSRC-L, including postings from the Virtual Law Library submissions robot, NET-LAWYERS, TEKNOIDS, LAW-LIB, LEGAL-WEBMASTERS, and INT-LAW.

Indexes to foreign and international primary and secondary sources

As I mentioned earlier in this chapter, GLIN (http://lcweb2.loc.gov/law/GLINv1/GLIN.html) is a spectacular resource for 50 jurisdictions as of the year 2001. Its index is free. The actual database is available in full text only to participating governments, supporting organizations, and libraries sustaining GLIN. Global Legal Information Network locates the law and provides an English abstract and the official citation of the document, usually from domestic official gazettes. Here is an example of how the GLIN "linking" works in the cyberlegal research process.

I was asked to locate Lithuania's ratification protocol to the European Convention for the Protection of Human Rights and Fundamental Freedoms Concerning the Abolition of the Death Penalty of 1999. The patron wanted to verify the accuracy of title and date of ratification, and also hoped to get the full text of the document in the vernacular. Knowing that Lithuania is a GLIN participant, I went to the database, logged in as guest, selected Lithuania from the country list, consulted the GLIN Thesaurus, and found CONVENTIONS as the searching word. I retrieved, along with other records, the following information:

Law Summary Display

Country: Lithuania **Title:** **Summary ID:** 86414

Instrument

Class: Law **Number:**VIII-1250 **Issuance Date:**22 June 1999

Publication

Title: Valstybes zinios **Number:**61 **Date:**14 July 1999 **Publication Specifics:**

Summary

Law No.VIII-1250 "On Ratification of Protocol No.6 to the European Convention for the Protection of Human Rights and Fundamental Freedoms concerning the Abolition of the Death Penalty". Ratifies Protocol No.6 signed by the Republic of Lithuania on 18/01/1999 at Strasbourg. Text of the Protocol not included (1 provision, p.4).

Subject Terms

Conventions
Human rights
Criminal law
Penalties
Capital punishment

The second step was to go to the Lithuanian Parliament Seimas of the Republic of Lithuania database (http://www.lrs.lt/inter/plsql/www_viewer.home?p_kalb_id=2). I chose the English version to find the entry for Legal Documents. Then I selected and searched Legal Acts of Lithuania. I searched by the law number given by GLIN, VIII-1250. I retrieved from Document Search Number the bibliographical record I needed:

Search Conditions
Number: VIII-1250
Date: since 01/01/1883 *till* 12/31/2001

***Documents found*: 1**

1. Dėl Europos þmogaus teisiø ir pagrindiniø laisviø apsaugos konvencijos 6 protokolo dėl mirties bausmės panaikinimo ratifikavimo ĮSTATYMAS
(Seimas of the Republic of Lithuania|Law|VIII-1250|06/22/1999|Enters into Force since 07/14/1999|Valstybės þinios'1999 No.61-1975)

New Search

© Information Technologies department of Seimas of the Republic of Lithuania.
Comments and suggestions - webadm@lrs.lt

This led me to the full text in the vernacular.

NATLAW—The Inter-American Database (http://www.natlaw.com/index.htm) is a full-text database offering free access to search the records for Latin American countries. For example, if you search for Codigo Civil Federal for Mexico you retrieve all bibliographic records related to these Keywords. A password is required to see the full text of the non-consolidated code:

CODIGO CIVIL
Cómav25: Código Civil de la Federación prmx2.htm, May 29 1997
CODIGO CIVIL PARA EL DISTRITO FEDERAL EN MATERIA COMUN Y PARA TODA LA REPUBLICA EN MATERIA FEDERAL
CODIGO Civil para el Distrito Federal en Materia Común y para toda la República en Materia Federal.
REFORMAS AL CODIGO CIVIL PARA EL DISTRITO FEDERAL EN MATERIA COMUN Y PARA TODA LA REPUBLICA EN MATERIA FEDERAL
Código Civil: parte 3o. de 4 partes, May 29 1997
CODIGO CIVIL PARA EL DISTRITO FEDERAL EN MATERIA COMUN Y PARA TODA LA
CODIGO Civil para el Distrito Federal en Materia Común y para toda la República en Materia Federal.
REFORMAS AL CODIGO CIVIL PARA EL DISTRITO FEDERAL EN MATERIA COMUN Y PARA
Código Civil: parte 2o. de 4 partes, May 29 1997
CODIGO CIVIL PARA EL DISTRITO FEDERAL EN MATERIA COMUN Y PARA TODA LA
CODIGO Civil para el Distrito Federal en Materia Común y para toda la República en Materia Federal.
REFORMAS AL CODIGO CIVIL PARA EL DISTRITO FEDERAL EN MATERIA COMUN Y PARA
Código Civil: parte 4o. de cuatro partes, May 29 1997
CODIGO CIVIL PARA EL DISTRITO FEDERAL EN MATERIA COMUN Y PARA TODA LA
CODIGO Civil para el Distrito Federal en Materia Común y para toda la República en Materia Federal.
REFORMAS AL CODIGO CIVIL PARA EL DISTRITO FEDERAL EN MATERIA COMUN Y PARA
Código Civil: parte 1o. de cuatro partes, May 29 1997
CODIGO CIVIL PARA EL DISTRITO FEDERAL EN MATERIA COMUN Y PARA TODA LA
CODIGO Civil para el Distrito Federal en Materia Común y para toda la República en Materia Federal.
REFORMAS AL CODIGO CIVIL PARA EL DISTRITO FEDERAL EN MATERIA COMUN Y PARA

Here is a sample taken from the first record:

Copyright 1997

InterAm Database

National Law Center for Inter-American Free Trade

26 de mayo de 1928

Diario Oficial de la Federación (México)

CODIGO CIVIL PARA EL DISTRITO FEDERAL EN MATERIA COMUN Y PARA TODA LA REPUBLICA EN MATERIA FEDERAL

TEXTO VIGENTE

El C. Presidente Constitucional de la República se ha servido dirigirme el decreto que sigue:

"PLUTARCO ELIAS CALLES, Presidente Constitucional de los Estados Unidos Mexicanos, a sus habitantes, sabed:

Que en uso de la facultad que ha tenido a bien conferirme el H. Congreso de la Unión por Decretos de 7 de enero y de 6 de diciembre de 1926 y de 3 de enero de 1928, expido el siguiente

CODIGO Civil para el Distrito Federal en Materia Común y para toda la República en Materia Federal.

Disposiciones preliminares

Artículo 1.

At the end of the document are given all amendments:

REFORMAS AL CODIGO CIVIL PARA EL DISTRITO FEDERAL EN MATERIA COMUN Y PARA TODA LA REPUBLICA EN MATERIA FEDERAL

REFORMAS: 34 PUBLICACION: 26 DE MAYO DE 1928

Reformas aparecidas en el Diario Oficial de la Federación en: 31-III-1938, 20-I-1940, 14-I-1948, 27-II-1951, 9-I-1954, 15-XII-1954, 31-XII-1954, 30-XII-1966, 17-I-1970, 17-I-1970, 28-I-1970, 24-III-1971, 4-I-1973, 14-III-1973, 28-XII-1973, 23-XII-1974, 31-XII-1974, 22-XII-1975, 30-XII-1975, 29-VI-1976, 29-XII-1976, 3-I-1979, 31-XII-1982, 27-XII-1983, 27-XII-1983, 7-II-1985, 10-I-1986, 7-I-1988, 7-I-1988, 23-VII-1992, 21-VII-1993, 23-IX-1993, 6-I-1994, 10-I-1994, 24-V-1996.

Copyright 1997 Inter-Am Database

My library has a subscription to NATLAW, so in order to see the last amendment I was able to go back a few screens to the *Diario Oficial* in full text from November 1994. I also remembered that InfoJus (http://www.juridicas.unam.mx/infjur/leg)—Legis lación federal—contains a consolidated version of all Mexico's codes and recent laws in full Spanish text (free access).

SCADPlus (http://europa.eu.int/scadplus) is the free bibliographical database of European Community legislation, official publications, articles, and recent documents on the activities of the EU. To locate documents on the subject "electronic signature", I chose General Search; Words from title or abstract ; Title and Abstract; and Term "electronic" With term "signature".

Here is one of the records I retrieved:

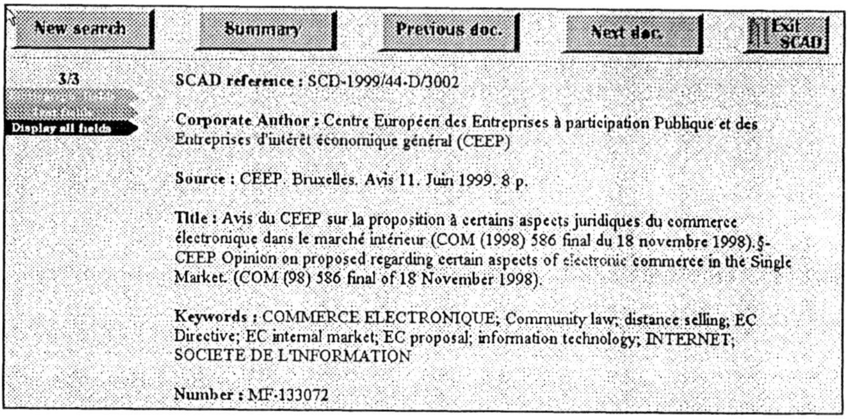

However, pursuant to a reorganization of European Commission services, SCAD is no longer being updated as of March 1, 2001. The Commission's Central Library has taken over responsibility for articles from periodicals, which are now indexed in the ECLAS database. This transfer will probably take some months. In the meantime, sources, subjects, and language cover will remain unchanged, so that all articles can be found in the same database. Links are being created from the Central Library's homepage to SCAD and vice versa, and SCAD will remain available at least until the end of the transfer. Responsibility for the other sectors of SCAD, including SCADPlus, has been assigned to the Commission's Press and Communication Service

A search in Pre-Lex (http://europa.eu.int/prelex/apcnet.cfm?CL=en) for COM (98) 586 final of 18 November 1998 provided the history of the document and a Celex Number (NUMERO CELEX) link that brought me to the full text of the document. COM documents may be found as tif files on EUDOR (European Union Document Delivery Service, http://www.eudor.com/):

18-11-1998	**Adoption by Commission**
Primarily responsible	DG15
Associated	DG01; DG02; DG03; DG04; DG05; DG07; DG10; DG12; DG13; DG19; DG21; DG23; DG24; Secretariat-General
Mandatory consultation	Economic and Social Committee
Addressee for formal act	Council; European Parliament
Documents:	COM/1998/586/FINAL Bulletin/1998/11/ 1.2.24 C4/1999/20/ OJ C/1999/30/ 4
Procedures:	Codecision procedure
Type of file:	Proposal for a Directive
Legal basis:	100aCE ; 57,2CE , 66CE
NUMERO CELEX	51998PC0586

READEX (http://infoweb.newsbank.com) is a fee-based index to United Nations documents and publications. Indexing of the bilateral and multilateral treaties in the UN Treaty Series is one of its unique features. Full-text resolutions from the General Assembly, the Security Council, and the Economic and Social Council are added to the bibliographic citations.

Current Legal Information (www.sweetandmaxwell.co.uk/digital/cli/interneto/index.cfm) by Sweet and Maxwell is a fee-based resource extensively used by European scholars. CLI Complete Service incorporates the Legal Journals Index, Financial Journals Index and CLI Current Law Service (containing the BADGER Grey Paper Index, the CL Case Citator, and the CL Legislation Citator).

Index to Legal Periodicals and Books (http://wilson web2.hwwilson.com) is a fee-based bibliographic database, covering mostly the common law area; it cites articles from legal periodicals, and indexes law books published since 1993. Index to Legal Periodicals and Books (http://www. hwwilson.com/newDDs/WZ.htm) covers all areas of jurispru-dence, including recent court decisions, new legislation, and original scholarship. The above-cited URL (http://www.hw wilson.com/newDDs/WZ.htm) lists sample searches that could be helpful for working with the database.

Index to Foreign Legal Periodicals (http://eureka.hudson.rlg.org) ; fee-based; published by The Research Libraries Group (http://www.rlg.org/toc.html) is considered the leading source for international and foreign legal research. Multilingual and multinational, the Index to Foreign Legal Periodicals (http://www.rlg.org/cit-flp.html) indexes articles and book reviews appearing in over 500 legal periodicals. Also analyzed are the contents of approximately 80 individually published collections of legal essays, festschriften, mélanges, and congressional reports. Coverage extends from 1985 to present. As it covers legal literature mostly outside the common law area, the index has different subject headings than Index to Legal Periodicals. Searchers must be aware of these implications; that is why I have always recommended keyword searches as a starting point until the right record is retrieved. For example, in ILP "prostitution" is a subject heading. In IFLP, that search will not retrieve anything; as IFLP reflects the conceptual structure of civil law, the subject heading for this law topic is "offenses against morals". A legal professional searching IFLP for a subject such as "administrative law" will retrieve a great deal of bibliographic records, but nothing will come up using the same subject in ILP. In civil law countries there are civil and administrative courts with parallel procedure, whereas in common law countries parallel courts do not exist. This example shows how important it is to be familiar with legal jurisdictional structures.

Index to Canadian Legal Literature (ICLL in Quicklaw America) (http://quiclawamerica.com) is an excellent fee-based source for Canadian secondary sources.

Legal Journals Index (LJI in Westlaw) is focused on United Kingdom secondary sources. The LJI database indexes articles from legal journals published in the United Kingdom and Europe and journals covering topics pertaining to the laws of the European Community and of its Member States.

Legal Resource Index (Electronic Companion to Current Law Index) (LRI in Westlaw) contains indices to articles that have appeared in journals from the United States, Canada, Great Britain, New Zealand and Australia.

LegalTrac (http://infotrac.galegroup.com/) by Gale Group is a fee-based major source for law reviews and bar association journals. It is an index to more than 900 law journals, newsletters, and legal newspapers published from 1980 to the present, with full text of articles from selected law journals. LegalTrac corresponds to the print Current Law Index, and to the Legal Resource Index on Westlaw.

UNIQUE (http://www.un.org/Depts/dhl/unique/index.html) (UN Info Quest) is a free ready reference file created by the

Dag Hammarskjöld Library to respond to frequently asked questions. It is designed to provide quick access to document symbols/sales numbers for UN materials (from 1946 to present). It does not give full bibliographic details, nor does it replace existing bibliographic databases (UNBISnet, UNBIS Plus on CD-ROM). UNIQUE focuses upon documents and publications of a recurrent nature: annual/sessional reports of committees/commissions; monographic series; journals; annual publications; reports periodically/irregularly issued; reports of major conferences; and statements in the General Debate.

Seeking a report on the assistance mission for Rwanda (UNAMIR), I searched simply for: report Rwanda. The retrieved files contained citation to UN documents. To find them in full text, I went to the UN database—UN Documentation Center (http://www.un.org/documents/).

UNBIS (http://unbisnet.un.org) is a free catalogue of UN publications and documentation indexed by the United Nations Dag Hammarskjöld Library and the Library of the UN Office at Geneva. It is widely used for its voting records and index to speeches.

Online legal journals

EBSCO Information Services (http://www-us.ebsco.com/home/default.asp) provides serials access and worldwide delivery through subscription. EBSCO Online: Electronic Journal Access and Management (http://www-us.ebsco.com/ess/Services/online.stm) offers simplified identification, access, acquisition and management of hundreds of full-text electronic journals.

Electronic Legal Journals (http://info.library.yorku.ca/depts/law/linksJournal.htm) at the York University Libraries provides an alphabetical listing of full text e-journal lists compiled by different law schools.

Hieros Gamos (with German, French, Spanish, Italian interfaces) provides links to free-of- charge legal and law-related journals (http://hg.org/hierosgamos.html), including newsletters and bulletins (abstracts, tables of contents only, or full text).

Oxford Journals (http://www3.oup.co.uk/jnls) provides access to free-of-charge tables of contents and, through subscription, access to the full texts of 170 currently published journals, covering a wide range of academic disciplines.

The fee-based Northern Light (http://www.northernlight.com) contains about 7,100 full-text publications. Citations, summaries and Web results are free. The full text of articles is delivered for a modest price.

JSTOR (http://www.jstor.org) is a fee-based database containing backfiles of 117 journal titles from 15 academic disciplines, a collection numbering nearly 5,000,000 pages, and growing.

Legal Journals by Hein Online (a retrospective collection of major law reviews in full text) (http://heinonline.org) contains early years of legal journals (for example, *Yale Law Journal* from 1891 to 1925). A few of them are up to 2000. New journals are added on a regular basis. It is fee-based.

Proquest.umi.com (http://www.bellhowell.infolearning.com/proquest) is one of the world's largest collections of information, including articles from over 8,000 publications. Most are summarized, but many are in full text, full image format. It is fee-based.

ScienceDirect (http://www.sciencedirect.com/) is a database of mixed abstract and full-text documents, with in-depth coverage across a wide spectrum of disciplines. To view specific journal titles, go to the ScienceDirect Web site and click on Tour Journals if you are a guest. If you are already a ScienceDirect subscriber, click on Journals.

UnCover Reveal (http://uncweb.carl.org/reveal) is a fee-based automated current awareness service that delivers the tables of contents of journals by e-mail. Reveal creates search strategies for "favorite" topics. Keyword or author searches result in a list of individual article citations. Articles may be ordered from UnCover by e-mail or by fax.

UnCoverWeb (http://uncweb.carl.org/) is a fee-based database of current article information taken from over 18,000 journals in many disciplines. UnCover contains brief descriptive information for over 8,800,000 articles which have appeared since Fall 1988. Recently, the combined database

Ingenta/uncover (http://ingenta.com/home/login/fs_ingen tanews. htm) offers access to over 20,000 scholarly journals.

The fee-based Westlaw (http://www.westlaw.com) and Lexis (http://www.lexis-nexis.com) containthe richest collection of tull-text electronic legal journals in the world. The coverage starts in the late '70s, but it differs for almost every journal. Comprehensive descriptions of holdings can be found at the Westlaw and Lexis main entry points.

Dictionaries

The former database 50 Dictionaries moved recently to YourDictionary.com (http://www.yourdictionary.com). It includes language dictionaries (English, Spanish, French, German, Japanese, Chinese, Hindi, Arabic, Russian, etc.), multilingual dictionaries, and law dictionaries (http://www.yourdictionary.com/diction5.html#law). Merriam-Webster Online (http://www.webster.com) has a free interface. There are also many law dictionaries at the Institute of Advanced Legal Studies (http://ials.sas.ac.uk) under Law dictionaries (http://ials.sas.ac.uk/Diction.htm).

Eurodicautom (dictionary for EU legislation) (http://euro dic.ip.lu/cgi-bin/edicbin/EuroDicWWW.pl) is a friendly web query system for words/phrases/abbreviations, giving legal equivalents in eleven official EU languages.

French Private Law Dictionary (Dictionnaire du Droit Privé), by Serge Braudo (http://juripole.u-nancy.fr/braudo/dictionnaire/cadre.html) is an excellent tool for French legal research.

International Law Dictionary and Directory (http://au gust1.com/pubs/dict/index.shtml) by Ray August provides definitions of words and phrases used in private and public international law with cross-references to related words and phrases.

Oxford English Dictionary (http://dictionary.oed.com), which is fee-based, contains as of February 2001 the complete A to Z sequence of the second edition, its three-volume additions series, and also draft material from the revision program, which represents the latest progress towards the third edition.

Library catalogs

ECLAS(http://europa.eu.int/eclas/) is the Catalog of the European Commission Libraries. The database is free. ECLAS contains hyperlinks to the full text of official documents, accessed via Celexplus with the Celex Numdoc/Docnum. Here is an example of an ECLAS search (I specified "Title only"; "electronic signature"), and I retrieved:

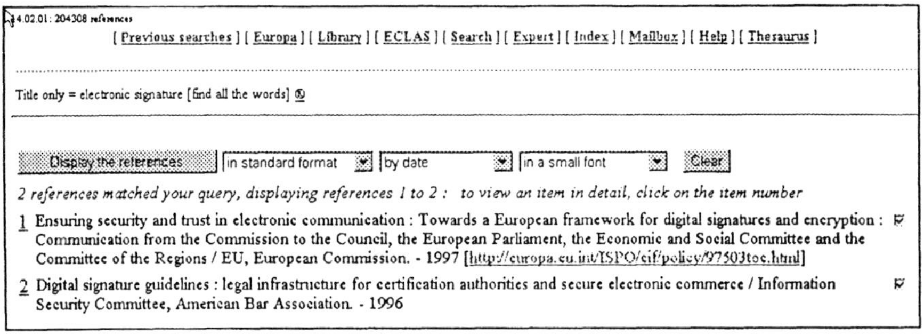

14.02.01 : 204308 references

[Previous searches] [Europa] [Library] [ECLAS] [Search] [Expert] [Index] [Mailbox] [Help] [Thesaurus]

Title only = electronic signature [find all the words]

Display the references | in standard format | by date | in a small font | Clear

2 references matched your query, displaying references 1 to 2 : to view an item in detail, click on the item number

1 Ensuring security and trust in electronic communication : Towards a European framework for digital signatures and encryption : Communication from the Commission to the Council, the European Parliament, the Economic and Social Committee and the Committee of the Regions / EU, European Commission. - 1997 [http://europa.eu.int/ISPO/eif/policy/97503toc.html]

2 Digital signature guidelines : legal infrastructure for certification authorities and secure electronic commerce / Information Security Committee, American Bar Association. - 1996

If you search using "electronic" in the Title/Author/Subject field, the results are more impressive. Links to hypertext documents are present. Records from online journals are delivered, such as this one:

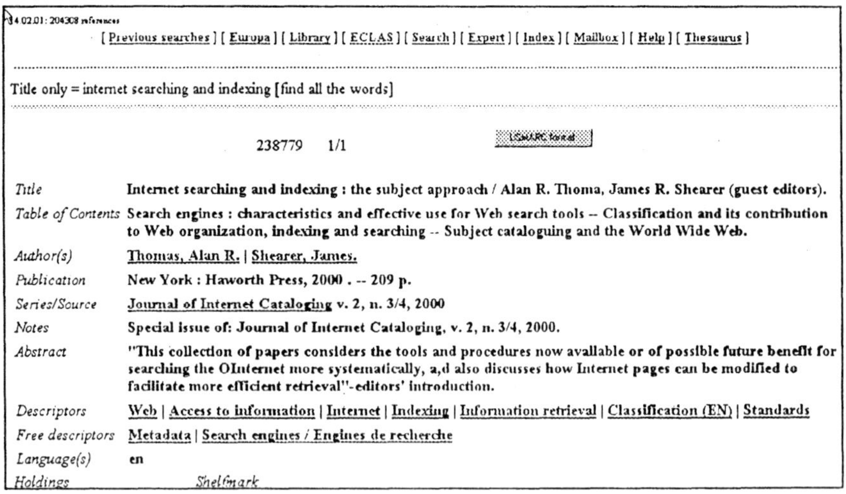

14.02.01 : 204308 references

[Previous searches] [Europa] [Library] [ECLAS] [Search] [Expert] [Index] [Mailbox] [Help] [Thesaurus]

Title only = internet searching and indexing [find all the words]

238779 1/1

Title	**Internet searching and indexing : the subject approach / Alan R. Thoma, James R. Shearer (guest editors).**
Table of Contents	**Search engines : characteristics and effective use for Web search tools -- Classification and its contribution to Web organization, indexing and searching -- Subject cataloguing and the World Wide Web.**
Author(s)	**Thomas, Alan R. | Shearer, James.**
Publication	**New York : Haworth Press, 2000 . -- 209 p.**
Series/Source	**Journal of Internet Cataloging v. 2, n. 3/4, 2000**
Notes	**Special issue of: Journal of Internet Cataloging, v. 2, n. 3/4, 2000.**
Abstract	**"This collection of papers considers the tools and procedures now available or of possible future benefit for searching the OInternet more systematically, a,d also discusses how Internet pages can be modified to facilitate more efficient retrieval"-editors' introduction.**
Descriptors	**Web | Access to information | Internet | Indexing | Information retrieval | Classification (EN) | Standards**
Free descriptors	**Metadata | Search engines / Engines de recherche**
Language(s)	**en**
Holdings	*Shelfmark*

"Gabriel" Gateway to Europe's National Libraries (http://www.konbib.nl/gabriel/en/union.html) contains the National Union Catalogues maintained by Europe's National Libraries (Austria, Czech Republic and Slovakia, Denmark, France, Germany, The Netherlands, the UK, and others). Gates to similar catalogs are The British Library (http://portico.bl.uk) and the HYTELNET Library Catalogs (http://www.lights.com/hytelnet/sites1.html) maintained by Peter Scot.

RLIN–The Research Libraries Group (http://www.rlg.org) is a membership database of over 160 university libraries, national libraries, archives, historical societies, and other institution catalogs around the world.

OCLC (http://www.oclc.org/oclc/menu/home1.htm) is a nonprofit, membership, library computer service and research organization dedicated to the public purposes of furthering access to the world's information and reducing information costs. Searches are fee-based. The WorldCat database (http://www.oclc.org/oclc/about/brief.htm) and other OCLC products and services make this a tool of worldwide librarianship. OCLC Europe Libraries (http://www.oclc.org/oclc/europe/libs.htm) and OCLC Latin America Libraries (http://www.oclc.org/america_latina/new_libs.htm) give legal information specialists the opportunity to search almost all the world's online catalogs.

HELVETICAT (http://www.snl.ch/helveticat/english) is the online catalog of the Swiss National Library. The library's task in this project is "to preserve this material for posterity and make it available to the public. We use the term 'Helvetica' to denote the entire literary production of the country stored on all kinds of information media (handwritten manuscripts, printed, digitized, in pictorial form or as sound documents), all works published abroad with a bearing on Switzerland, its population, its past, present and future works (including translations of them) by Swiss authors. The term 'Helvetica' also includes all publications of associations and official bodies, musical scores, daily newspapers, dissertations and even telephone and address directories." The total number of documents is around 4 million, and growing. Total shelf length is currently more than 40 kilometers.

COPAC (http://www.copac.ac.uk) provides unified access to the catalogues of some of the largest university research libraries in the UK and Ireland. COPAC is a union catalogue which gives free access to the merged online catalogues of members of the Consortium of University Research Libraries (CURL). There are 23 Members of CURL, of whom 19 are current contributors to COPAC. The remaining CURL libraries' catalogues are in the process of loading. COPAC records represent documents dating from c. 1100 AD onwards, in many languages. A variety of materials is included, and some records display links to the document in full text.

KATALOG DER UB KARLSRUHE UNIVERSITÄTSBIBLIOTHEK (http://www.ubka.uni-karlsruhe.de/hylib/suchmaske.html) assembles 23 online catalogs from Germany, including university, court, and institutes online catalogs. The searcher must select the specific catalog.

Library consortia

The border between shared catalogs or union catalogs and library consortia is hard to define. Many of the European and US catalogs discussed above originated as projects initiated by library consortia and developed as ways of sharing resources and ensuring survival in the electronic environment. This trend is growing. Consortia are located on all continents, but I will list here only a few, based in the USA. A researcher working in a library that is a member of a powerful consortia enjoys access to more research tools and discounted databases, as well as research privileges such as interlibrary loan services.

The Center for Research Libraries (CRL) (http://www.crl.uchicago.edu) is an international not-for-profit consortium of colleges, universities and libraries that makes available scholarly research resources to users everywhere. CRL is governed by the major research libraries of North America and is funded by fees, grants and contributions. Its catalog (http://wwwcrl.uchicago.edu/info/crlcat.htm) includes over 500,000 records, virtually all of the bibliographic and authority records in CRL's cataloged collections.

The Research Library Group (RLG) (http://www.rlg.org/rlg.html) is a not-for-profit membership corporation devoted to the mission of "improving the access to information that supports research and learning." Founded in 1974 and incorporated in 1975 by Columbia, Harvard, and Yale universities and The New York Public Library, "RLG became and is today a pioneer in developing cooperative solutions to the problems that research collections and their users face in the acquisition, delivery, and preservation of information". RLG is an international member alliance including universities and colleges, national libraries, archives, historical societies, museums, independent research collections, and public libraries.

The New England Law Library Consortium (NELLCO) (http://www.nellco.org) assembles 25 libraries in a cooperative sharing of resources, pooling "our strengths to add to and enhance the essential services and vitality of our member organizations."

Subject-oriented databases

Human rights, environment, international criminal law, treaties, international trade, international organizations (WTO, NAFTA, MERCOSUR, EU, Council of Europe, etc.), are discussed in the Appendix—International and Foreign Law Databases.

Foreign Collections and International Implications

Finding domestic cases or laws with international implications—e.g., a human rights decision of a foreign constitutional court, or the implementation act of a multilateral treaty on the domestic level—presents a major challenge. In Germany, landmark decisions are published by courts and available at German Case Law (GLAW, http://www.uniwuerz burg.de/dfr) in full text, sometimes with an English abstract. Some countries—e.g., Lithuania, Russia, and Ukraine—have bilingual databases, but English translations from, e.g., France, Spain, or Italy are virtually nonexistent.

THOMAS (http://thomas.loc.gov), for example, is an excellent source of US treaty information, but without interfaces in other languages. Go to the Congressional Record Index. Select Congress; Browse; List of Major Topics; T—Treaties and Agreements. You will find subheadings such as agreements, lists, and memoranda, with hypertext links to full texts of everything. You can also choose Browse (List of all index topics) and select a subject. For Australia, the Australian Treaties Library (http://www.austlii.edu.au/au/other/dfat/) contains multilateral and bilateral treaties in full text, including treaties not yet in force (http://www.austlii.edu.au/au/other/dfat/treaties/notinforce). For France, the Ministry of Foreign Affairs database called BASE PACT (http://www.doc.diplomatie.gouv.fr/pacte) contains all multilateral and bilateral treaties in force or concluded in the past in full French text. The South African Cyber Treaty Series (http://home.earthlink.net/~apronto/treaties/trindex.htm) by Arnold Pronto gives a comprehensive and and up-to-date list of the treaties South Africa has entered into, with, where possible, links to full text as well as to ratification information.

Almost all governments and international organizations have a presence on the WWW. In some cases, such as the USA (http://www.gpo.gov), Australia (http://www.austlii.au), and Canada (http://www.droit.umontreal.ca), these sites are very sophisticated and complete. But this is not the rule. I was happy when, for example, I saw that the Italian Ministry of Justice (http://www.giustizia.it/index.htm) had posted an Index to Supreme Court cases, as well as cases in full text from 1999 (http://www.giustizia.it/cassazione/giurisprudenza/giuris.html), as the Italian Supreme Court database is expensive and difficult to manage. Although the presence of a foreign government in the cyberlegal culture may sometimes be nothing more than an online library, a national newspaper, or a simple interface describing the legal system, such a source could contain a thread leading to the required information. You don't always have to subscribe to an expensive service to get the information you need.

USA jurisdiction information is increasingly available in government databases and awareness services on the Internet such as LLRX (http://www.llrx.com), FindLaw (http://www.findlaw.com/index.html) or the THOMAS (http://thomas.loc.gov/) or GOP (http://www.access.gpo.gov/su_docs/gils/index.html) databases. However, if many great Web resources are for free, many others are not. LOISLaw (http://www. loislaw.com), VersusLaw (http://versuslaw.com), and Jurisline (http://www.jurisline.com) offer value-added content by subscription or pay-as-you-go credit card. Worldwide, a developing network of government document sources parallel to Westlaw and Lexis is the most important ongoing development in the global legal documentation system. Unless the legal specialist needs value-added features such as shepardizing or code annotations, such free databases often have the answer to a research question.

In France there is a growing trend to provide legislation free of charge, as can be seen in government databases such as Admifrance (http://www.admifrance.gouv.fr/cgi-bin/multitel/admifrance/accueil) and Legifrance (http://www.legifrance.gouv.fr/). The latter contains the Constitution of 4 Octobre 1958; Declaration des droits de l'Homme et du Citoyen of 1789; the Preambule of 1946; *Journal Officiel*, codes, and links to all courts. However, if a law office or a library decides that access to French materials is necessary and that updating, case law and legal commentaries are vital, a subscription to Jurifrance (http://www.jurifrance.com/) is advisable. The same is true for Austria, comparing the free-of-charge Republic Oesterreich Bundeskanzleramt Rechtsinformatiossystem RIS (http://www.ris.bka.gv.at/) with the fee-based Die Rechtsdatenbank RDB (http: //www.rdb.at/).

As of this date, UK legislation is not consolidated. The UK Acts are online in full text on the government legislation database from 1988, but without amendments. In the United Kingdom, where the free-of-charge databases of statutes and cases are fragmentary and not updated at all, other services are required to supplement the missing information. These include the Court Service (http://www.courtservice.gov.uk), Smith Bernal's Casetrack (http://www.smithbernal.com/), Butterworths LEXIS Direct (http://butterworths.com), Westlaw (http://www.westlaw.com), and Lawtel (http://www.lawtel.co.uk/). Similarly, EC free databases do not link or update all judgements, legislation, or cases, so CELEX (http://europa.eu.int/celex/) is usually the right choice if there is a significant need for European Union legal materials. Help in locating EU materials may be found on SCAD (http://europa.eu.int/scad plus/) or ECLAS (http://europa.eu.int/eclas/). Again, what is missing and needed in civil law countries is online legal literature in full text. The skyrocketing cost of printed services, as well as the difficulty in dealing with foreign vendors, is compelling libraries to rely on online databases, both free and fee-based. Although many valuable legal documents are available for free, most countries (including Russia and Japan, and to a large extent Spain, Italy, Germany, Argentina, and many others) do not offer much reliable information free of charge.

The legal information professional gets substantive information quickly, and in the requested format, with subscriptions to fee-based databases. But this can be costly, especially if a database is not comprehensive. In any case, however, the database may be used as an updating tool for the printed collection, which does not make legal research cheaper and easier. For major academic libraries, the cost of servicing patrons is included in tuition. Special academic subscription rates add another advantage. Private libraries, however, despite their expansion into the international arena, must often buy at higher rates every legal document, or even parts of documents, if the information specialist can't (or doesn't know how to) get it for free or for a reasonable price. So the broader the business, the more databases must be acquired.

Databases and General Search Engines

The logic of database structure is clearly analyzed by Ned L. Fielden and Maria Garrido,[24] who explain database records' arrangement, search logic, and various means of submitting queries, keyword searching, combining search terms, refining search terms, limiting a search and so on. Those of us familiar with Lexis and Westlaw can apply the search strategies of those databases to WWW research. However, almost every foreign and international database search engine or general search engine requires a specific strategy in order to retrieve records. As the database structure varies, so does the search engine. Methods of searching for information on the World Wide Web and in proprietary databases can vary considerably.

More and more, Boolean searching ("and", "or", "not" operators) is complemented by algorithms that analyze search terms. A few metasearch engines already use these artificial intelligence tools. Retrieved records with AskJeeves (http://www.askjeeves.com) reveal the precise importance accorded to any word typed in the search box. Controlled vocabulary or

[24] Fielden, Ned L., and Garrido, Maria, *Internet Research: Theory and Practice*. McFarland & Company, Inc., 1998.

thesaurus term search is becoming common in vortals, subject-oriented databases or subject-oriented search engines with an online thesaurus. The structure of these records is displayed in the retrieved records. Because records may be differently structured in databases, using this information can help you refine your search.

Legal databases have emerged and changed with a speed that has sometimes exceeded our updating tools, so keeping informed in the development of the cyberlegal domain has been a general task. In order to retrieve quality information in the proliferation of content on the Internet, labeling content with assigned metadata helps the search process considerably. Projects such as Dublin Core Metadata Initiative criteria of selection (http://purl.oclc.org/dc) develop a controlled vocabulary which improve communication with the database content in the retrieval process. In my searches I always combine databases using the Internet as a primary and unique carrier with proprietary databases such as Lexis/Nexis (http://www.lexis.com), Westlaw (www.westlaw.com), Butterworths in Australia (http://www.lexislegal.com/aus/butterworths/butterworths.asp) or Butterworths Direct UK focused services (http://www.butterworths.com/) .

That Internet interfaces and free information services to the legal community at large are now available is a major accomplishment. Lexis.com/lawschool (http://lawschool.lexis.com) provides reference tools (http://lawschool.lexis.com/reference), online tutorials, search support, and other products for free. Westlaw (http://www.lawschool.westlaw.com) also supplies the legal researcher with free tutorials, search assistance, legal literature, etc. Butterworths LexisDirect (http://www.butterworths.com) has almost the same features. LAWDIRECT Daily Update (http://macdonald.butterworths.co.uk/updates/update.asp) offers valuable information about English cases, statutes in force, and so on for free (http://macdonald.butterworths.co.uk/inforce/inforce.htm).

How old is your document?

Pre-1979 legal documents are difficult to find online. There are some online archival databases such as JSTOR and HEIN Journals, covering backfile archives of the scholarly journal literature. JSTOR Phase I database includes the backfiles of 117 journal titles from 15 academic disciplines. Hein Online, another provider of law reviews in full text, and scanned pdf documents, will have access to more than 225,000 law review articles and 3.5 million pages by the end of 2001. As of February 2001 *University of Chicago Law Review* is online from volume 1 right up to the December 2000 issue. This law review joins *Cornell Law Review*, *Northwestern Law Review*, *Notre Dame Law Review*, *Harvard Journal of Law and Technology*, *Texas Law Review*, *Virginia Law Review*, and a few others with full texts of the entire law review contents from volume 1 to the end of 2000. Some other titles, however, have a "moving wall" of only one year for the full contents of the journal. In these circumstances we must continue to rely on microfiches, books, bound journals, and other print-based resources.

Other historical international law collections, besides JSTOR and Hein Online, include the Avalon Project (http://www.yale.edu/lawweb/avalon/avalon.htm); the Digital National Security Archive (http://nsarchive.chadwyck.com/ and http://www.gwu.edu/~nsarchiv); the American Memory Collection (http://memory.loc.gov/ammem/amhome.html); the Swiss Diplomatic Documents database (http://www.admin.ch/bar/dds/e_dds1.htm); the Early Canadiana Online (ECO) database (http://www.canadiana.org/eco/english/abouteco.htm), a digital library of primary sources in Canadian history from the first European contact to the early 20th century; the German Law Archive, in English (http://www.iuscomp.org/gla/index.html) at the Comparative Law Society (http://www.iuscomp.org/), and in German at the Political Archives (http://www.auswaertiges-amt.de/www/en/infoservice/politik) of the German Foreign Office (http://www.auswaertiges-amt.de/www/en/index_html); the Australian War Memorial Website at The Journal of the Australian War Memorial (http://www.awm.gov.au/journal/j3); and other online sources. The field is growing rapidly. (See more at page 160).

Search engines

Much substantive information is proprietary and available only through database vendors requiring a password. Search engines and metasearch engines cannot search password databases. Moreover, other databases, many of them access-free, do not permit search engine "spiders" to index the information in the database because fire walls protect the content. A successful search must often combine three approaches: a metasearch engine or a general search engine (such as Go.com or Google), an index (such as GLIN), and a specific database search engine (such as HUDOC for the European Court of Human Rights).

I know from practice that legal information specialists, highly-trained users, start always with a portal or a gateway in order to avoid wasting time. But this is not the rule. Although there are good indexes by subject and guides to different subjects, most users prefer search engines as their access point to the Internet for topical information. A study published in March 2000[25] supported the conclusion of another study run at the State University of New York at Albany in 1996.[26] Both studies found that search engines are the predominant means of searching the Internet. This outcome acknowledged the crucial task of "providing users with guidance to proven online databases, especially during course-integrated instruction. A well-developed information resources instruction program is needed in conjunction with the one-on-one instruction that takes place every day at the reference/information desk." The challenge is to integrate "information resources instruction into the lives of end users."

A common database problem arises when a document contains a meta-tag with words that have no relevance to the content. If search terms or the searching "formula" are not focused, a metasearch engine will retrieve trash records or non-relevant records, and a legal specialist without experience of this problem would waste time and energy. Search engine spiders index Internet documents according to meta-tags hidden in the code of HTML documents, the titles, or the full text of HTML documents. They pay attention also to the frequency of words within a text and grade these texts accordingly—a time and energy-consuming procedure that is

[25] Kibirige, Harry N., and Lisa DePalo, "The Internet as a Source of Academic Research Information: Findings of Two Pilot Studies," 19 *Information Technology and Libraries* 1 (March 2000), 11-16.

[26] Wei Peter He, "What Are They Doing on the Internet? Study of Information Seeking Behaviors," *Internet Reference Services Quarterly* 1 (1996), 31-51.

often of no value whatsoever.

Another difficulty arises from the preference accorded by search engines to specific domains (business, health, etc.), and the way webmasters describe databases or documents. The legal information specialist should be aware of the politics behind search engines, including webmasters' practice of buying first-entry places in the ten first retrieved records of a search engine.[27] Search engines are not neutral. They have preferences in indexing. Sometimes they like one subject more than another. We can often perceive their politics/policies behind the façade, but this is difficult or impossible when they do not disclose their indexes and subject preferences.

Lately, "general search engines are getting smarter," in the words of Diana Botluk[28] in her review of six popular search engines: AltaVista, Excite, Go, Google, HotBot, and Lycos. This means that many search engines attempt "to anticipate what it is the researcher wants". Botluk's comparison chart has as its main evaluation features the following criteria: inclusion of words, alternative words, proximity, exclusion of words, phrases, case sensitivity, truncation/wildcard, nesting, date, language, location, media type, title, URL, search restrictors, other search features (such as translations, media filter, basic search ranked by relevancy, etc.), results display, subject directory, and other special features. From my experience, the relevancy consists in the capacity of a search engine to deliver the answer to the query in a few seconds and in the first five records.

This is why a particular innovation in the domain of search engines is not very feasible. A French and Canadian group launched in the fall of 2000 a new type of search engine: search with human help. This is http://www.webhelp.fr in which, purportedly, any question is answered by an actual human being. To get results to the query, the searcher must to fill out

[27] Introna, Lucas and Helen Nissenbaum, "Defining the Web: The Politics of Search Engines," *Computer*, Vol. 33, No. 1, January 2000 [Online]. Available HTML and PDF in WWW: http://computer.org/computer/co2000/r1054abs.htm [October 24, 2000].

[28] Botluk, Diana, *Update to Search Engines Compared* [Online]. (Published July 15, 2000.) Available WWW: http://www.llrx.com/features/engine3.htm [October 20, 2000].

a questionnaire, give his or her email address, etc. The answer is sent by email and also displayed. The time and privacy issues alone make this service questionable.

A good online searcher is like a piano player. Search analysis based on practice of patterns, and being present in the cyberlegal culture, are the keys to understanding cyberlegal domain searching structure.

Search engines for international and foreign law

Although the decentralization of the WWW predisposes the use of search engines as a major tool of a searcher, no search engine is truly comprehensive. Accordingly, searching requires a combination of search engines in order to obtain the best result. Discussions arise today regarding the collection and indexing methods and retrieval and ranking methods of search engines. Many analysts feel that a wider adoption of field searching, proximity searching, and relevance feedback would improve the quality of search results.[29] The recent appearance of topical search engines or specialty search engines built within vertical portals, or vortals, may ease this process in the future.

Many WWW search engines do not provide search fields such as author, title, subject, and so on, which are so valuable in proprietary databases. Limiting and refining results is also a problem. The default is poor. Results briefly displayed often contain the beginning of full records. The improvement of search engine retrieval, and especially the retrieval of legal concepts, has been very much discussed.[30] Results have been applied in some portal search engines in the UK.

If proximity search is not always available, searching within retrieved results helps to narrow the number of records. Infoseek, found today under another name, Go.com (http://www.go.com/), is still in my opinion the most powerful, accurate and current search engine in finding the precise answer to a

[29] Clarke, Sarah J., "Search Engines for the World Wide Web: An Evaluation of Recent Developments," 2 *Journal of Internet Cataloging* 81 (No. 3/4), 2000.

[30] De Mulder, R.V. and M.J. van den Hoven, "The Concept in Conceptual Legal Information Retrieval," 3 *Law Technology Journal* 1 [Online]. Available WWW: http://www.law.warwick.ac.uk/ltj/3-lc.html [November 10, 2000]. This article provides an extensive bibliography on this issue.

legal query. Go.com provides the capability of translating six languages; however, it cannot search through customized interfaces in the vernaculars for Denmark, Germany, Spain, France, Italy, Sweden, or The Netherlands, among other countries.

Google (http://www.google.com) has also emerged as an excellent search engine. Its speed is attributed in part to the efficiency of its search algorithm. The heart of Google is PageRank (http://www.google.com/technology/index.html), a system for ranking web pages developed by founders Larry Page and Sergey Brin at Stanford University.

HotBot, owned by Terra Lycos (http://www.terralycos.com/about/au_1_2_1.html), is one of the most popular Internet networks in Europe and Asia and a leading portal to Spanish- and Portuguese-speaking markets.

AltaVista (http://altavista.digital.com) allows searching in 25 languages with eight distinct search dimensions (see About AltaVista http://doc.altavista.com/company_info/about_av/background.html). AltaVista has created local sites in France, Germany, Italy, the Netherlands, Sweden, and the UK.

FindLaw (http://www.findlaw.com/) is actually the Law Crawler Web search engine (http://lawcrawler.lp. findlaw.com/); LawCrawler is powered by Alta Vista (Digital Equipment Corporation) under license. LawCrawler added LawCrawler International (http://web.lawcrawler.com) for searching legal information within individual country domains. From the onset of the query, FindLaw narrows its search according to the country or the world region. From the Main Index: Foreign & International Resources, choose the region or the country (Individual Country Search Pages). FindLaw refines the query with Boolean and proximity operators and other property value information including file size and an abstract. Recently, FindLaw launched FindLaw for Legal Professionals. Library Search (http://library.lp.findlaw.com) is a good source for legal news, USA cases and codes, forms, and articles on different topics of law.

Askjeeves (http://www.askjeeves.com) guides searches through questions displayed on the screen, providing intuitive, intelligent Web interactions. Ask Jeeves (http://www.askjeeves.com/docs/about/whatIsAskJeeves.html) allows users to interact on the Web in natural language. Users pose questions in plain English and receive links to Web sites containing relevant information.

LawRunner (Internet Legal Resource Guide) (http://www.ilrg.com/search.html) is an index allowing search by country (even with the suffixes of particular countries, i.e., .fr for France) using the AltaVista search engine. ILRG uses Boolean operators and an "exclude" field. "About the ILRG Search" stipulates that when one enters a search term or terms into the ILRG search box, the ILRG will return the URLs from its database of 3100+ web sites that match the specified key words, and not simply just a list of web pages. Running a query through FindLaw and LawRunner, you may discover that both retrieve almost the same URLs in the same order. This is not coincidental, as both use the same search engine program.

For international and foreign law research I would rank HotBot (http://hotbot.lycos.com/) as the third-best search engine, the first and second being Infoseek (Go.com) and Google.

Running the same query (Corte di Cassazione—Italian Supreme Court) through a few search engines already mentioned, and judging the quality of the engines according to the relevance of the first five entries, I received the following results: Infoseek (Go.com) had the right record as the first entry; Askjeeves displayed a few questions related to Corte di Cassazione jurisprudence; HotBot had it as the first entry; AltaVista had the answer within the five first records; Google had the answer as the first entry. Neither FindLaw nor LawRunner provided relevant entries among the first five.

To verify the accuracy of my findings I ran a second search through the above mentioned search engines plus The Northern Light (http://www.northernlight.com). I wanted to find U.N. Doc. CCPR/C/49/D/469/1991 (1994) on the issue of Ng extradition from Canada to the United States. This was a U.N. Human Rights Committee decision. Of search strategies, I most warmly appreciate the Boolean one. So I searched very broadly using the "and" connector: Ng and extradition.

Go.com displayed as the first entry the case *Chitac Ng v. Canada*, Communication No.469/1991, U.N. Doc CCPR/C/49/D. Google had the same document as the third entry. HotBot displayed the same decision at the second record. Askjeeves asked a question related to the "Canadian sentences death penalty", and provided a link to the *Ng* case. AltaVista produced records related to the case but not a link to the decision. NorthernLight produced 626 items in 447 sources for the same queries—articles and general information in French and English from Canadian and American sources, a precious bibliography on this matter.

Search engine logic

Search engine structure or logic is manifested by the search form, by the way the search must be constructed, and by the structure of the retrieved records and their inner organization. Queries can be submitted in Boolean formula, legal terms, or truncated elements. Unless coupled with experience in the cyberlegal culture, the impact of searching for legal information online could be frustrating. Some search engines such as AskJeeves support queries in natural language, words being sorted according to their importance. Google does almost the same thing. Searching for an institution, legal organization, or legal term, it is not necessary with these engines to write the words in quotes as it is with some other search engines.

Ex: Corte di Cassazione

Go.com permits limiting the search, narrowing results according to new criteria/words. But in many other search engines, such as WebCrawler (http://www.lawcrawler.com) and FindLaw (http://lawcrawler.lp.findlaw.com), the same search has to be done in quotes:

Ex: "Corte di Cassazione"

Otherwise the result doesn't match the request.

Another issue is related to what kind of vocabulary the search engine supports. The searcher can manipulate this situation to his/her advantage. Keywords, keywords in Boolean formula, legal terms in quotes are all good strategies. Many database search engines are built to support only legal concepts or only controlled vocabulary search.

Database search engines

When a search engine browsing the Web locates a

database, the database search engine then logically locates relevant documents within its records. Any serious and reliable database has its own search engine. A file on the search engine's features is available to guide the user. The online access training booklet[31] at the US Government Printing Office is an excellent example of user instruction. Unfortunately, the two-hundred-page pdf file is extremely inconvenient to use unless it's printed. A chapter-by-chapter reading, and a more flexible HTML version, would better help users to benefit from it.

Controlled vocabulary and a built-in thesaurus are main features of many search engines. The GLIN (http://lcweb2.loc.gov/law/GLINv1/GLIN.html) searching form allows only subject terms from the GLIN thesaurus. In Brazil, Senado Federal de Brasil (http://www.senado.gov.br/web/secsdefa/principa.htm) has an excellent built-in thesaurus, WEBTHES (http://webthes.senado.gov.br/thes), to help find legal terms (http://webthes.senado.gov.br/thes/navthes.htm). The United Nations Treaty Collection provides a Treaty Reference Guide (http://untreaty.un.org/english/guide.asp) and definition of key terms, as well as a glossary of terms relating to treaty actions, etc. SOSIG (Social Science Information Gateway, http://www.sosig.ac.uk) has a HASSET Thesaurus linked to the search engine. A recent database, TOB-EUR-OPA (http://tob-eur-opa.com), specializing in consultancy, information and news on European law about takeover bids (in French and English), has a great Definitions + Keywords file in English, French, Spanish, German, Italian, and Portuguese, containing the most-used terms.

Almost every database search engine has its own configuration. Rambler (http://www.rambler.ru/), a Russian search engine, searches using Latin characters in English and Russian. The Universal Database of Russian Newspapers (http://www.eastview.com/) allows searches in Cyrillic or in transliteration using the Library of Congress Transliteration Guide. EUROPA (http://europa.eu.int/) has more than one search engine with a specific configuration for each searchable directory: there is a general one (http://europa.eu.int/geninfo/

[31] GPO Access Training Booklet: A Service of the Government Printing Office. Washington, D.C.: Office of Electronic Information Dissemination Services, Electronic Access, June 1998. GPO Publication 500.8 (September 25, 2000). Available WWW: http://purl.access.gpo.gov/GPO/LPS2636.

query_en.htm), and Rapid (http://europa.eu.int/rapid/start/welcome.htm) for news only. Latin American database search engines are different in comparison with the US, but close to European database search engines in their structure and logic.

There are also search engines that specialize in jurisdictions within a language, such as the "Francophone" search engines. These include Chez.com (http://chez.libertysurf.fr); Ecila-Moteur de Recherche (http://www.ecila.nomade.fr), which includes a file on searching methods (http://www.ecila.nomade.fr/french/guide/introduction.html); Francité (http://www.i3d.qc.ca/), which lists search examples (http://www.francite.com/aide/option_recherche.htm); MégaFrancité (http://mega.francite.com/fr/mega_fr.asp); Lokace (http://www.lokace.com/); Nomade (http://www.nomade.fr); and Euroferret (http://euroferret.com/old_version.html). Derecho (http://derecho.org/), recently changed to V-Lex (http://vlex. com/), is a great index and an excellent search engine for Spanish-speaking territory. Cadê? (http://www.cade.com.br/) covers Brazil; searches must be done in Portuguese.

Online translation

With few exceptions, online translating services provide word-by-word translation, but fail to match corresponding legal terms. For example, "tax code" will become "code de taxation" in French while the correct French legal term is "code des impots". In the same way, "supreme court" might shown as "court supreme" in French, while the correct legal term is "cour de cassation".

To some extent, however, this difficulty can be overcome. For instance, *Eurodicautom* is of real help in finding the correct legal term in European Union country languages. *Eurodicautom* is an electronic dictionary of terminology presenting terms, acronyms and abbreviations from all aspects of European Union activities in 11 official languages (http://eurodic.ip.lu/cgi-bin/edicbin/EuroDicWWW.pl). Online translation assistance may also be found at the Terminological Information System—TIS (http://tis.consilium.eu.int/utfwebtis/frames/introfsEN.htm) of the Council of the European Union. TIS is a simplified version of the terminological database used by terminologists and translators working in The General Secretariat of the Council.

More general translation service is available at Legal Language Services (http://www.legallanguage.com), which provides "certified translation in more than 150 languages and dialects". LLS also provides direct assistance on specific translation projects such as patent translations, cataloging for international document discovery, and research of foreign legal texts.

Issues of legal translation are rampant, and the scarcity of reliable legal translation services on the Internet is obvious. Do not rely on AltaVista or similar services; they merely offer word-by-word translations without contextual meaning. However, some new online translation services, such as InterTran (http://secure.worldlanguage.com/world/online1.htm), are improving rapidly. I find the rate of failure (in the correct translation of legal concepts) to be about 50 percent currently but getting better. Systran (http://www.systransoft.com) and Berlitz GlobalNET (http://www.systranet.com/systran/html) are almost in the same category. All three are powered by Systran, a new translation software.

How to evaluate your search

Is this the best result? Are these the best records? Have I chosen the right words and legal terms? How can I refine my search? Would it be better to change the database, modify the search terms, or search within the results already obtained? Is this the best search engine to use?

General search engines present different problems than database search engines or controlled vocabulary full-text databases and indexes' search engines, such as SCAD, ECLAS, IFLP, or ILP. During the search process you must decide the best terms to use, and how to structure them to correspond with the database record fields. I keep model searches for databases I visit infrequently. For example, whenever I search Sistema Argentino de Informatica Juridica (SAIJ, http://www.saij.jus.gov.ar), a comprehensive fee-based database in Spanish that is user-friendly but also difficult, I look in my file to remember SAIJ search engine features.

In the constantly changing world of legal databases, researchers must also develop a strong sense of reliability criteria. But this is another story, which I will discuss in the next chapter.

Search strategies : some practical examples

As it is helpful to present practical examples that illustrate the application of the search strategies described in this chapter, I will here present a few.

I needed an English text of the MERCOSUR Treaty or the Treaty of Asuncion (March, 1991), a regional trade treaty in Latin America. First I visited the main MERCOSUR databases (http://www.guia-mercosur.com/ and http://www.mercosur.com/) to examine the authentic Spanish text. I did not have time to search other legal portals and indexes on international trade, so I chose the Google search engine and constructed a search in the simplest Boolean formula: MERCOSUR and treaty and English. The first record retrieved was the organization of American States Trade Unit OSCE home page (http://www.sice.oas.org/) containing the Treaty of Asuncion in English, Spanish, and Portuguese.

Yahoo hired a lawyer in New York for their lawsuit in France in the fall of 2000, in which the Union des Étudiants juifs de France (UEJF) had sued Yahoo for selling Nazi merchandise over the Internet. The lawyer, a professor of international law and an internationally-known expert, needed the decision issued by a French tribunal in this case on May 22, 2000. As such cases are becoming common, and as I knew from experience that subject-oriented databases are valuable sources of legal materials, I went to Juriscom (http://www.juriscom.net) and Lex-elec tronica (http://www.lex-electronica.org), both well-known for publishing cases and legislation on Internet subjects. Not only did I find the decision using the databases' search engines, but also extremely helpful commentaries on similar decisions in France and all over the world. Juriscom pointed me to another database, Imaginons un Réseau Internet Solidaire (IRIS, http://www.iris.sgdg.org), containing legal literature and commentaries on similar sentences adopted by different courts and magistrates in France.

In another assignment, I was asked to find a case from the German Constitutional Court limiting organ donation. Bundesverfassungsgericht, BverfG (http://www.bundesverfassungs gericht.de) had ruled against petitioners under the Organ Transplant Law of 1997. The decision was published in 1999. First, I accessed the German Constitutional Court cases (Entscheidungen, http://www.bundesverfassungsgericht.de/cgi-bin/lin k.pl?entscheidungen) and searched as a default Tematische Suche for Transplant. The very first result was the one I needed, in full German text:

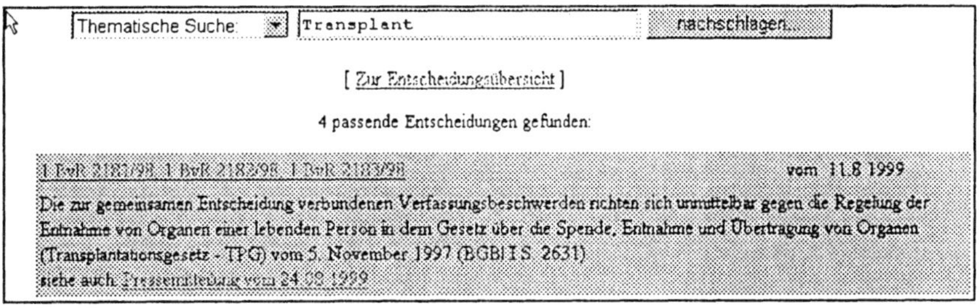

Thematische Suche | Transplant | nachschlagen...

[Zur Entscheidungsübersicht]

4 passende Entscheidungen gefunden:

1 BvR 2181/98, 1 BvR 2182/98, 1 BvR 2183/98 vom 11.8.1999

Die zur gemeinsamen Entscheidung verbundenen Verfassungsbeschwerden richten sich unmittelbar gegen die Regelung der Entnahme von Organen einer lebenden Person in dem Gesetz über die Spende, Entnahme und Übertragung von Organen (Transplantationsgesetz - TPG) vom 5. November 1997 (BGBl I S. 2631)

siehe auch: Pressemitteilung vom 24.08.1999

As I also needed a commentary or an abstract in English, I went to Lexis; International Law directory; Legal News; International Law Update file, and searched for Germany and Transplant and 1999. There I found an English abstract (a note from *The Washington Post*):

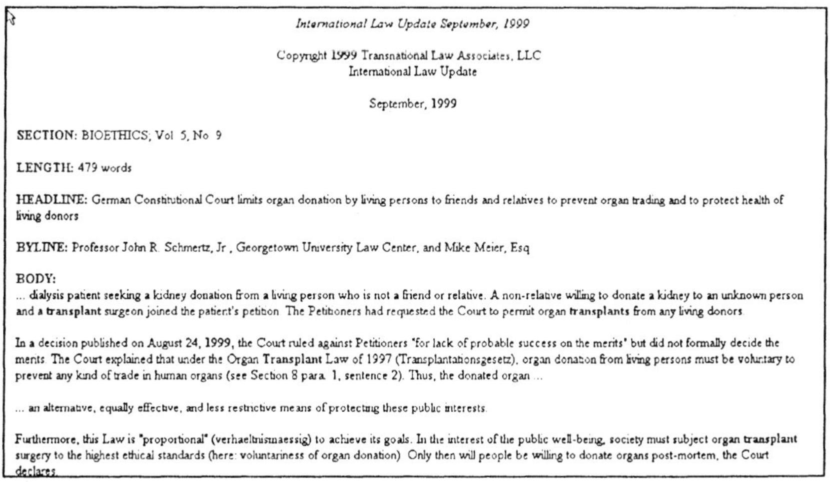

International Law Update September, 1999

Copyright 1999 Transnational Law Associates, LLC
International Law Update

September, 1999

SECTION: BIOETHICS; Vol 5, No 9

LENGTH: 479 words

HEADLINE: German Constitutional Court limits organ donation by living persons to friends and relatives to prevent organ trading and to protect health of living donors

BYLINE: Professor John R. Schmertz, Jr., Georgetown University Law Center, and Mike Meier, Esq

BODY:
... dialysis patient seeking a kidney donation from a living person who is not a friend or relative. A non-relative willing to donate a kidney to an unknown person and a **transplant** surgeon joined the patient's petition. The Petitioners had requested the Court to permit organ **transplants** from any living donors.

In a decision published on August 24, 1999, the Court ruled against Petitioners "for lack of probable success on the merits" but did not formally decide the merits. The Court explained that under the Organ **Transplant** Law of 1997 (Transplantationsgesetz), organ donation from living persons must be voluntary to prevent any kind of trade in human organs (see Section 8 para. 1, sentence 2). Thus, the donated organ ...

... an alternative, equally effective, and less restrictive means of protecting these public interests.

Furthermore, this Law is "proportional" (verhaeltnismaessig) to achieve its goals. In the interest of the public well-being, society must subject organ **transplant** surgery to the highest ethical standards (here: voluntariness of organ donation). Only then will people be willing to donate organs post-mortem, the Court declares.

In March 1999 a professor teaching business in China needed the new January 1999 Chinese securities law. The law was not included yet in *Commercial Laws and Business Regulations of the People's Republic of China* or *China Laws for Foreign Business*. I tried World News Collection (http:// wnc.fedworld.gov/), choosing the structured search form limited by region (China), by title (securities law), and by the period of time (January-March 1999). The law was there in full English text (unofficial translation) from the Chinese newspaper *Beijing Xinhua*.

A patron preparing a paper on women's rights and violence against women urgently needed all UN covenants and basic documents on this matter, as well as some legal literature. My first choice was Project DIANA, the Toronto mirror (http://www.law-lib.utoronto.ca/Diana/) of the Yale Law School Project Diana (http://diana.law.yale.edu/). The Toronto mirror provides human rights conventions and landmark commentaries on every related issue (such as annotated bibliographic references to scholarly articles with links to full text where available; and annotated references to conventions and UN Reports, NGO reports, case law and legislation with links to full text where available).

The draft of the new Venezuelan constitution was requested at the beginning of the year 2000. The Wuerzburg database had no news about the newly-enacted Constitution or the draft. First, I searched the web with a general search engine using Spanish keywords. One of the records I retrieved was the Congreso de la Republica de Venezuela—Novedades Legislativas (http://www.internet.ve/sail/sv/nove.html) where I found the draft of the Constitution as well as other new laws such as Ley del Sufragio, extremely important in the Venezuelan political context, where on 28 May 2000 the general election was stopped by the Supreme Court (http://www.uni-wuerzburg.de/law/ve_indx.html).

I was asked to find Russian Constitutional Court cases on the freedom of religion, and any relevant articles in Russian and if possible in English too. The first step was to go to theRussiaSite.org (http://www.therussiasite.org/legal/laws/ccrulings/list.html), where I looked through the English abstracts of the all court rulings. I found that it was actually one case with two plaintiffs as follows:

> No. 16-P of November 23, 1999 On the Case Testing the Constitutionality of Paragraphs Three and Four of Clause 3 of Article 27 of the Federal Law of September 26, 1997 "On Freedom of Conscience and on Religious Associations" in Connection with Complaints from the Jehovah's Witnesses Religious Association in the City of Yaroslavl and the Christian

Church of Apotheosis Religious Association."

The second step was to go to the list of cases of the Russian Constitutional Court (http://ks.rfnet.ru/pos/postan.htm) and to locate the full text of the decision in Russian:

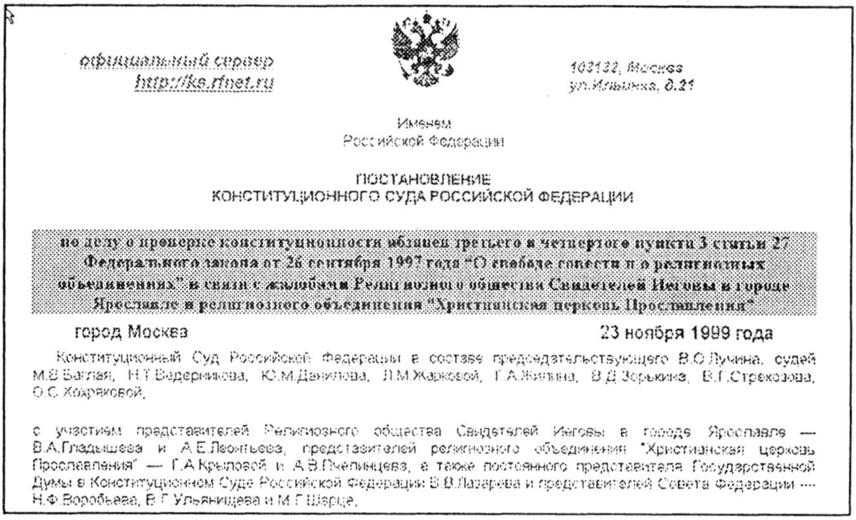

официальный сервер
http://ks.rfnet.ru

103132, Москва
ул.Ильинка, д.21

Именем
Российской Федерации

ПОСТАНОВЛЕНИЕ
КОНСТИТУЦИОННОГО СУДА РОССИЙСКОЙ ФЕДЕРАЦИИ

по делу о проверке конституционности абзацев третьего и четвертого пункта 3 статьи 27 Федерального закона от 26 сентября 1997 года "О свободе совести и о религиозных объединениях" в связи с жалобами Религиозного общества Свидетелей Иеговы в городе Ярославле и религиозного объединения "Христианская церковь Прославления"

город Москва — 23 ноября 1999 года

Конституционный Суд Российской Федерации в составе председательствующего В.О.Лучина, судей М.В.Баглая, Н.Т.Ведерникова, Ю.М.Данилова, Л.М.Жарковой, Г.А.Жилина, В.Д.Зорькина, В.Г.Стрекозова, О.С.Хохряковой,

с участием представителей Религиозного общества Свидетелей Иеговы в городе Ярославле — В.А.Гладышева и А.Е.Леонтьева, представителей религиозного объединения "Христианская церковь Прославления" — Г.А.Крыловой и А.В.Пчелинцева, а также постоянного представителя Государственной Думы в Конституционном Суде Российской Федерации В.В.Лазарева и представителей Совета Федерации — Н.Ф.Воробьева, В.Г.Ульянищева и М.Г.Шарце.

The following step was the Universal Database of Russian Newspapers (http://news.eastview.com/) and the Universal Database of Parliamentary Publications (http://news.east view.com/duma/) where I searched for Constitution, case, and religion (in Russian) using the Russian keyboard:

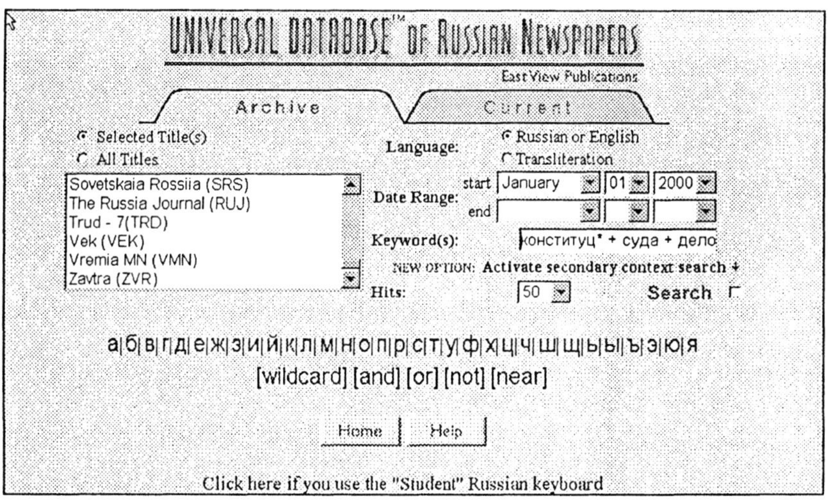

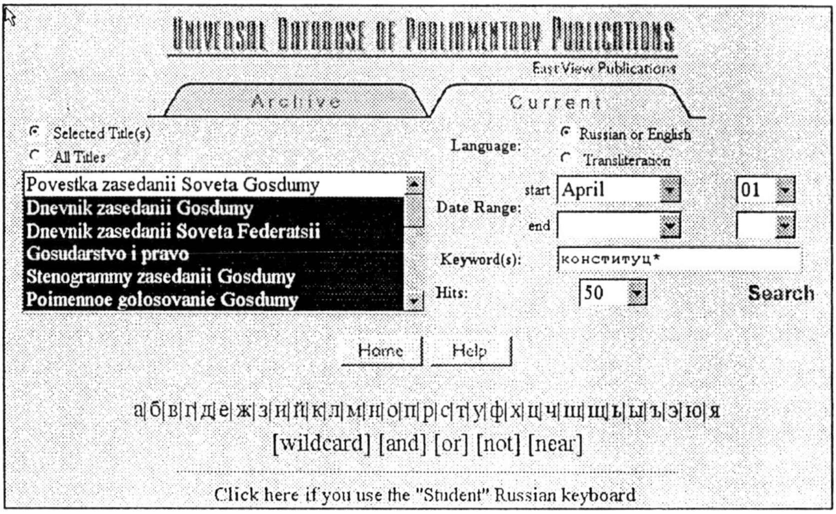

For more full-text laws and legal commentaries, I searched KonsultantPlius in Russian (http://www.consultant.ru/go.phtml?Mode=Section&Section=Online&Page=/Online/Systems/) and used the search form (http://www.consultant.ru/dbs/nbu.phtml?B0CKQ). To become familiar with Konsultant Plius I looked first at the demo version (http://www.kadis.net/kplus/demo.php3).

A student with a citation to the "FLR" was trying to find a case. "FLR" turned out to be the Fiji Law Reports. I found the decision at AUSTLII (http://www.austlii.edu.au), which contains Fiji cases and links to Fiji courts (http://www.austlii.edu.au/fj/cases/FJC/) using a combination of Google and AUSTLII search engines.

A decision of the French Conseil d'Etat from July 26, 1996 was required. I had the number of the decision (170106). Jurifrance (http://www.jurifrance.com/) provided the full text of the administrative decision:

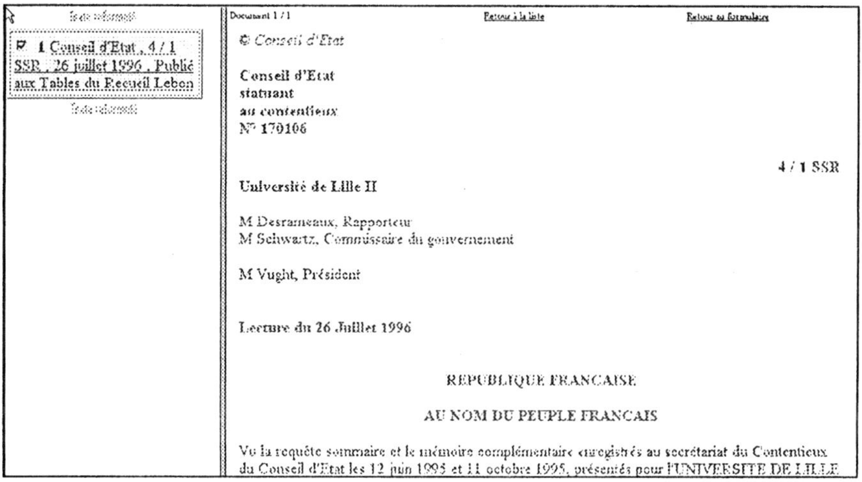

The European Union Commission issued a document related to the European Union-United States Dispute on Bananas in July 2000. The easiest way to find it was to go to Europa (http://europa.eu.int) and try the general search: banana commission. I retrieved an overview of dispute settlement cases, an article on the banana case and, of course, the Commission document related to the dispute in Europa's Trade Directory (http://europa.eu.int/comm/trade) under Multilateral Issues—Dispute Settlements.

Pursuing a tax issue related to Germany I accessed REFACT (http://www.refact.de/rda_inh.htm), a database specializing mainly on taxation. It is important to remember that REFACT contains tax cases. I needed the German Foreign Tax Credit Act. I went to Steuerrecht (Taxation); Außensteuergesetz (AStG) (Fiscal Code); and Suche Wort (Word Search) for "Foreign Tax Credit Act" in German using "Freistellungsverfahren". For the box "Das gesuchte Wort soll" I selected as default "mit den gesuchten Zeichen beginnen"; from the retreived records I chose Einkommensteuergesetz 1997 [EStG 97] and got § 50d Besonderheiten im Fall von Doppelbesteuerungsabkommen. I found the full text of the law:

REFACT - Fundstellen

Fundstellen in: **Einkommensteuergesetz 1997** (EStG 1997)
Gesucht: **FREISTELLUNGSVERFAHREN**

Hinweis: Die Texte werden gewichtet nach der Anzahl der gefundenen Worte oder Wortverbindungen dargestellt. Der Text mit den meisten Fundstellen steht an erster Stelle.

Texte, die das Suchwort enthalten:

- § 50d [Gültige Fassung bis 31.12.2000]
- § 50d Besonderheiten im Fall von Doppelbesteuerungsabkommen
- § 43b Bemessung der Kapitalertragsteuer bei bestimmten Kapitalgesellschaften
- § 44d [Gültige Fassung bis 31.12.2000]

Klick zur Homepage www.refact.de Inhalt A-Z Suche Wort Gehe zu § Stichwort Urteile/Schreiben

REFACT

Here is a sample taken from the second record:

Gesucht: **FREISTELLUNGSVERFAHREN**

Buch: Einkommensteuergesetz 1997 (EStG 1997) [Register]
Stand: BGBl. 2000, S. 1978 vom 21.12.2000
Herkunft: IX. Sonstige Vorschriften, Bußgeld-, Ermächtigungs- und Schlußvorschriften

§ 50d Besonderheiten im Fall von Doppelbesteuerungsabkommen

[Fassung ab dem Gesetz zur Senkung der Steuersätze und zur Reform der Unternehmensbesteuerung (Steuersenkungsgesetz - StSenkG) vom 23.10.2000 BGBl. I 2000 S. 1433]

[Inkrafttreten: 01.01.2001]

(1) Können Einkünfte, die dem Steuerabzug vom Kapitalertrag oder dem Steuerabzug auf Grund des § 50a unterliegen, nach § 43b oder nach einem Abkommen zur Vermeidung der Doppelbesteuerung nicht oder nur nach einem niedrigeren Steuersatz besteuert werden, so sind die Vorschriften über die Einbehaltung, Abführung und Anmeldung der Steuer durch den Schuldner der Kapitalerträge oder Vergütungen im Sinne des § 50a ungeachtet des § 43b und des Abkommens anzuwenden. Unberührt bleibt der Anspruch des Gläubigers der Kapitalerträge oder Vergütungen auf völlige oder teilweise Erstattung der einbehaltenen und abgeführten Steuer; der Anspruch ist durch Antrag nach amtlich vorgeschriebenem Vordruck geltend zu machen. Für die Erstattung der Kapitalertragsteuer gilt § 45 entsprechend. Der Schuldner kann sich im Haftungsverfahren nicht auf die Rechte des Gläubigers aus dem Abkommen berufen.

When I urgently needed to send by email the India Citizenship Act of 1955, I went to the free-of-charge India Code Information System (INCODIS)(http://164.100.10.12/) and searched by keyword: citizenship. I retrieved a list of citizenship acts, including the consolidated text I needed. The trouble with this database is that articles can only be viewed one by one, as you can see from this example:

Short Title: THE CITIZENSHIP ACT, 1955

Act No. of Year: ACT NO. 57 OF 1955 1*

Enactment Date: [30th December, 1955.]

Act Objective: An Act to provide for the acquisition and termination of Indian citizenship. [30th December, 1955.] BE it enacted by Parliament in the Sixth Year of the Republic of India as follows:-

CLICK_For_SECTION_TEXT: Click Here

If you click on the section text link, a table of contents with links to the full text is displayed:

Documents	Section Title
1	Short title.
2	Interpretation.
3	Citizenship by birth.
4	Citizenship by descent.
5	Citizenship by registration.
6	Citizenship by naturalisation.
7	Special provisions as to citizenship of persons covered by the AssamAccord.
8	Citizenship by incorporation of territory.
9	Renunciation of citizenship.
10	Termination of citizenship.
11	Deprivation of citizenship.
12	Commonwealth citizenship.
13	Power to confer rights of Indian citizen on citizens of certaincountry.
14	Certificate of citizenship in case of doubt.
15	Disposal of application under sections 5 and 6.

A reference query was related to the 1997 Netherlands land law related to agriculture. First of all I consulted an English-Dutch dictionary; after that I went to the fee-based Wettenbank (http://wettenbank.sdu.nl/), searched Woorden uit de titel for agrarische, and retreived 5 records:

Overzicht gevonden wet- en regelgeving in de Sdu Wettenbank

Op basis van uw zoekopdracht zijn de volgende resultaten gevonden:

Resultaat 1 tot en met 5 van 5

- Besluit bekostiging agrarische innovatie- en praktijkcentra 1997
- Besluit sociaal beleidskader inzake de vorming van agrarische opleidingscentra
- Lozingenbesluit open teelt en veehouderij
- Wet machtiging tot deelneming Nederland in de Eerste Aanvulling der Middelen Internationale Fonds voor Agrarische Ontwikkeling (IFAD)
- Wet machtiging tot deelneming Nederland in de Tweede Aanvulling der Middelen Internationale Fonds voor Agrarische Ontwikkeling (IFAD)

... and the full text of the 1997 law:

Besluit bekostiging agrarische innovatie- en praktijkcentra 1997

Besluit van 28 januari 1997, houdende voorschriften voor de bekostiging van agrarische innovatie- en praktijkcentra (Besluit bekostiging agrarische innovatie- en praktijkcentra 1997)

(Besluit bekostiging agrarische innovatie- en praktijkcentra 1997 [Versie geldig vanaf: 19-02-1997])

Wij Beatrix, bij de gratie Gods, Koningin der Nederlanden, Prinses van Oranje-Nassau, enz. enz. enz.

Op voordracht van Onze Minister van Landbouw, Natuurbeheer en Visserij, van 20 november 1996, nr. J. 9611314, Directie Juridische Zaken;
Gelet op *artikel 2.2.12 van de Wet educatie en beroepsonderwijs* ;
De Raad van State gehoord (advies van 20 december 1996, No. W11.96.0552);
Gezien het nader rapport van Onze Minister van Landbouw, Natuurbeheer en Visserij van 16 januari 1997, nr. J.97180, Directie Juridische Zaken;

To find the same result without a fee, you can search the free Overheid.nl—Officiële Publicaties (Official Publications) (http://www.overheid.nl/op/) for agrarische innovatie and get the law (record 22) :

In onderstaand overzicht zijn de Officiële Publicaties 21 t/m 34 van 34 gesorteerd op publicatiedatum weergegeven, die beantwoorden aan uw zoekopdracht en die van 1-1-1995 t/m 15-2-2001 aan Overheid-OP zijn toegevoegd.

21. 17-07-1997, Staatsblad 1997, 310 (39 Kb)
Wijziging Aanwijzingsbesluit verplicht-verzekerden Ziekenfondswet en Besluit beperking kring verzekerden ZFW
22. 18-02-1997, Staatsblad 1997, 66 (21 Kb)
Besluit bekostiging agrarische innovatie- en praktijkcentra 1997
23. 23-07-1996, Staatsblad 1996, 397 (35 Kb)
Wet educatie en beroepsonderwijs e.a.; wijz. ivm decentralisatie rechtspositieregeling educatie en beroepsond

The text was published in pdf by *Staatsblad*, the Official Gazette.

Chapter 3

Guiding Principles on the Evaluation of Legal Databases*

During the last five years of the twentieth century legal documents began to appear at a dramatic rate on the Internet. Law librarians and legal researchers quickly discovered that they could expand and enhance their collections beyond what their library's space limitations could accommodate, and even beyond budget restraints. Numerous excellent free and fee-based legal databases on many subjects, many of them sufficient for meeting a library's selection or collection development policy, were now available and accessible. Legal professionals also discovered that they could have ongoing access to old and reputable services, such as the United Nations Treaty Collection (http://untreaty.un.org/), as long as they maintained their subscriptions. They also realized that paying the access fee to the content didn't mean they owned that content. In many cases, the amount of the online information, downloading it, and even viewing it might be subject to charge. Terms also had changed their meanings. If "piracy" for the traditional media meant making and selling large numbers of counterfeit copies, in the electronic era "piracy" seems to describe any unlicensed activity at all. "The borders between legitimate and illegal behavior are subject to bitter dispute" as new wars on the digital media take place in the courtrooms.[32] In addition, free and reputable online services such as the USA Government Printing Office (http://www.access.gpo.gov/) did not provide legal documents as easily as Lexis or Westlaw, and the search strategy was completely different and sometimes painful.

*An early version of this chapter was previously published in the February 1, 1999 issue of LLRX.com, and updated in the October 2, 2000 issue (http://www.llrx.com/features/evaluating2.htm).

[32] Litman, Jessica, "War Stories." Early Draft, 2/19,01. Lecture delivered at New York University School of Law, 2001 Innovation Policy Colloquium.

Was this suitable or not? Acceptable or not? First, specialists applying almost the same standards as those used for print data closely analyzed the reliability of electronic sources. It was essential to achieve the highest quality, both of access to information and of the information itself, throughout the WWW virtual legal library.[33]

A huge number of articles on evaluation of electronic information is currently posted on the Internet. Searching the World Wide Web with different search engines I have retrieved hundred of guides, tutorials, recommendations. The best starting points to these Internet articles is probably the WWW Virtual Library Evaluation of Information Sources (http://www.vuw.ac.nz/~agsmith/evaln/evaln.htm).

The fact that so many of these contributions duplicate the same information is actually reassuring. As in a forum, authors agree on certain patterns of evaluation. Repetition and absence of originality are WWW features in any event. The Web is a public place where individuals are free to express their thoughts, and where one may publish freely without the restrictions or rules of composition required by journals.

The shortcomings of literature on this topic arise from the failure to understand the newness of Internet publishing and Internet technology, so crucial in accessing, viewing, and delivering content. The domain is precisely the "interface" of librarianship and computer science. The information specialist/librarian must bridge this gap and learn to understand the specific features of the Internet source in order to evaluate its performance. In a printed text, a publisher is judged by the published content. A book is good or bad, and the librarian, holding it in his or her hands, is able to decide. But when servers, special software, document formats, transaction protocols, passwords, and internal search engines are the core of a publisher's features, the role of database protocols is as important as the content. Between the librarian/information specialist/end user and the database, there is a chain of protocols to be understood.

[33] Ciolek, T. Matthew, *Information Quality WWW Virtual Library. The Internet Guide to Construction of Quality Online Resources* [August 22, 2000] Available WWW:http://www.ciolek.com/WWWVL-InfoQuality.html.

A library can subscribe to or buy a database, but it might not be able to locate or even "see" any document if the computer's software, server configuration, or browser don't match the publisher's database requirements. There are even databases that can be viewed only with a specific browser. This was the case with Legal Journals by Hein Online (a retrospective full-text collection of major law reviews, http://heinonline.org), which, after a lot of criticism, was restructured. As I write, the Penelope Project (http://www.penelope.gr) and the Commonwealth Constitutions (http://www.echr.net/const/default.asp) from the EchrNet Human Rights (http://www.echr.net/) database are accessible only with Microsoft Internet Explorer (MSIE) version 5 or greater, although the possibility of viewing and searching the content with Netscape is promised shortly. The same is true for some Russian databases. Access and content disclosure are also a problem. A fee-based Spanish database, Aranzadi (http://www.aranzadi.es/nueva/index.html),will not allow you to browse the directories and find out about pricing and access issues.

Other databases reject proxy servers. This is the case with Lexis/Nexis (http://www.lexis.com) and with BAILII (http://www.bailii.org/), an excellent access-free database containing full texts of United Kingdom statutory materials and case law. Both of these major databases are useless in Moscow, for instance. Almost all legal centers and law libraries in former Soviet Union Countries use proxy servers with very high access control lists (they are useful for filtering/ censoring access to the Internet). Moscow's very important Library for Foreign Literature Legal Center has no access to Lexis. A proxy server is a WWW server that "acts as the sole web server" for the entire domain or whatever clients are "behind the firewall, a logical block between your clients and the rest of the Internet" (http://www.cedpa-k12.org/databus-issues/v36n1/proxy.html). If the requested web page or web database is on the control list, the user receives a message indicating that the URL is not accessible or not valid.

Host servers also act differently regarding the IP address of the guests. Accessing a database is quite different in America than it is in Europe. When a law firm with offices all over the world subscribes to a database, a server analysis must be run for every location.

Another issue is the accessibility of the publisher's server. What is the best access time for CELEX in Europe? Definitely not between 9AM and 5PM European time. The CELEX server is down very often, mainly because CELEX (http://europa.eu.int/celex) and SCAD (http://europa.eu.int/scadplus) do not have their own servers but are directories of the EUROPA (European Union) server (http://europa.eu.int). A server has a limited number of access ports. EUROPA's server hosts many directories and is almost always very crowded. Only a few ports remain available for CELEX, SCAD, ECLAS, EUR-Lex, and Pre-Lex. As long as this situation persists, it might be wiser to use CELEX via Westlaw in Europe, or to restrict use to the hours between 6AM and 8:30 AM or after 8PM in Europen time. It seems that CELEX access problems will be alleviated by July 2001 when a new law portal is scheduled for release. This new portal (or perhaps vortal) will eventually be an integrated system, an interface between four databases—CELEX, EUR-Lex, EUDOR, and Curia. The searcher will be able to search them all at the same time or individually. Simultaneously, EUROPA will launch a search engine with a built-in thesaurus using metadata standards. This restructuring seeks to address the problem of access to EU resources, and to provide a more comprehensive gateway to EU primary and secondary materials.

Some database servers give preferential access, or reject connections based on location (region) and/or type of server (.edu, .org, .com, .net). A server from Portugal rejected the .edu and (implicitly) any US connection. One Japanese database even discloses that its content is not available outside Japan. Even if you buy the database in Japan, you will not be able to use it in the USA or Europe. NACSIS-IR (http://www.nacsis.ac.jp/ir/ir-e.html), a Japanese provider, sells Japanese Laws in Force for "domestic service only".

Although there is a vast literature on the evaluation of databases, ultimate guidelines have yet to be formulated. Not only are databases surfacing at a dramatic rate, but the factors of evaluation are considerably more numerous and growing in complexity. The continuing rapid development of WWW technology and the WWW decentralization of information must both be taken into consideration.

Important relevant projects include the Argus Clearinghouse Ratings Systems,[34] NELLCO's very complicated procedure which is not realistic in a workable environment (see Criteria Worksheet for Electronic/Intranet Acquisitions at http://www.nellco.org/criteria.htm and the form http://www.nellco.org/CRITERIA/EntryForm.CFM), Evaluation of Internet Medline for OMNI database guidelines (http://www.omni.ac.uk/general-info/intmedeval.html), and Principles for California State University Acquisition of Electronic Information Sources (http://seir.calstate.edu/EIR.prin.html). The famous Scout Project (http://scout.cs.wisc.edu/index.html) publishes four electronic newsletters and reviews and describes new databases of interest to the academic community according to a specific set of criteria. The Signpost database (http://www.signpost.org/signpost) offers descriptions for metadata records. At the end of the year 2000 Signpost included more than ten thousand records. Behind this work related to cataloging and acquisition criteria there are library standards and rules coming from projects such as Dublin Core Metadata Initiative criteria of selection (http://purl.oclc.org/dc) and the Dublin Core Metatag Generator (http://bridges.states.mn.us/taggen.html); SOSIG (http://www.sosig.ac.uk/law); and RENARDUS (http://www.renardus.org) criteria of selection and evaluation of WWW databases in order "to find quality networked information". The SOSIG Internet Catalogue points to resources selected and described by librarians or academic contributors. To this list may be added BIBLINK standards (http://www.ukoln.ac.uk/metadata/biblink), which are designed to establish authoritative bibliographic information; DESIRE standards (http://www.desire.org), which focus on enhancing existing information networks for research users across Europe through research and development; ROADS project criteria (http://www.ilrt.bris.ac.uk/roads), a tool to set up subject gateways of Internet based resources now ended; LINNEA's criteria of selection (http://linneaw.helsinki.fi/indexen.html), a gateway to European Union Databases maintained and developed by Helsinki University Library; Eagle-i Service (http://ials.sas.ac.uk/eagle-i.htm), which provides electronic access to global legal information hosted in London at the Institute of Advanced Legal Studies (http://ials.sas.ac.uk).

[34] The Argus Clearinghouse Ratings Systems [August 22, 2000]. Available WWW: http://clearinghouse.net/ratings.html.

Criteria of selection and evaluation of WWW databases are not always very explicit or comprehensive. Scout Internet Project (http://scout.cs.wisc.edu/report/sr/criteria.html) lists only the basic criteria of content, authority, information maintenance, presentation, availability, and cost. Links to two articles (published in 1996 and 1997) of a Scout editor found on this page do not shed more light on this matter as of October 2000. SOSIG (http://scout18.cs.wisc.edu/sosig_mirror/about.html) has an entry to the SOSIG selection criteria (http://scout18.cs.wisc.edu/sosig_mirror/desire/ecrit.html) (evaluating resources for SOSIG). The main headings listed are Content Criteria, Form Criteria, and Process Criteria; subheadings are Validity, Ease of Navigation, Information Integrity, Authority and Reputation of Source, Provision of User Support, Site Integrity, Substantiveness, Use of Recognized Standards, System Integrity, Accuracy, Appropriate Use of Technology, Comprehensiveness, Aesthetics, Uniqueness, Composition, and Organization. As of October 2000, this is the most comprehensive approach to the WWW database evalua-tion process, despite the fact that not all factors are discussed and not all technicalities are covered.

Evaluation checklists written by information professionals are abundant. Laura Gordon-Murnane's article[35] and Hope N. Tillman's recommendations[36] show the same broad approach, offering no solutions to important information technology related problems. A few guides (http://www.swem.wm.edu/resources/search/evaluation.htm) merely repeat the same criteria gathered together. One of the earliest guides to evaluation, initially published in 1996 by Esther Grassing,[37] discussed elements of publishing in the new electronic environment. An interesting article by Marie Stefanini Newman, paying attention to designing and improving "legal Internet sites", was

[35] Laura Gordon-Murnane, "Evaluating Net Evaluators," 7 *Searcher* 57 (February 1999).

[36] Tillman, Hope N, "Quality Librarian Web Sites," *Information Outlook* 1 (March 1997), pp. 25-26, 46. Available WWW (September 22, 2000): http://www.sla.org/pubs/serial/io/1997/mar97/marnet.html.

[37] Grassing, Esther, *Thinking Critically about World Wide Web Resources*,(September 22, 2000.) Available WWW: http://www.library.ucla.edu/libraries/college/instruct/web/critical.htm.

unfortunately restricted to a particular database.[38] Jeanne Merrill failed to design a paradigm in her promising article on evaluating sites on classical civilization.[39] Karen McLachlan's "WWW CyberGuide Ratings for Content Evaluation"[40] is good for elementary schools, but has little further value. Jan Alexander and Marsha Ann Tate, in their slide presentations published on the Internet and recently in a book, presented a combination of mainly traditional criteria and some WWW features.[41]

A crucial issue lying at the heart of legal research is raised by the continuing appearance of books on electronic legal research that mention legal databases but do no indicate their research value. Robert Watt, for instance, in his concise *Legal Research*, an otherwise excellent book on legal research in Australia, New Zealand, Canada and India,[42] reviews many databases but offers no practical evaluation. Other books I have already mentioned, such as *Legal Research in a Nutshell* by Cohen and Olson,[43] remain at the most general level in order to avoid potential mistakes. They list only a few databases generally accepted by the legal community (i.e., United Nations, World Trade Organization, Jurifrance, etc.), which gives a false impression of the scarcity of reliable legal databases. To speak about Internet databases as research tools, without discussing their configuration or reliability, is a way of not confronting the subject. In this connection, Fielden and Garrido's book, although one of the best on discussing computer and Internet skills, the nature of research, Internet tools, information retrieval, and Internet subject resources, contains almost

[38] Marie Stefanini Newman, "Evaluation Criteria and Quality Control for Legal Knowledge Systems on the Internet: A Case Study," 91 *Law Library Journal* 1, 9 (Winter 1999).

[39] Jeanne Merrill, "The Internet and Classical Civilization," 23 *Acquisitions Librarian* 97 (2000).

[40] McLachlan, Karen, *"WWW CyberGuide Ratings for Content Evaluation"* (September 22, 2000).Available WWW:http://www.cyberbee.com/guide1.html.

[41] Alexander Jan, and Marsha Ann Tate, *Evaluating Web Resources* (September 20, 2000). Available WWW: http://www2.widener.edu/Wolfgram-Memorial-Library/webevalution/webeval.htm.

[42] Watt, Robert, *Legal Research*, Third Edition. Sydney, Australia: The Federation Press, 1997.

[43] Cohen, L. Morris, and Kent C. Olsen, *Legal Research in a Nutshell.* Saint Paul, MN: West Group, 2000.

nothing new on database evaluation.[44] The authors take into consideration the difficulties of the matter and remind us that "the tradition of research in academic and other arenas has built a framework of professionalism that is more identifiable than in the world of Internet."[45] Their guidelines of evaluation are address stability and resource authority (the reliability of information related to its accuracy). The last criterion includes "worthy origin of information" as the standard of authenticity, adding the location of information or publisher. All other possible concerns must be resolved by the "evaluative skills" of the researcher, which are improved "over time and are part and parcel of any good research effort." One might ask why it is taking so long to develop standards for online legal resources. The answer is that it has not been possible to adapt traditional evaluation criteria because the very newness of electronic sources demands new standards. I must also confess that many librarians will not read or fill out a form whenever they are asked to evaluate a database. Ultimately, however, legal and information science skills, the experience coming from intense reading of literature on this topic, searching skills on the WWW, and a solid understanding of what is needed and what is good for his/her working environment will all contribute to the sound growth of this area.

I keep a file for every highly used database in which I record observations about coverage and changes, search strategies, and so on. This has proven over the years to be of tremendous help, especially when working with databases from many diverse foreign jurisdictions.

Databases

There is a distinct difference between a "site" and a "database". An Internet "site" can be any URL on the Internet which contains one or more documents (e.g., treaties, decisions, laws), an index of some sources, links to other sites, and/or other information, often gathered by some good-hearted persons. There are many good Samaritans on the Internet. By contrast, "database" means subject-oriented data gathered and main-

[44] Fielden, Ned L, and Maria Garrido, *Internet Research: Theory and Practice*. London: McFarland & Company, Inc., 1998.

[45] *Op. cit.*, p.32.

tained in a server by an official entity, displaying a high interactivity with the user as well as search engine capability, data record files, query or sales transactions, product catalogs, and other kinds of information. A database is a front-end mechanism providing access to information stored in corporate or other organizational information system. The Hague International Court of Justice official database (http://www.icj-cij.org/icjwww/icj002.htm), the United Nations data-base (http://www.un.org), the UN Optical Disk System (http://www.ods.un.org/), the European Union (http://europa.eu.int/) database, the World Trade Organization (http://www.wto.org/) database, and major foreign databases such as AUSTLII-Australasian Legal Information Institute (http://www.austlii. edu.au/) are built according to this structure.

A database is a collection of data organized in such a way that its content can be easily accessed, managed, and updated. Generally, a database has its own server, hosting HTML, PDF, RTF, CGI, and other file formats. In practice, legal professionals work mainly with databases and not with Internet sites. In fact, "the Internet" often has a pejorative connotation in our profession. In summary, it is more accurate to say that we evaluate legal databases than legal sites on the Internet.

I should add that the process of monitoring and evaluating foreign and international legal databases from so many jurisdictions is also a question of content expertise, and requires certain skills. They include weighing and authenticating documents found (to use Richard Danner's words from his article "Redefining a Profession")[46] identifying value-added features, engaging in the establishment of database policies, the ability to recognize and understand copyright issues, maintaining links, implementing mirror sites, and dealing with different languages and various formats. Some consider that "source evaluation is an art",[47] achieved by first acquiring an extraordinary level of understanding. As we know, reference librarians for foreign and international law must work with databases located in faraway servers, different jurisdictions, in many languages, and

[46] Richard A. Danner, "Redefining a Profession."[1998] Available WWW:http://www.law.duke.edu/fac/danner/paper1.html.

[47] Robert Harris, "Evaluating Internet Research Resources."17 November 1997. Online Internet [August 28, 2000]. Available WWW: http://www.sccu.edu/faculty/R_Harris/evalu8it.htm.

in various formats, displaying a great diversity of thinking as well as understanding of different copyright issues. All of this contributes to the complexity of our task.

Though we are still in the process of creating a full set of necessary standards, guidelines are available to guide us to the right information, from the right source, at the right time, and in the form most suitable for use. In addition to the evaluation forms I have designed and use on a daily basis, and which are available at the home page of New York University Law Library—Guide to International and Foreign Legal Databases (http://www.law.nyu.edu/library/foreign_intl/index.html), I would like now to bring your attention to a more comprehensive checklist for evaluating foreign and international legal databases.

Criteria of Evaluation

There are commonsense guidelines for doing this job, such as currentness, accuracy, reliability and others, that are brought on by the newness and peculiar features of the electronic publishing environment. The caveat of "buyer beware" has never been more true.

In his *Introduction to Reference Work*, William A. Katz[48] discusses the evaluation process for print reference sources, taking into consideration criteria such as purpose, authority, scope, currency, audience, cost, format, objectivity, annotated indices, and guides to reference. In a comment on "Evaluation of Databases"[49] found in the same book, he emphasizes that "effective evaluation of databases depends on methods similar to those employed for evaluating printed works, such as purpose, authority and scope." In addition, he makes reference to various formats for storage of database data, means of access, frequency of updating, "what hardware and software is necessary to make use of the database to its fullest," and to the speed and efficiency of search. However, because of many unexpected factors, these criteria have unfortunately proved insufficient, and sometimes actually impossible, to apply to

[48] Katz, William A., *Introduction to Reference Work. Vol. 1: Basic Information Sources*. Sixth Edition. New York: McGraw-Hill, Inc., 1992, p. 23.

[49] *Ibid.*, p. 50.

legal sources online, as the Internet carries both non-professional and professional information. In the former case, a "site" may contain almost any type of data, with home pages usually not disclosing either author or publisher; the source of the information may be uncertain (for example, neither the reliability nor the authority for the data may be specified). Reliable legal databases fall in a different professional category.

Product description and main user identification

Database name; Database subject; Database address; Date of evaluation; Name of the person evaluating and monitoring the database; Official citation; Database contact person.

Despite the fact that databases are cataloged today, not all of them are found in online catalogs and not all of the above elements are included in the online records even when they do exist. In this transitional and still turbulent period of time, we need to watch the above-stated elements carefully and act promptly to accommodate the changes that occur frequently. The address of a database could change as well as its name and features. New content could be added. Coverage and even the language could change (abstracts in other languages than the vernacular, or even full interfaces in other languages than the official one, can appear overnight). Other confusing situations exist, such as that at the University of Southern California's collection of electronic journals (http://www.usc.edu/isd/elecresources/subject/j_a.html), where full-text journals and abstracts appear together with mere tables of contents. The searcher must spend a lot of time to find out what is what.

In the case of fee-based databases with only one available password, these changes need to be shared with all other potential users. In this category fall databases such as the Inter-American Database for International Trade (NATLAW at http://www.natlaw.com) with no IP access, and very dynamic changes in the content. In fact, all international databases load old content continuously, build up mirror servers, and migrate to more accurate URL addresses consistent with the content and server requirements.

Completeness of content

Is this a full text database? Or index and abstracts? Or index only? Many databases are still under construction or in the process of expanding their amount of information. The fee-based Congressional Information Service—CIS (http://www.cispubs.com) databases are an example. In the USA the CIS Congressional Universe, the States Universe, the Indexes, and the Statistical Universe are unsurpassed for their depth, thoroughness of coverage, and the speed at which they acquire comprehensiveness. This is true also of the European Union databases, where nearly every month new data is added.

Content completeness is important even for the established databases in the legal information business, such as Lexis and Westlaw. For example, recent disputes concerning the content of the US treaties database caused relevant changes of which a legal information specialist should be aware. In this regard, a comparison of Lexis and Westlaw made in the summer of 2000 revealed that the US Treaties directory in Lexis contains recent treaties and international agreements released by the US Department of State but not yet printed in TIAS, while Westlaw contains the Senate treaty documents of ratification since the 103rd Congress.

Although partial text databases are unsatisfactory, an index or abstract can often be very helpful in obtaining the citation to an official gazette and locating a source for the full text of a law in electronic or print format from a foreign jurisdiction. Fee-based databases are not always available at our discretion, but they may nevertheless be valuable tools because of their free-to-see indices. Foreign databases that display a summary or an index of laws should be taken into consideration. The following databases are useful in this regard:

Magnus (http://www.magnus.dk/ajour/framdd.htm), a comprehensive fee-based Danish legal database in the vernacular, with prices ranging from $300 to $450 per month. Magnus allows free access to its valuable daily index of legal news.

COLEX-DATA (http://www.colex-data.es), a fee-based database offering free access to a valuable index of new Spanish laws (the last month's laws), followed by a helpful abstract. (See Ultimas Novedades en las Bases de Datos—Jurisprudencia; Legislacion; Derecho Fiscal at http://www.colex-data.es/men unove.htm).

GLIN (http://lcweb2.loc.gov/law/GLINv1/GLIN.html), although fee-based, permits users to search its content. Its citations to official gazettes or other foreign legal documents are always of great help. Unfortunately, GLIN doesn't give us any idea about data coverage by jurisdiction.

Who is the author/publisher

Does the database have standing authority, and if so of what kind—government, university, a legal institution, a private vendor, a Samaritan provider? Does the electronic publisher have a commitment to publish data in the event that data becomes freely available on the Internet? Is there electronic "added value"?

In the case of foreign and international substantive law published by legal databases on the Internet, the ideal situation occurs when both author and publisher are the same entity, for example, a government, a parliament, a department of justice, an international organization, or a legal institute working under government supervision. A fee-based database of a private vendor providing guarantee for the authenticity of legal documents should be viewed as preferable to a database which may be free but does not provide such guarantee. The quality and reputation of the publisher is a guarantee in "creating quality controlled collections".[50] In the field of Internet databases, publisher and author are often the same, and information from such sources should be compared where possible with printed legal documents. It is also becoming common for printed services to rely on, or refer to, online databases. A recent example is *The Handbook of WTO/GATT Dispute Settlement* by Pierre Pescatore and published in the US by Transnational Publishers. In July 2000 the editors stated that "in light of the enormous number of pages of findings in recent WTO Panel and Appellate Body Reports, the editors of the *Handbook* have expanded their Summaries of the Panel and Appellate Body Reports and direct readers to the WTO web site—www.wto.org—under 'trade topics'—'dispute settlement'—for the full text of the decisions."

[50] Emma Worsfold, "Questioning the Quality of Internet Information," 64 IFLA General Conference, August 1998. [Online Internet] Available WWW:http://www.ifla.org/IV/ifla64/worsfold.pdf.

Going one step further, there are situations when a direct question to the Webmaster of a database is the best approach under the circumstances. For me, this was the case with The South African Cyber Treaty Series by Arnold Pronto (http://home.earthlink.net/~apronto/treaties/trindex.htm). To be sure about the reliability of the database, I directly asked the Webmaster about his credentials and the sources of his data. His answer (http://home.earthlink.net/~apronto/treaties/trindex.htm) was satisfactory, so I included his database in my annotated guide to South African legal resources (http://www.law.nyu.edu/library/foreign_intl/southafrica.html).

Despite the fact that many data are freely available, private vendors nonetheless provide this data at a cost. This is not as contradictory as it seems. Electronic publishers play a major role, even in a "free information environment", because they "add electronic value" by competition, enhanced software, data quality, support and training .[51] Money is paid for "the value added to the source". We witness this process today in many jurisdictions, from international organizations to foreign country databases. Free databases coexist with fee-based ones, and the information specialist has to decide which is suitable and proper in the structure of his or her job's working environment.

Source verification is a major concern. Is there a guarantee of content authenticity, e.g., an electronic signature on imaged pages such as we find at (for example) Republick Osterreich (http://www.ris.bka.gv.at/), The Australasian Legal Information Institute (AUSTLII) (http://www.austlii.edu.au), Sistema Argentino de Informatica Juridica (SAIJ) (http://www.saij.jus.gov.ar/), and Deutschland REFACT (http://www.refact.de/rda_inh.htm)? A scandal on Wall Street (August 2000) was related to sensitive information published by Internet portals that misled shareholders and caused the bad investment of thousands of millions of dollars. This event brought to international attention the hot issue of source verification. The ensuing series of law suits is certain to enforce this criteria as

[51] Robin Williamson, "Free Access to Electronic Law?" CTI: New Directions in Legal Information Systems. A one-day seminar for academics, librarians, and legal practitioners, Friday 20th February 1998. Scarman House Conference Centre, University of Warwick, Coventry. (September 25, 2000). Available WWW: http://www.law.warwick.ac.uk/seminars/sem98-1b.html.

a requirement for reliable commercial and news databases. As the evaluation of databases must follow general guidelines, as applied to any databases on the Internet, these developments will affect legal databases too.

Does the database indicate the page of the printed document?

More and more databases now indicate the actual pagination of the printed legal document, as well as the citation to the official code, gazette, or reporter. The German database REFACT (http://www.refact.de/rda_inh.htm) does this; the UN Treaty Collection (http://untreaty.un.org/) displays the image page of the UNTS series. In Canada, QUICKLAW (http://www.quicklaw.com/) and a new database recently launched by eCarswell, LAW.PRO (http://ww1.ecarswell.com/law.pro) are disputing the rights of pagination of the Carswell Law Reports. eCarswell also announced that it will offer legal documents in both html and pdf (the imaged page of the reporter with the printed pagination).

Do we have the imaged version of the official page in pdf or other formats ? Is there also an HTML version? Or are there both pdf and html versions, such as may be found in UN ODS (http://www.ods.un.org/) and the Swiss Systematische Sammlung des Bundesrechts—Recueil Systematique du Droit Federal (Swiss Federal Law) (http://www.admin.ch/ch/f/rs/rs.html)?

The ideal, of course, is to obtain the original version in the vernacular in pdf format (image of the original text) together with a translation in another language (English or French or Spanish would be preferred whenever Chinese or Japanese or Russian are the language of databases). This ideal is usually hard and expensive to acquire, although some international organizations such as the UN, supranational organizations such as the European Union, and governments such as the German and Swiss are already providing data in this way. Nevertheless, it is preferable to have the original version of a legal document, rather than an English translation which may be without guarantee of accuracy.

Language

Is the vernacular the only version available? Or is there an English, French, Spanish, or German abstract, or an abstract in any other widely-known language?

Full-text databases containing foreign laws in English are an important requirement for English-speaking information specialists. Constitutions at Wuerzburg University (http://www.uni-wuerzburg.de/law/index.html), tax treaties of the world at Taxbase (http://taxbase.tax.org/), laws from all jurisdictions in unofficial translations at World News Connection, commercial and licensing laws at EIU (http://store. eiu.com/), Latin American countries' laws at NATLAW (http://www.natlaw.com/index.htm)—these are a few examples of good English -language sources. I would add international organization databases, as well as international courts and criminal tribunals.

In general, however, most foreign legal databases offer no information about the content in any other than the vernacular. They display it in the country or confederation languages, or perhaps in another language historically close to that legal culture. This is the case with Confederatio Helvetica, the Swiss government database (http://www.admin.ch/), which offers legal documents in French, Italian, and German, the official languages of the Confederation. Belgian databases provide legal documents in Dutch and French, the official languages of Belgium. On the other hand, many Chinese databases, such as Ceilaw (http://www.ceilaw.com.cn) and Great China Web (http://www.gcw.net) do not give us any hint about the content in any other language, but you may find Macao laws in Portuguese. The same is true of the Russian databases such as KonsultantPlius (http://www.consultant.ru/). If you don't know the Cyrillic alphabet you cannot understand the content or even the names of the legislative materials in the database. Some databases provide an English service (Juristisches Internet Project Saarbrucken, http://www.jura.uni-sb.de/), or English abstracts. This is the case with GLAW (German Case Law Project, http://www.uni-wuerzburg.de/glaw), which has moved recently to Bayerische Julius-Maximilians-Universität Würzburg (http://www.uni-wuerzburg.de/dfr/index.html).

Accuracy

Is the information correct? Fully or partly? Is it comprehensive? Is the content as reliable as its print counterpart? Does the resource have an organization or expert backing it? Are there any obvious errors or omissions in the documents? Is the information of consistent quality?

When both are available to me, I always compare online documents with the printed ones. This exercise helps me see the differences or even the gaps. Gene L. Wilkinson emphasized the importance of objectivity of recognizing "indications of careless or hasty preparation". [52] D. Scott Brandt considered as important points of source evaluation the ways in which "information gets filtered"[53]—e.g., whether it is written and/or issued by an authoritative source (such as a federal government or other reliable organization); authenticated as part of an editorial or peer review process by a publisher; or evaluated by experts, reviewers or subject specialists/librarians as part of a collection development. Aimee Glassel[54] highlighted the importance of selection criteria to filter resources and recom-mended starting "with a site recognized for its authority; look for references to new resources; evaluate new resources as either a potential site to review, or as a new source for further scouting."

In any case, it is worthwhile whenever possible to obtain the views and opinions of scholars from different coun-tries concerning their own country's databases. INT-LAW and EUROLEX listserv members (over two thousand scholars from more than 60 countries) are of great help in maintaining the critical review process.

An outstanding example of high quality regarding all evaluation criteria is the US Government Printing Office Access (http://www.gpo.gov/gpoaccess/). At this moment, it would seem natural for the databases published by the US government or US legislative bodies to become accepted by the legal community as documents fully as reliable as their printed counterparts (which will in fact be discontinued soon) or as the texts available on Lexis and Westlaw. I see no reason why a document published by the US GPO is not as authentic as the Westlaw or Lexis document. We can see here a sort of

[52] Gene L. Wilkinson, "Evaluating the Quality of Internet Information Resources." [August 23, 2000.] Available WWW: http://itech18.coe.uga.edu/faculty/gwilkinson/webeval.html.

[53] Scott D. Brandt, "Evaluating Information on the Internet." [1st May, 1998.] Available WWW:http://thorplus.lib.purdue.edu/~techman/evaluate.htm.

[54] Aimee Glassel, "Finding Quality Resources on the Internet: Filtering and Selecting for the Internet Scout Project: http://scout.cs.wisc.edu." [August 20, 2000.] Available WWW: http://www.ifla.org/IV/ifla64/glassel.pdf.

conservative attitude, fueled by commodity and prejudice. The use of the databases on the Internet versus conventional sources is no longer a real issue, but merely a mental attitude.

Currency and Timeliness

Currency is an important consideration, emphasizing the inherent advantage Internet databases have over print sources. Currency involves the answers to such questions as: Is the document page or home page dated? When was it last revised? Are statutes and cases updated? How often? How timely is the content? [55] Does the electronic publisher have a commitment to the ongoing maintenance and stability of the resource? How current are the links? What percentage of them are dead and misdirected?

Some work is timeless, explains Robert Harris, like the classic novels and stories; other work has a limited useful life because of advances in the discipline; and some work is quickly outdated, as in the field of common law. Therefore, we must often decide whether the database information is still of value, and of how much value. Harris stressed: "An important idea connected with timeliness is the dynamic, fluid nature of information and the fact that constant change means constant changes in timeliness. The facts we learn today may be timely now, but tomorrow will not be."

Often a document includes the date when the information was gathered, or clearly refers to dated information, or to a "publication date or a last updated date," or to a date of copyright.[56]

Determining the date of the last updating of a database or of a legal document is a very difficult task, especially when dealing with civil law jurisdictions where no date is displayed on the home page. Often there is a date, but it refers to anything rather than the question of updating the legal content. In many cases, however, even when webmasters do not care to inform us about this issue, the machines themselves can be very informative, because they can neither lie nor ignore this issue due to

[55] Harris, Robert, *ibid.*

[56] Kirk, Elisabeth E."Evaluating Information Found on the Internet."August 28, 2000] Available WWW:http://milton.mse.jhu.edu:8001/research/education/net.html.

their built-in software. The Hypertext Transfer Protocol (HTTP) is the language which Web clients and Web servers use to communicate with each other. The server can "tell" about the currency of data whenever there is a doubt related to a database or a document. This can be done through Telnet.

Telnet is the standard for character-based network communications. It is a part of TCP/IP, the networking protocol of the Internet, used to connect to the Internet and wide-area networks. Computer users on local area networks and on the Internet use Telnet to connect to a remote host and execute programs on the host. Telnet server is a server application that runs on a host computer and allows remote users to "Telnet in" to a host. Telnet client is a client application that allows a user to "Telnet out" from his system to run a program on remote hosts. In trying to learn when a database was last updated, it is wise to use the HTTP protocol. When we "talk" directly with the server, we operate through telnet within a personal email account on a UNIX server. Otherwise the remote server cannot be approached. We must identify ourselves in order to gain access to a server's data.

Here is what I have done in order to find out the updates of Confederatio Helvetica (http://www.admin.ch), the Swiss government database. First, I went to my Telnet port i5.nyu. edu, logged in, and at the prompt typed "telnet". The technique is to omit http:// from the beginning of the URL but to add 80, which is the standard port for any server in the world, at the end of the address. Here is how this procedure works: at the prompt: telnet, enter the name of the host you wish to connect to: www.admin.ch 80, and press the enter key:

```
mr24 @ i5 /home1/m/mr24 % telnet www.admin.ch 80
Trying 193.5.216.31...
Connected to adminsrv.admin.ch.
Escape character is '^]'.
```

At this prompt type the following command (^ means leave a space):

HEAD^/^ HTTP/1.0

Now hit the enter key twice to leave a blank line. This is what I received:

```
mr24 @ i5 /home1/m/mr24 % telnet www.admin.ch 80
Trying 193.5.216.31...
Connected to adminsrv.admin.ch.
Escape character is '^]'.
HEAD / HTTP/1.0

HTTP/1.1 200 OK
Date: Wed, 21 Feb 2001 15:45:14 GMT
Server: Apache/1.3.17 (Unix) tomcat/1.0 PHP/4.0.4pl1 mod_perl/1.21 mod_frontpag3
Vary: accept-language
Last-Modified: Mon, 19 Feb 2001 08:04:19 GMT
ETag: "1de3e1-20f2-3a90d383;4507c-23b-37ccc415"
Accept-Ranges: bytes
Content-Length: 8434
Connection: close
Content-Type: text/html
Content-Language: de
Expires: Wed, 21 Feb 2001 15:45:14 GMT

Connection closed by foreign host.
```

To find more about a specific file (Ex: http://www.admin.ch/ch/f/rs/rs.html), follow the same steps with the difference that at step no. 2 you type in the specific directory's address:

1. Telnet—the same as above.

2. Type in the file's address containing links to Recueil systématique du droit fédéral :

HEAD^/^rs.html/HTTP/1.0

3. Hit the enter key twice to leave a blank line:

```
Escape character is '^]'.
HEAD / re.html/HTTP/1.0

HTTP/1.1 200 OK
Date: Wed, 21 Feb 2001 15:51:12 GMT
Server: Apache/1.3.17 (Unix) tomcat/1.0 PHP/4.0.4pl1 mod_perl/1.21 mod_frontpag3
Vary: accept-language
Last-Modified: Mon, 19 Feb 2001 08:04:19 GMT
ETag: "1de3e1-20f2-3a90d383;4507c-23b-37ccc415"
Accept-Ranges: bytes
Content-Length: 8434
Connection: close
Content-Type: text/html
Content-Language: de
Expires: Wed, 21 Feb 2001 15:51:12 GMT

Connection closed by foreign host.
```

The server revealed that the French directory of the database was updated on the same day as the entire database. Also, comparing my previous attempts to find the same information, I discovered that the database is updated twice a week, specifically on Mondays and Wednesdays. The shortcoming of this technique is that, even though the server indicates the date of change in the physical file, this may not necessarily reflect the currency of information.[57] Moreover, some pages are updated automatically in databases using artificial intelligence. The date is updated every time *any* change is made to the file, no matter how insignificant, as for example adding a comma.

The above example may appear somewhat extreme. Another way to evaluate currentness is by checking the occurrence of dead and misdirected links. The bigger the percentage, the less reliable the database. The age of links is also important. Links that point to out-of-date databases suggest that the database in question is not credible.

Free databases such as AUSTLII are considered standard tools in their jurisdiction, even though the statutes are updated in AUSTLII only once a year. In order to check the latest developments, ScalePlus (http://law.agps.gov.au/) should be used as an updating tool. Other free databases (in the UK, for example) are fragmented or not updated at all, so other services try to supplement the missing information. One of these is the Court Service by Smith Bernal's Casetrack (http://www.smithbernal.com/). In the EU law free databases, not all judgements or laws are linked or updated. The legal information specialist must be aware of all these issues while doing legal research. Annotations, headnotes, and linkage are all available in fee-based databases such as CELEX, Westlaw, Lexis, and Butterworths (http://www.butterworths.com/).

Coverage

One of the major problems in evaluating Internet full-text databases is that the records are very dynamic. The scope and

[57] Alastair G. Smith, "Testing the Surf: Criteria for Evaluating Internet Information Resources," 3 *The Public-Access Computer Systems Review* 8 (1997). [August 28, 2000] Available WWW:http://info.lib.uh.edu/pr/v8/n3/smit8n3.html.

the coverage can change overnight. The FAQ file and the description of the database should be visited once in a while. Same databases cover in full text only the last few weeks of a legal publication—such as the French Official Journal (official version: http://www.journal-officiel.gouv.fr/)—others are trying to be complete, such as the International Court of Justice database (http://www.icj-cij.org/icjwww/icj002.htm). ICJ continuously loads legal data. As of March 2001, the database contains all contentious cases and advisory opinions referred to the Court since 1946 and the unpublished pleadings of selected cases. United Nations ODS (http://www.ods.org) has formally announced that the full texts of documents dating back to 1992 are now accessible in Portable Document Format(PDF) in all official languages of the United Nations—Arabic, Chinese, English, French, Russian and Spanish. The database has an English and a French interface. UN documents are stored in two databases: UN Documentation, which includes documents since 1992, and UN Resolutions, which includes resolutions of the General Assembly, Security Council, and Economic and Social Council and Trusteeship Council since 1946.

Archiving

How long will the provider keep data ? Is accumulation limited to certain types of data? Will the data be archived by another provider, and if so who? Does the database state archival duty ? Does the database permit users to make/obtain digital copies of content for archiving and for use in perpetuity ?

For example, EUR-Lex (http://europa.eu.int/eur-lex/) keeps EU Official Journal issues (http://europa.eu.int/eur-lex/en/oj/index-list.html) only for 45 days after the date of publication. After that they can be found in EUDOR (http://eudor.eur-op.eu.int). EUDOR informs users that the Official Journals of previous years (back to 1952) will gradually be made available from the time the site is made public (as of March 2001, EUDOR is a fee-based database, providing also some documents free of charge). Norway's legal database Lovdata (http://www.lovdata.no/eng/index.html) offers Supreme Court decisions shortly after release by the Court, but each decision remains available for about two months only. Many much-relied-upon databases have no archiving commitment. CELEX (http://europa.eu.int/celex) and WTO (http://www.wto.org), for instance, do not mention an archiving commitment anywhere, so we must remain aware of the possibility of the disappearance of some data from these databases. In order to prevent loss in such an event, we must always have alternative parallel sources.

Search quality/findability

Is there a link to an external search engine, or is there a search engine embedded in the database? Is there a built-in thesaurus? Are these features easy to use? What kind of logic does the search engine depend on—Boolean logic? Fuzzy logic? Natural language processing? Concept-based searching? Is searching restricted in its criteria—date, kind of legal document, citation, region?

Senado Federal de Brasil (http://www.senado.gov.br/), with its built-in thesaurus WEBTHES (http://webthes.senado.gov.br/thes), has an excellent search engine. CELEX (http://europa.eu.int/celex/htm/celex_en.htm) has an online glossary of terms. To see it, go to "About CELEX", "Online User Guide" and "Glossary of Terms". United Nations Treaty Collection provides a guide and definitions of key terms to use with its search form, as well as a glossary of terms relating to treaty actions (http://untreaty.un.org/english/guide.asp).

Serena Fenton rates "Search Engine Intelligence" as one of the most important criteria in evaluating a database.[58] In fact, "findablity" is important not only for new users but for experienced ones too.[59] The ability to find the needed document quickly is a big advantage. In some major databases, such as GLIN (http://lcweb2.loc.gov/law/GLINv1/GLIN.html) and READEX (http://infoweb3.newsbank.com)(Index to United Nations microfiche system), searching is quite difficult. GLIN has real problems with the search engine form. READEX search engine form fields are very peculiar. You must know very well to which field of the form the searching terms might apply. In the beginning ODS (UN Optical Disk System) was in the same cate-

[58] Serena Jardine Fenton, "Information Quality: Is the Truth Out There?"[23 April, 1998.] Available WWW:http://ils.unc.edu/~fents/310/.

[59] Karen R. Diaz, "The best of the best: ranking and rating digital reference sources," 39 *Reference and Users Services Quarterly* 17 (Fall 1999).

gory, but the database's dialog with its users and its openness and willingness to change finally made ODS a product whose findability may be rated as good. An opposite example is the Minnesota Human Rights database search engine (http://www1.umn.edu/humanrts/). The previous search engine was better. The new one has the ambition to be comprehensive, to search at once all possible human rights databases. Its authors are violating the principle of decentralization, crucial in the WWW environment at this stage of its development.

Another issue related to findability is the terminology[60] used for services. European and Asian databases use names different than we are used to to label the same services. Linguistic "obscurity" coming from different legal concepts, or from word-by-word translation into English of foreign legal terms, is a problem the information specialist should be aware of.

Workability

Alastair Smith[61] uses this term to describe the resource convenience and its effectiveness of use. Workability can include user friendliness; resource access with standard equipment or special viewing and downloading instructions (an example could be seen at EUDOR databases where instructions are displayed for decompressing files and all other technical maneuvers, http://www.eudor.com:8444/EUDOR/DISPLAY/faq.htm/897688068); password; network and software requirements; browsability and organization; and a logical manner to locate the resources/ the site navigation/the site legend.

In this respect, the Eur-Lex site map (http://europa.eu.int/eur-lex/en/map.html) is outstanding. A "site legend" is a "website feature that contains the descriptive documentation information essential for making an initial assessment about the website and the worth of its content."[62] A good organi-

[60] Barbara I. Dewey, "In search of services: analyzing the findability of links on CIC university libraries' Web pages." 18 *Information Technology and Libraries* 210 (December 1999).

[61] Alastair Smith, "Criteria for evaluation of Internet Information Resources." [August 29, 2000.] Available WWW: http://www.vuw.ac.nz/~agsmith/evaln/index.htm.

[62] Robert M. Weiler and Lisa N Pealer, "The Site Legend: Twelve

zational scheme (e.g., categorized by subject, format, chronology, etc.) is also helpful.

An example of all these difficulties can be experienced at the Italian Supreme Court database, Corte Suprema di Cassazione (http://www.giustizia.it/cassazione/), a fee-based database that costs $1,500/year for one password and is very frustrating to work with. EasyFind is the software that has to be downloaded in order to access the database. The downloading is possible only with a special password, which is different from the one given for accessing the database. The browser and the computer configurations must be changed every time a user accesses the database. This downloading process and the connection to the database took me more than one week, including back-and-forth email to Italy. Special assistance from the library's computer support was needed. All information regarding the database was in Italian only. The database handbook, written in 1996, did not cover all user questions. In order to be of real value for the legal community at large, Corte Suprema di Cassazione must adjust to the features of the new electronic environment. The difficulties in accessing the database are high, and the required configurations are time-consuming and primitive.

More and more, access to databases requires software applications (plug-ins)[63] such as Adobe Acrobat Reader, Shockware, Real Audio Player, and others. To read and search Chinese and Japanese databases Asian Suite, a very effective interface, is required. Similar software downloaded for free will not allow the searcher to write in the search box, so only Asian Suite helps to search these databases.

As a courtesy, some webmasters provide links to databases containing plug-ins that are easy to download. The necessary software is not always free, however. In some cases, software comes with the package. This is the case with JUDIS

Components of a New Strategy for Providing Website Documentation," 70 *The Journal of School Health* 148 (April 2000).

[63] Plug-ins allow a browser to display multiple media types such as animation and sound, or to perform other functions in a manner clear to the user. For example, there is a plug-in that allows sound files to be played directly from the browser window, without downloading the files in the computer and using another software.

(http://www.judis.nic.in/), which contains all reportable judgments of the Supreme Court of India since 1950. From 1950 to 1998 they are on CD-ROM. From 1998 to date they may be obtained online. A special device is necessary in order to access the CD-ROM. Moreover, for security and licensing reasons, the CD-ROM can be installed only once in one computer. If the computer has to be replaced for any reason, a new CD-ROM is required.

Stability/server reliability/malfunctions

Is there a mirror site? Does database use fluctuate at different times of day? A study from the Internet Research Group indicates that 85 percent of the largest Web databases will have multiple hosts by the year 2001.[64] As the Internet grows, the practice of having two or more hosts for one database is becoming more prevalent. This procedure speeds the delivery of content to end users (downloading), and also improves traffic management (congestion that must to be avoided).

As I have already indicated, servers have a limited numbers of ports, which means that there is a limited number of users able to access the server at the same time. An example of extreme congestion is seen at the CELEX database. In this case, one may be better off using more than one location/publisher whenever possible. This can be done, for instance, when CISG (United Nations Convention on Contracts for the International Sale of Goods) documents are needed. The CISG Online Project (http://www.jura.uni-freiburg.de/ipr1/cisg/title.htm) is maintained by the Institute of Foreign and International Private Law at the University of Freiburg, Germany. It provides the status of the convention, text, cases, bibliographic references and German case law on the CISG. However, the International Trade Database at Pace University (http://cisgw3.law.pace.edu/) provides the same content. The International Court of Justice official database (http://www.icj-cij.org/icjwww/icj002.htm) has three mirror servers: the Cornell mirror database (http://www.lawschool.cornell.edu/library/cijww); the French mirror (http://www.u-paris2.fr/cij); and the UK Glasgow mirror (http://www.icj.law.gla.ac.uk). The United Nations Optical Disk sys-

[64] Brian Quinton. "Road maps to content: Akamai debuts service to route users to distributed Web sites." 238 *Telephony* 26 Nr.23 (June 2000).

tem (ODS) (http://www.ods.un.org) has a mirror site in Geneva under a slightly different title: Documents of the United Nations. Geneva Optical Disk system Web Server (http://www.undocs.unog.ch).

Open to any kind of problems, many databases list any possible errors encountered by the searcher. Malfunctions range from server malfunction during some periods of time (European databases and United Nations databases both have their pick hour problems) to situations where similar searches in the same database in the same period of time bring different results. As Karen Diaz remarked in her above-mentioned article on "The Best of the Best", a great database that can not be reached "is as useful as a great reference book that is nowhere to be found".

Interactivity with the user

Are there interactive files such as forms for queries and/or comments? Are they helpful? Is it easy to request documents or order publications (using, e.g., cgi scripts, perl programs)? Is online user support available?

The length of time it takes to respond to an email message submitted to a database is a good way to gauge the quality of a web-based relationship. Speaking from my own experience, I can recommend databases such as WTO based in Geneva, SAIJ based in Argentina, Wettenbank from The Netherlands, Hong Kong and China legal portals, and AUSTLII located in Australia, from all of which I have received prompt responses to my email. The time lag must be taken into consideration when dealing with overseas databases.

Cost: online versus print format

Are there hidden costs? Other costs that are not hidden? How much cost above and beyond the actual cost of the document is attributable to licensing of the content and providing access?

My belief is that a subject-oriented database should cost no more than its print analog. Ideally, a legal specialist should maintain one paper copy in addition to the electronic version. In this transition period, however, end users may actually be helping to fund a database that is still incomplete or growing (e.g., UN ODS). But it is always important to remember that the database has the advantage of being more timely than the printed service. Indeed, it is preferable to rely primarily on database sources for several reasons: because electronic databases represent the future format in which legal documents will exist; because today electronic databases offer the most up-to-date legal information; and because the user is not a prisoner of a library's collection anymore. The user can access electronic collections of laws from any location in the world.

Almost every fee-based database has a different approach to pricing. Many offer a subscription specifying a particular number of records and require further payment for additional records. This is the case with the Chinese CEIlaw database (http://www.ceilaw.com.cn). European databases such as Jurifrance (http://www.jurifrance.com/) offer a specific amount of information for a flat fee, and charge for each additional use. I receive an invoice from France each time I look at or print a document from Jurifrance. LAWSITE (http://www.lawsite.co.nz/law/ct_frame.htm) from New Zealand charges per view, per search, per data services products, such as recent decisions, $5.00 (PDF format); Environmental News Bulletin, $5.00 (PDF format); Environmental Digest, $3.00 per section; $20.00 per statute; $15.00 per PDF decision downloaded; etc.

The Russian database Garant (http://www.garant.ru), which provides documents in Russian and selected documents in English, charges about $250 per month for unrestricted access, but also offers a flat rate subscription with charges for additional use. However, speaking in Moscow with Garant representatives, I learned that the database actually charges $1 per Kilobyte of information. I also learned that Garant was unaware that Cyrillic documents can take up to five times more K than documents in the Roman alphabet, and that consequently it is unfair to charge the same rate per K for an English document and a Russian document. This was a very unexpected perspective, and the Garant representatives promised to establish a more equitable pricing policy.

Copyright stipulations

Information related to the copyright aspects of using legal information published by a foreign or international database is indispensable. It is common for legal specialists to address this issue while buying a new database. Most databases maintain a file listing the permissions to reproduce and the protocols to be followed in such a situation. Some databases, in an effort to discourage aggressive users from downloading huge amounts of information, restrict downloading to a limited amount. On the other hand, free databases need to have some control over unrestricted use, so registration, or a request for permission to reproduce a particular document, may be required. Recent discussions have brought to international attention the possibility of web-linking agreements[65] in order to protect databases against misuse. This idea is somewhat unrealistic, as the World Wide Web is, in essence, "a protocol that exists only to link sites to each other," and it is "hard to see how anyone could claim the right to restrict site access only to those receiving specific information to do so."[66] There may also be copyright issues regarding the "structure, sequence, and organization of those links"; copying them could constitute a copyright infringement.

An interesting "web-linking" idea has emerged in the OpenURL (http://www.sfxit.com), a protocol between an information resource and a service component which offers localized services in an open linking environment. OpenURL (http://www.sfxit.com/OpenURL/openurl.html) is built on the idea that links should lead a user to appropriate resources. It transports metadata, or keys to access metadata, via an Institutional Service Component (ISC). This development could be of value in enhancing the librarian's ability to define the library's electronic collection, including both licensed and freely available resources, and to determine the manner in which the component resources can be linked to best suit the library's users.

New copyright laws applicable to the Internet are in force or in the process of being enacted in many jurisdictions of the world. WIPO, the USA and the European Union have been very active in this area. Information technology and the WWW have given rise to extensive discussions in the international arena on this field of law, as well as a growing corpus of cases. In the

[65] American Bar Association. *Web-Linking Agreements: Contracting Strategies and Model Provisions*. Book Publishing ABA: Chicago, 1997.

[66] Rosenoer, Jonathan. *CyberLaw: The Law of the Internet*. New York: Springer, 1997 (See the Chapter on Copyright, pp. 1-93.)

cyberlegal environment, viewing, copying, distribution, public performance and display, and Internet transmission are extremely important. For the most part, databases charge only for viewing, and it is unclear to what extent downloading the information to a disk file requires a licence.[67]

An example of a copyright permission statement appears in EUR-Lex (http://europa.eu.int/eur-lex/en/copy right.html):

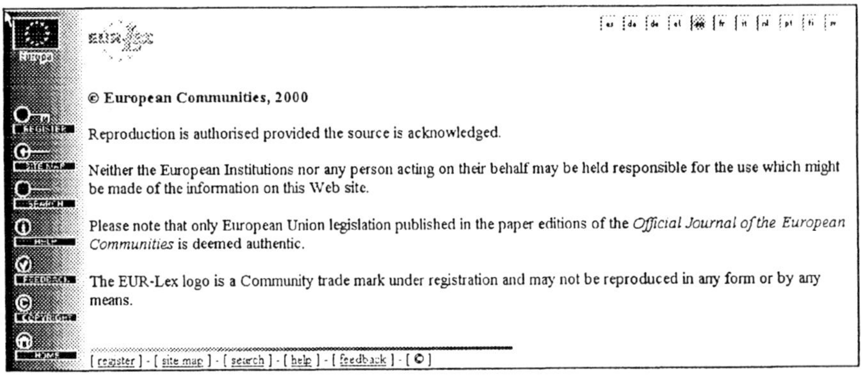

Copyright is also related to the amount of information available and to updating concerns. In the UK, the government databases post statutes as published; they do not contain further amendments. Privatization of government services (HMSO, http://www.official-documents.co.uk/menu/uk.htm), and the debate over Crown Copyright which "provides a property right in government information" is being pursued by private agencies and commercial vendors of information. An ongoing debate in the UK suggests that HMSO must abolish licences for legislative and judicial material in order to provide public access to primary legal information.[68]

[67] Street, F. Lawrence and Mark P. Grant. *Law of the Internet.* Charlottesville,VA: Lexis Law Publishing, 2000, p. 484. See Chapter 5 for analysis of copyright laws all over the world.

[68] Andrew Charlesworth. "Primary Legal Information on the Internet—Vision and Reality." CTI. New Directions in Legal Information Systems. A one day seminar for academics, librarians, and legal practitioners, Friday 20th February 1998. Scarman House Conference Centre, University of Warwick, Coventry (September 25, 2000). Available WWW: http://www.law.warwick.ac.uk/seminars/sem98-1b.html.

Licensing

Does the database permit fair use of all information for non-commercial educational, instructional and research purposes by authorized users, including unlimited viewing, downloading, and printing ? Is the number of simultaneous users limited ?

Licensing agreements for digital content have become more prominent in the electronic era. A licensing agreement should cover those circumstances which a content owner and user/purchaser agree upon for the use of certain specified content in a digital environment. First, we must understand the nature of licensing content for appropriate use. After that, we must decide upon an appropriate type of arrangement. The licensing provisions involving copyrights must be understood in order to use a database.[69] Relevant issues that concern legal information specialists working with electronic databases include the evaluation of licensing agreements, minimizing the risks in licensing electronic resources, strategies to protect the organization interest while working with consortia, strategies to overcome negotiations, basic principles on pricing, impact of electronic delivery, and cost recovery (i.e., publisher's obligations, user's obligations, who may access the content, how much is charged for the content).

There is no consistency in the way this matter is handled. At one time TAXBASE (http://www.taxbase.tax.org) accepted multi-users for one password. A single annual subscription gave unlimited access to any tax professional in a company, which meant that one "tax professional" could make his password available to more than 10 persons working with him or her. Today, however, TAXBASE offers portions of the database for a specified price. Multiple user subscriptions use a different rate. LoisLaw (http://www.pita.com) uses flat rate pricing and offers monthly payment programs. A single user Internet license can be shared among multiple users. In contrast, ODS (http://www.ods.un.org) and CELEX (http://europa.eu.int/celex/) allow only one access per password at a time, while the United Nations Treaty Collection (http://untreaty.un.org) and the Eu-

[69] See an interesting review in Kurz, Raymond A., *Assignment and Licensing:Internet and the Law. Legal Fundamentals for the Internet User.* Rockville, Maryland: Government Institutes, 1996.

ropean Journal of International Law (http://www.ejil.org) accept IP address.[70]

In addition, the term "fair use" (see AALL Copyright Committee Report—Fair Use Guidelines at: http://www. aall net.org/committee/copyright/fair_use.html) does not have the same meaning in Europe as it does in the US (see the Copyright Act, 17 U.S.C. Section 107). In recent years, US case-law and statutory law related to the Internet have developed strongly.[71] The fair use exemption in Europe is, generally speaking, more limited than in the US. For example, in the U.K. it appears that there is no "educational" fair use.

Databases monitoring intellectual property and copyright issues in Europe may be found at the European Union Information Society Website (http://www.ispo.cec.be/Wel come.html), the Legal Advisory Board (http://www.ispo.cec.be/legal/en/lab/lablab.html), the Legal News (http://www.ispo.cec.be/legal), and the Internet Action Plan Promoting Safer Use of the Internet (http://www.ispo.cec.be/iap).

"The law governing electronic commerce, software licenses, and published information content over the Internet is in larval stage both in the United States and around the globe."[72] This reality sometimes makes the task of dealing with cross-border procedures and restrictions and norms of foreign jurisdictions difficult or even impossible.

Structural considerations/database performance

The record structure and the index structure of databases with built-in search engines reveal the structure of the database.[73] The evaluation must estimate the record structure and the subject hierarchy structure. Greg R. Notess recommends comparison of the subject structure to a traditional thesaurus.

[70] IP address is the numeric address of a particular computer connected to the Internet. TCP/IP software (SLIP or PPP) allows computers to access the Internet via a modem or telephone line.

[71] See Rosenoer, *CyberLaw: The Law of the Internet, ibid.*, pp. 1-93.

[72] Hoffer, Steven. *World Cyberspace Law.* Juris Publishing, Inc. (2000), p.12-1.

[73] Greg R Notess, "Tips for Evaluating Web Databases," 21 *Database* 69 (April/May 1998.)

In databases with powerful search engines, the full stored text is directly available through search results. When retrieved records only display extracts of the full texts, the searcher doesn't know which are the searchable fields. The retrieved records offer the only guidance. Because indexes of internal search engines cannot be browsed and the search engines do not offer full records, the searcher must know in depth how the database search engine manages the search.

The duration of transactions[74] (search and content delivery) is another point to be considered as a key measurement of database performance. Any eventual barriers to accessing information at its entry point must also be considered. Nor can ongoing research to continuously refine the database be overlooked. Some databases, such as WTO, are changing so quickly that we must be aware of this process. Changing database features means a new configuration and database structure, which is not comfortable at all. Database managers often have no idea of the shock they provoke for end users. Sometimes a whole new training is required in order to familiarize users with the new features. The issue here involves "real-time communications services over the Internet" and the need for "a new architecture to meet their required quality".[75] It is an inevitable consequence of improvements in types of networks and servers. In the short term, however, it can interrupt the performance of quality services .

Conclusion

It is becoming clear that, in the provision of legal information (especially statutory law and caselaw), electronic format will predominate over, if not completely replace, print sources. In the traditional media era the publisher sent out individual copies of the same product/book that readers acquired for their instructional, educational, etc., needs. The dissemination of information was centrifugal. In the electronic age the dissemination of information is centripetal. Users access

[74] Terry Sweeney, "Content delivery needs improved management tools," 776 *Informationweek* 166 (March 6, 2000).

[75] Ikda, Katsuyoshi, Kenji Kawahara, and Yuji Oie, "Performance Evaluation of the Architecture for End-to-End Quality-of-Service Provisioning," 38 *IEEE Communications Magazine* 76 (No. 4, April 1, 2000).

the information published in a server through an Internet connection. Therefore, it is critically important from the outset to establish clear standards for publication and access over the Internet. These standards must be agreed upon among Internet database publishers and users. The information and research environments make the evaluation process a problem involving content, access, point of view, and server and database configuration.

The evaluation depends on our patrons' needs, the realities of our workplace, and our technological surroundings. The main concerns in the evaluation process are the quality of information found on the Internet and the ways of accessing it. Criteria of evaluation are equally valuable as starting points in building electronic resource collections, developing Internet-based information services, or instructing users in the effective use of digital information. Value-added features will continue to make fee-based databases as popular as the free ones. These two phenomena will coexist as long they respond to different user profiles (ranging from citizens to information specialists) and to different needs (from finding a statute to the case law related to it).

Chapter 4

Teaching versus Reference versus Teaching: Restructuring the Mission of the Law Library

Experience shows that a law librarian (especially in an academic environment), if he or she is to survive in the dynamic circumstances of the cyberlegal culture, must build self-sufficient faculty, lawyers, and students through training. *Dis-intervention* and *disintermediation,* explained in Chapter 2 of this book, require the creation of independently skilled patrons through the instruction of high technology information resources. The fact that the law librarian's task is greater today at the teaching level is proven by the degree to which research overlaps teaching. There is a point where research is simply impossible if the patron cannot work comfortably in the cyberlegal world. And in order to do that he or she must be taught.

Teaching foreign and international law research in both the WWW environment and the traditional one means building a non-linear mode of thinking able to decipher and adjust to the configuration of information contained in electronic, print, and microform resources as well as to the paradigms that lie behind them. This task must be accomplished through various teaching styles and communication skills, including flexibility, interconnectivity, synergy, and knowledge of artificial intelligence patterns and structures. Law librarians who perform as teachers themselves learn, and pass to others via the instruction process, the ability to instantly recognize the shortcomings of the virtual reality generated by and pertaining to cyberlegal culture as well as the trends of its developments. And they also learn and teach its specific logic, with its vagueness or "fuzzy" quality, the logic of cybernetics. As logic is the science of reasoning, fuzzy logic is the science of reasoning with imprecise concepts.

In the cyberlegal culture there are no black-and-white realities or answers, but another kind of apprehension that is comparable to human thought, which cannot be nailed down to easy concepts. Within cyberlegal research and teaching there is not a two-valued logic of "yes" and "no" with the Aristotelian excluded middle. The cyberlegal domain is rather a set of infinite resources. And the infinite cannot be handled with yes-and-no Aristotelian logic.[76] In a "fuzzily" perceived world, qualitative questions may be answered quantitatively.

For example, a researcher working on a representative environmental case decided by the International Court of Justice might find the *travaux préparatoires* on the home page of an English scholar; the regional treaty related to the case could be in the AUSTLII database in Australia; legal articles on the case might be hosted by Jean Monnet's Working Papers database at Harvard (USA); commentaries referring to national implications of the decision might be found in *The New York Times* (USA), *Le Monde* (France), and *The Times* (UK) newspapers; pertinent observations on different interpretations of the case might be discovered in INT-LAW and EURLEX listservs; and social science, environmental, or other discipline-oriented scholarly journals might discuss the matter, as might different groups on habitat and quality of life all over the world.

Legal research instruction in US library schools and law schools emphasizes the fee-based services Lexis, Westlaw, and Dialog, as well as indexes such as the *Index to Legal Periodicals*, the *Index to Foreign Legal Periodicals*, LegalTrac and so on. Professors who are fond of these products usually avoid free-of-charge databases because they tend to believe that whatever is free is not reliable, and in any event it is easier to move along already-explored and comfortable paths. We see the same facile distinction between free and fee-based in the teaching process in Europe, Australia, and South Africa. These enemies of free databases also tend to overemphasize the offer of value-added features, forgetting that they are teaching content and not format.

The legal community all over the world actively discusses the role of the law library and its possible development models

[76] Negoita, Constantin Virgil, *Fuzzy Sets*. Tempe, Arizona: New Falcon Publications, 2000, p. 55.

in the cyberlegal environment, the impact of information technology on legal education and law libraries, and emerging models of legal education and responses to change. This should be connected with what is happening at broader levels of society. In the UK, for example, a National Committee was appointed on 10 May 1996 to make recommendations on the shape, purpose, and structure of higher education over the next twenty years. The electronic environment was very much taken into consideration (http://www.leeds.ac.uk/educol/ncihe/docsinde.htm).

In October 1994, after extensive discussion about the future of adult learning in Alberta, Canada, the Ministry of Advanced Education and Career Development released its New Directions for Adult Learning in Alberta (http://www.aecd.gov.ab.ca/learning/vision/new_directions/new_ directions.htm). The policy paper identified goals and outlined strategies for the adult learning system. Among the strategies is an expansion of learning technology and alternate forms of delivery to create more learning opportunities. In September 1995, the department released *A Vision for Change: a concept paper for the development of a virtual learning system (*http://www.aecd.gov.ab.ca/learning/publications/system_funding/funding/*)*, which presents the concept of a "virtual" system for learning, reducing the barriers of time and place by linking teachers, students and curricula through technology, thus serving learners in ways, times and places suited to their needs.

In 1998, the US Congress amended the Higher Education Act to establish the Web-Based Education Commission. The Commission (http://www.webcommission.org) presented its final report to Congress in November 2000. The Commission evaluated the World Wide Web's potential for transforming and improving learning and teaching. Questions and testimonies (http://www.hpcnet.org/cgi-bin/global/a_bus_card.cgi?SiteID=154797) covered such issues as access, equity, teacher training and support, standards, accreditation, and new learning institutions.

There are three notable trends visible in the use of the electronic environment in teaching today: distance learning education via WWW, computer-assisted education, and interactive courses in classrooms with access to the virtual world.

Distance learning education is much discussed and still contested. The most-cited criticism is that existing technological devices are incapable of creating a complete and sustainable learning environment. The three WWW layers—content (information, exercises, tests), interface (browser, email, word processor), and infrastructure (computer, operating system, Internet connection)—must work in a synergy when "using the Internet to deliver instruction".[77] An examination of state-of-the-art software programs designed to facilitate distance learning education and migration to e-classes shows that further development is needed before we have a truly effective education process. Video conferencing does not yet "allow the same experience as the classroom experience".[78] "Teaching at an Internet Distance: The Pedagogy of Online Teaching and Learning", the report of a 1998-1999 University of Illinois faculty seminar (http://www.vpaa.uillinois.edu/tid/report/tid_report.html), responded to faculty concern about the implementation of technology for teaching. The report concluded that "online teaching and learning can be done with high quality if new approaches are employed which compensate for the limitations of technology, and if professors make the effort to create and maintain the human touch of attentiveness to their students." Participants agreed that it would be inappropriate to provide an entire undergraduate degree program online at this time. They also conceded that "the ongoing physical and even emotional interaction between teacher and students, and among students themselves, was an integral part of a university education."

There is a great deal of literature on this issue. Suffice it here to cite a few commentaries of various authors from different European countries published by the *Journal of Information, Law and Technology* at Warwick University (http://elj.warwick.ac.uk/jilt),[79] the IRISS Internet Research and In-

[77] Harris, Dave, "Creating a Complete Learning Environment," in *Internet Based Learning: An Introduction and Framework for Higher Education and Business*, edited by Deanie French, Charles Hale, Charles Johnson, and Gerald Farr. Sterling, Virginia: Stylus, 1999.

[78] *Ibid.*, p. 151.

[79] Herberger, Maximilian *et al.*, *Collaborative Learning via WWW in Legal Education.* [October 2000.] Available WWW: http://elj.warwick.ac.uk/jilt/cal/98-2kauf/kauffman.htm; Smith, Alan and Michael Walpole, *An Australasian Experience of the Use of Selected Technologies in the Delivery of a Legal*

formation for Social Sciences International Conference papers,[80] and the *E Law Murdoch University, Western Australia Electronic Journal of Law* (http://www.murdoch.edu.au/elaw). A colloqui-um at JURIST, the Law Professors' Network (http://www. jurist.law.pitt.edu) fueled a lot of controversies.[81] In June 1999, *Deconstructing the Law School Classroom: Workshop on Distance Learning in Law Schools* (http://www.cali.org/dlwork shop/resources.html), sponsored by Chicago-Kent College of Law, CALI, and Lexis, discussed technological news such as the Next Generation Internet, software applications to dramatically enhance any video program, and the networks required to support local and distance learning. *The American Center for the Study of Distance Education* (ACSDE; http://www.ed.psu.edu/acsde/), established in 1988, has become a center for the dissemination of distance education information through a journal (both printed and electronic) and other publications.

Well-researched articles on distance learning and the integration of the WWW into the classroom have appeared in recent years,[82] including guides to managing the assimilation of the WWW into the classroom[83] and evaluations of interactive tutorials and computers in legal education.[84] *The Chronicle of Higher Education* (http://www.chronicle.com/distance/) offers daily updates on e-learning and distance learning, as well as news on aspects of computer assisted learning such as Web-based training and the electronic classroom.

Despite criticism, however, external degree programs are already being offered at (for example) the Continuing Education

Education Program. [October 2000.] Available WWW: http://elj.warwick.ac.uk/jilt/98-3/smith.html; Bloxham, Sefton, *CommonLaw I: WWW-based Negotiation Exercises.* [October 2000.] Available WWW: http://www.warwick.ac.uk/seminars/98-2-sb.html.

[80] IRISS International Conference, 25-27 March 1998, Bristol, UK [November 2000] Available WWW: http://www.sosig.ac.uk/iriss/papers/proceed.html.

[81] See debates at http://www.jurist.law.pitt.edu/colloq1.htm.

[82] Jones, Richard and John Scully, "Effective Teaching and Learning of the Law on the Web." [November 2000.] Available WWW: http://webjcli.ncl.ac.uk/1998/issue2/jones2.html. See also the impressive bibliography on this topic.

[83] Cartwright, Martin J., *The Wolverhampton Experience.* Seminar: Using the Internet to Teach Law. [November 2000.] Available WWW: http://www.law.warwick.ac.uk/seminars/98-2-mc.html.

[84] Collins, Hugh. *The Place of Computers in Legal Education.* [Online] Available: http://www.law.warwick.ac.uk/ltj/3-3b.html.

Division of the University of Montana (http://www.umt.edu/ccesp/external). The Knowledge Catalyst (http://www.elementk.com/home.asp) offers online courses on topics such as office productivity, computer skills, business, and management, and provides free guides and tutorials on using the Internet for education and training; screening, evaluating, and selecting an online education provider; training teachers in essential technology; and so on.

"NetVision: Helping Teachers Teach With The Internet" is a service offered by a group of educators in Maryland working with the Northeast Regional Technology in Education Consortium (NetTech). Its puropse is to help "schools utilize the emerging availability of the Internet to enhance student learning, with a focus on staff development." The database offers "Spring-Into-The-Net" teacher training materials, a collection of K-12 web sites (http://www.inform.umd.edu/netvision/netv.html), and other related services. The 3Com database (http://support.3com.com/index.htm) offers courses for small businesses around the world, training (http://www.3com.com/training/index.html), and 3Com Certification "for e-business solutions" that "prepare [the user] for success with the next wave of emerging high-growth technologies." 3Com University's e-campus has "authorized select companies to deliver additional instructor-led training on 3Com products".

The database Australian Correspondence Schools (http://www.acs.edu.au/) delivers short courses, certificates, diplomas, and advanced diplomas on a variety of subjects including horticulture, agriculture, photography, business, writing, supervision, computers, and tourism. Such "virtual universities" and consortia claim to promote "Cybereducation" and "Cyberschools".

Other groups and organizations engaged in "creating education for the 21st century" include the Open University of the United Kingdom (http://www.open.ac.uk/frames.html), the Satellite Educational Resources Consortium (SERC) (http://www.serc.org), Education SATLINK (http://www.satlink.msba.gen.mo.us), WestEd Distance Learning Resource Network (DLRN) (http://www.wested.org/tie/dlrn.html), and the Pacific Resources for Education and Learning (PREL)(http://www.prel.hawaii.edu/).

Portals to electronic education promote new teaching and learning features. The World Wide Web Virtual Library: Distance Education (http://www.cisnet.com/~cattales/Deduca tion.html) is a useful starting point on this matter. Cyber LEARNERS (http://www.cyberlearners.com/) claims to be an online educational portal. The *American Journal of Distance Education* (http://www.ed.psu.edu/acsde/ajde/jour.asp) contains a rich literature related to the performance and perceptions of distance learners in cyberspace, perceptions of image transmissions during Internet-based training, case studies, etc. Distance Education Resources (http://cuda.teleeducation. nb.ca/distanceed/) lists a broad index of resources and links to "open universities", in particular the British Open University, The Dutch Open University, and the Flanders EuroStudy Centre for Distance Education. The Distance Education Clearinghouse (http://www.uwex.edu/disted/home.html) maintains a wide range of information about distance education and related resources, as well as interesting articles. Also of value are *The Nature and Value of Interaction in Distance Learning* (http://www.gwu.edu/~etl/interact.html) by Greg Kearsley, and *The Political Economy of Cyberschool: Rethinking "Instructional Technology" and the Suitability of Cyberspace as an Educational Environment* (http://www.edfac.uni melb.edu.au/online-ed/tim luke.shtml) by Timothy W. Luke.

Components of Software-Realized Scaffolding (http://www.cc.gatech.edu/gvu/edtech/SRS.html), Educational Technology (http://www.cc.gatech.edu/gvu/edtech) on distance education for Eclasses (http://www.cc.gatech.edu/fce/eclass/cc102/index.html), Basic Support for Cooperative Work (http://bscw.gmd.de/) are all intensively occupied with enabling collaboration via the Web. World Lecture Hall (http://www. utexas.edu/world/lecture) advertises links to pages created by faculty worldwide who are using the Web to deliver course materials in any language. Some courses are delivered entirely over the Internet, while others are designed for students in residence, and many fall somewhere in between. World Lecture Hall provides links to 40 law courses such as constitutional law, entertainment law, international law and business, education law, alternative dispute resolution, American legal history, ancient law, and business law.

Computer-assisted legal education is highly developed in the US, the UK, and Australia. Computer-based lessons covering various subject areas of legal education are integrated with other course materials in teaching substantive law. In the US, The Center for Computer Assisted Legal Instruction (CALI) Library of Lessons (http://www.cali.org) offers a collection of over one hundred Internet and computer-based lessons covering thirty legal education subject areas at the The CALI Library in a nutshell (http://lessons.cali.org/catalog.html). Lessons range from a simulated trial to practice on the interpretation of statues and individualized tutorials. Students are guided through a series of questions which require them to identify relevant issues and apply the concepts they learn. CALI lessons can be accessed via Internet or CD-ROM. A feature called CALI URL Builder allows professors to include links to CALI lessons on their Web pages in order to enhance the teaching process. The Bridge (http://web.lexis.com/xchange/bridge/BridgeForm.asp)—a computer-based set of course materials designed (primarily) for teaching freshmen law students—has been developed by faculty members at the Harvard Law School. Interactive computer programs for online instruction on different topics of legal education have been also developed by Lexis and Westlaw. Commercial courseware for law professors and law students is offered by Lexis Virtual Classroom (http://lawschool.lexis.com/virtualclass/index.html). TWEN: The West Education NetworkSM (http://lawschool.westlaw.com/shared/whatistwen.asp?site=OH), introduced as "the electronic classroom extension of lawschool.westlaw.com", provides similar interactive courses.

In Australia, computer-based lessons are found in the Butterworths database (fee-based access). Warwick University (UK) is very active in this direction. The design and the use of courseware in the classroom was extensively discussed and explored here.[85] The Active Learning Home Page (http://www.cti.ac.uk/publ/actlea), promoting "educational innovation

[85] Paliwala, Abdul. *Preserving Educational Values* [Online]. Available WWW: http://www.warwick.ac.uk/ltj/4-2a.html [November 2000]. The *Law Technology Journal* contains a database of articles on this topic, many of them (essays and seminar slides) by Abdul Paliwala, Professor of Law at the University of Warwick and the Director of the Law Technology Center and the

and good practice in the use of learning technologies", has been passed on to the Institute for Learning and Teaching, which systematically publishes articles on computer assisted assessment, teaching with multimedia, embedding technology in teaching, and so on.

The third trend, that of the actual interactive class-room, is focused on the ability to manipulate knowledge regarding what WWW resources may be used and where they are to be found. Data retrieval, hypertext systems, and the manage-ment of information portals and vortals as well as the content are the principal tools. Teaching substantive law is thus connected to selecting content and building web applications. Interactive courses in classrooms having access to the virtual world have become popular in the US, the UK, Australia, and several European countries. New management tools for the virtual classroom have been developed. In the field of education, learning/teaching portals containing guides and tutorials of interactive classes on different subjects of law, and providing access to selected academic resources, have been created at the SOSIG Law Gateway (www.sosig.ac.uk/law/), Eagle-i Service Electronic Access to Global Legal Information (http://ials.sas.ac.uk/eagle-i.htm), TDN Resource Discovery Network (http://www.rdn.ac.uk), and Renardus (http://www.renardus.org). Similar developments are taking place at a few universities in France, The Netherlands, Belgium, and Germany. In the US, tutorials, as part of interactive training classes, are found on almost every law school home page and legal portal. Interactive courses have a broad range, covering subjects from basic Internet skills to substantive law. In 2000 vortals dedicated to e-classes began to appear. XanEdu (http://www.xanedu. com) proclaims that it has developed "a bold new vision for creating and delivering courseware materials and tools" and "for creating customized course materials". Ebrary (http://ebrary.com) claims to have "revolutionized the way people conduct research and acquire information on the web by combining a powerful discovery engine, full-text viewing, and state-of-the-art ref-

Law Courseware Consortium. See the essay on computer mediated communication, *Law Schools in the Courseware Era* [Online]. Available WWW: http://www.warwick.ac.uk/ltj/2-2a.html [November 2000].

erence tools with an extensive collection of books, periodicals, maps, and archival works."

Numerous books on e-education describe and analyze the spectacular changes stimulated by the growth of World Wide Web communication and information delivery. Some reactions to the reconstruction of legal teaching in the electronic world question the intellectual mutation that has been produced by the information revolution and its new patterns and structures, while others attempt to incorporate those patterns and structures into a new understanding of the nature of legal teaching. *Librarians as Learners, Librarians as Teachers: The Diffusion of the Internet in the Academic Library*[86] addresses issues such as the emerging structure of knowledge created by the Internet revolution, and how and why the Internet has radically changed the way we work and teach in the library. The contributors to this book consider the Internet to be a synthesis of all previous technologies, involving new skills that may constitute an extension of critical thinking. They discuss the construction of knowledge as interaction with new information builds the global electronic infrastructure that sets new standards and amounts to a new way of thinking. They evaluate the teaching process in the context of this new mental structure.

Another recent contribution is *Internet Based Learn-ing: An Introduction and Framework for Higher Education and Business,* a thorough analysis of the conceptual framework and a reliable guide for integrating the new Internet technologies with learning and education.[87] New styles of teaching discussed include "augmented teaching", which incorporates aspects of Internet-based learning. Learning is defined as "gaining new knowledge or new skills, or enhancing current knowledge or current skills."[88] Addressing the issue of "learning to learn in a WWW-based environment", the authors review skills for developing Internet-based learning classes as well as Internet-based

[86] *Librarians as Learners, Librarians as Teachers: The Diffusion of the Internet in the Academic Library.* Edited by Patricia O'Brien Libutti. Chicago, Association of College and Research Libraries, A Division of the American Library Association, 1999.

[87] *Internet Based Learning: An Introduction and Framework for Higher Education and Business.* Edited by Deanie French, Charles Hale, Charles Johnson, and Gerald Farr. Sterling, Virginia: Stylus, 1999.

[88] *Ibid.*, p. 87.

learning tools. A description of the virtual classroom is followed by one dealing with the creation of a complete e-learning environment. The authors agree that virtual learning/teaching is not yet developed and that the task is to integrate the existing technology into teaching, a process that forces both teachers and students to become "continual learners". The extensive discussion of cognitive restructuring ("changing the ways learners think"),[89] module components for developing self-directed learning versus "teacher-directed learning",[90] the breaking-down of learning-to-learn into component skills,[91] and teaching from hyperlinked material[92] make this book a worthwhile source for lecturers engaged in interactive education. Speaking from my own experience since the 1996/1997 academic year, I have independently explored many techniques dealt with in this inspiring book and employed them in the classroom. The confidence and strength I gained confirmed my sense that I had been and continue to be on the right path.

The New York University Law Library was in fact one of the first academic institutions in the US to train students and faculty in the use of Internet skills to conduct online foreign and international law research on WWW databases. It continues to do this through the articulation of the teaching and learning process in sequences of learning which are built into the training programs via differentiated modules. Pilot sessions on online international, foreign, and comparative law research were set up at the outset for foreign LLMs and MCJs students who needed foreign legal materials not available at the library. They also needed US primary sources for continuing their projects while back home in their own countries. The1996/1997 sessions were designed to augment Internet skills such as html (hypertext markup language) editing and building home pages, and also to develop strategies for evaluating and using legal databases for final projects. In more recent years, the advancement of computer skills has helped us to concentrate on teaching domestic, foreign, and international substantive online law research. The syllabus and teaching strategies, from basic

[89] *Ibid.*, p.4.
[90] *Ibid.*, pp.17-21.
[91] *Ibid.*, p.25.
[92] *Ibid.*, p.30.

to the most advanced, have been refined. Today, this training is also available to US JDs enrolled in comparative law classes.

Interactive teaching methods, from instructing students to learn in a WWW environment to traditional teaching with Internet-based options, are now used in the classroom. Separate classes, a portion of a class, or lectures in classes and presentations are delivered on a case-by-case basis. General tours or specialized tours to familiarize students and visiting faculty with traditional collections, general Internet training for large groups, and specialized training integrating presentations, hands-on sessions, and one-on-one sessions have become a matter of course. The traditional collection and online legal databases are introduced together. Electronic, print, and microfiche collections are presented as complementary sources. Research strategies and access protocols are taught also. Full-text primary sources, meta databases, indexes, and listservs (discussion groups) have all been introduced in the classroom. Students learn that selecting an electronic legal service is not the end of a decision; that legal research is a continue quest for resources; that the search itself may require a different structure and/or execution depending on the database. And, of course, the document or citation itself may sometimes "be the most difficult task".[93]

Teaching online domestic, foreign and international law research has been developed at the New York University Law Library in order to respond to the Law School's needs. Various modules have been implemented in the process. I will discuss several of these, as they may inspire other legal institutions involved in the instruction process.

Supporting the School of Law/Legal Institution Instruction

General training

It is important for newcomers entering a law firm, as well as for students and younger faculty at the beginning of the aca-

[93] Amy E. Sloan. *Basic Legal Research. Tools and Strategies.* New York: Aspen Law and Business, 2000. The chapter on Electronic Legal Research starts on page 291.

demic year, to familiarize themselves with online catalogs, available databases (in addition to Lexis and Westlaw which enjoy separate training), comparison of databases from case to case, and search strategies in general. Three modules, each of them two and a half hours, are offered twice at the NYU Law Library for this purposes. The three-part program is designed to teach students how to use the research tools available via the Law Library Home Page. The module "Finding Books" concentrates on instructing students how to find treatises, government documents, and other materials necessary for any subject. Resources covered included Julius (the Library's online catalog), Bobcat, RLIN, OCLC FirstSearch, Index Master, Library Catalogs, and so on.

The module "Finding Articles" demonstrates how to use indexes and web-based resources to locate journals, and highlights current awareness tools for students. Resources covered included Index to Legal Periodicals, LegalTrac, Legal Journals by Hein Online, EBSCO journals, JSTOR, Westclip, Eclipse, Periodical Abstracts with full text, Science Direct, Uncover Reveal, Uncover Reveal Journal Alerting Service, Proquest, SmartCLIP, CIS Congressional Universe, Lexis/Nexis Academic Universe, and so on.

The module "Databases for Foreign, Comparative, and International Law" highlights, through comparisons and examples of content, coverage, and search strategies, such databases as Index to Foreign Legal Periodicals; United Nations Indexes and databases; European Union Indexes, catalogs, and databases; subject-oriented international databases; and domestic databases in the vernacular and in English. Here is the structure of this particular module.

Databases for International, Foreign, and Comparative Law

<http://www.law.nyu.edu/library/foreign_intl>
Library's Home Page <http://www.law.nyu.edu/library>

1. Indexes
   Index to Foreign Legal Periodicals (from the Library's Home Page—Indexes/Databases)
   READEX (UN) (from the Library's Home Page—Indexes/Databases)
   Unique (UN)(http://www.un.org/Depts/dhl/unique/index.html)
   UNBISnet (UN) (http://unbisnet.un.org/)
   ECLAS (EU) (http://europa.eu.int/eclas/)
   SCAD (EU) (http://europa.eu.int/scadplus)

2. Public International Law
   International Organizations:
   The United Nations (http://www.un.org/) and ODS (http://www.ods.un.org/)
   The European Union : Eur-Lex, Prelex, CELEX (http://europa.eu.int/celex/), EU materials in Westlaw and Lexis, etc.
   The Council of Europe (http://www.coe.int/)
   Treaties (United Nations Treaty Collection http://untreaty.un.org/ , International Criminal Law, International Human Rights, International Environmental Law, International Trade, etc.
   More at: http://www.law.nyu.edu/library/foreign_intl/index.html
3. Foreign Databases
   Collections: (http://www.law.nyu.edu/library/foreign_intl/foreign.html)
   The following databases contain foreign laws in English and in the vernacular for specific countries or specific subjects (i.e.,tax, health, labor, social security, trade, etc):
   Global Legal Information Network (http://lcweb2.loc.gov/law/GLINv1/GLIN.html)
   International Labor Organization (http://www.ilo.org/)
   The National Law Center for Inter-American Free Trade NATLAW (http://www.natlaw.com/index.htm)
   Taxbase (http://taxbase.tax.org/)
   World News Connection (http://wnc.fedworld.gov/)
   World Health Organization (http://www.who.int/) and (http://www-nt.who.int/idhl/)
   By Jurisdiction: (http://www.law.nyu.edu/library/foreign_intl/country.html)
   Australia, Argentina, Austria, Belgium, Brazil, Canada, China, France, Germany, India, Italy, Japan, Mexico, The Netherlands, Norway, Russia, Spain, South Africa, Switzerland, the UK, the US.

The legal institution's special projects

Projects that require highly specialized research training for individual faculty, lawyers, visiting scholars and small groups of students and associates occur throughout the educational and business cycles. As an example, the International Law Commission Project developed at NYU Law School is offered to interns during the summer at the United Nations headquarters in Geneva. These advanced students needed a special training on foreign, comparative, and international law research, as do the School of Law interns at the International Court of Justice and students working for the New York University Journal of International Law and Politics.

The Global Law School Program requires training for individual scholars from all over the world. One-on-one training sessions are tailored according to immediate target projects.

Specialized training in international and comparative law research

The globalization of trade, commerce, trademarks, and patents has brought issues of international law and the domestic law of foreign jurisdictions to the forefront of legal practice. Law firms everywhere deal more than ever with foreign and international issues. Law schools curricula include more comparative and international law courses. In US law schools, foreign-trained students and lawyers have been increasing in numbers.

There are more than 400 non-US students at the NYU Law School, and from this number more than 250—mostly JDs and lawyers from foreign jurisdictions—enroll in the LLM programs almost every academic year. Specialized research sessions in substantive law areas such as aboriginal rights, business in Latin America, contracts, comparative civil procedure, human rights, international environmental law, international taxation, and international trade are conducted by international law librarians. *Fellows in Public International Law,* with a different topic or theme every year, is a course built on specialized individual studies requiring one-on-one research sessions. Students' research papers are published at the end of the academic year in a special number of the *Journal of International Law and Politics.*

The general structure of the specialized teaching modules is as follows:

1. Seminar support in one or multiple sessions
2. Class presentations (alternate explanation and demonstration) in "smart classrooms"
3. Sessions consisting of alternating hands-on sessions and hands-on exercises with explanation, demonstration, and handouts of exercises
4. One-on-one sessions
5. Recommending and creating guides (annotated and updated every year) such as LLRX.com guides (http://www.llrx.com/resources4.htm), ASIL Guides to Electronic Resources for International Law (http://www.asil.org/resource/Home.htm), and in-house guides such as the

United Nations Research Guide (http://www. law.nyu.edu/library/unguide.html) by Jeanne Rehberg, WTO/GATT (http://www.law.nyu.edu/library/wto_gatt.html) by Jeanne Rehberg, or International Treaties Guide (http://www.law.nyu.edu/library/treatiesguide.html) by Radu Popa.

Here is an example of one teaching module for a specialized course.

Together with Radu Popa, I have developed this module for the New York University School of Law LLM Program in International Taxation. It consists of a multi-part system of training. The succession of sub-modules is as follows:

1. Customized sessions on available printed resources and approaches to substantive law:
    - international law
    - foreign law
    - secondary sources
2. Hands-on sessions on international and foreign databases by jurisdiction
3. Individual sessions for assisting students with final projects
4. Creation of a home page, including the index to specialized online databases according to the students' country of origin
5. Publication of annotated research guides in the Library's Home Page
6. Discussion, recommendation, and encouragement of feedback from students and former graduates

A good example on how this training may be applied for the benefit of legal professionals is Steuerrecht im Internet (http://www.pinkernell.de/) by Reimar Pinkernell, a graduate from Germany. His home page is a unique directory of German tax sites and international tax sites containing information on the taxation of electronic commerce and on U.S.-German tax materials (U.S. tax glossary, U.S.-Germany tax treaties) in German and in English.

The NYU Law Library's general approach to case, statutory and administrative law research by jurisdiction and by database includes how and when to use the terms and connectors or the natural language search method, and how to build the query. Students' background—such as religion, legal culture, languages and political sensitivities—is also very much considered.

The computer lab provides each student with a workstation. Passwords of databases from different jurisdictions are provided to facilitate the quest for foreign legal materials. An LCD panel and a projector make the course home page, the syllabus, the WWW resources, databases, and the online presentation available. Questions for class exercises are always based on issues which need to be considered for some case study. During the class, students are expected to explore the tax database useful for researching his/her own country's tax law. For example, one assignment was related to taxation of royalties (find legislation, tax rulings, any new developments, treaty provisions and any other available documents that concerned the tax treatment of cross-border royalties of that specific country). Another assignment was related to building depreciation (research tax database of his/her own country to find legislation and/or tax rulings that provided for depreciation of the cost of commercial buildings, and try to discover if there were any special incentive regimes). The home page of the Taxation of International Business Transactions course (http://dev.law.nyu.edu/braunery/spring01/intlBusTrans/index.html) contains links for course description, course schedule, teams and advisors, case study, case studies, presentations, and research questions.

The following handout was distributed for two reasons: students can see the URLs which are hidden in the online version, and they also are able to follow me in case of Internet connection troubles or computer difficulties. At this stage of Internet and computer technology development, faraway servers might be hard to access during training, and malfunctions of particular workstations in the classroom are always possible.

Handout of Hands-on-Training for

INTERNATIONAL BUSINESS TRANSACTIONS SPRING 2000

Resources for Country and Planning Research

(http://www.law.nyu.edu/library/foreign_intl/taxint.html)

General International Tax Databases and Resources:

Foreign Tax (http://vls.law.vill.edu/prof/maule/taxmaster/taxfor.htm) Index to International and Foreign Country databases.

Guide to Foreign and International Legal Databases (http://www.law.nyu.edu/library/foreign_intl) Look at Foreign Databases—Collections and Foreign Databases—By Jurisdiction.

IBFD Tax News Daily. Fee-based database. To gain free and unlimited access for 30 days, simply fill out the form (http://www.ibfd.nl).

Lexis— worldwide Tax Daily (TNI); International Bureau of Fiscal Documentation (IBFD)—Tax Treaties & News; Tax Analysts Publication Library (TAXANA); Federal Tax Library (FEDTAX).

OECD Periodicals (http://www.sourceoecd.org/content/html/index.htm). Available to users from university locations only or by changing the browser's configuration.

TaxBase (http://taxbase.tax.org). Fee-based database. Password available. To gain free and unlimited access to TaxBase for 30 days, simply fill out the online form.

Taxman International (http://www.taxman.nl/). Gateway to Tax and Customs Administrations on the Internet. See also International Tax (http://www.taxman.nl/tax-links.html).

World News Connection (http://wnc.fedworld.gov).

Westlaw (http://www.westlaw.com). Federal Taxation (FTX-ALL) and FTX-Treaties.

Foreign Country Law Databases

AUSTRIA (http://www.law.nyu.edu/library/foreign_intl/austria.html)

Republic Oesterreich Bundeskanzleramt—Rechtsinformatiossystem—RIS (http://www.ris.bka.gv.at/) Republic of Austria—Office of the Federal Chancellor—Legal Information System. Published by the Austrian Government (Federal Chancellor's Office). Current. Official site with full text of laws and decisions in the vernacular, but no official pagination.

BRAZIL (http://www.law.nyu.edu/library/foreign_intl/brazil.html)

Courts (http://www.solar.com.br/~amatra/linkjur.html)

Legislation and Jurisprudence (http://www.cd-graf.com.br/legis.htm)

CANADA (http://www.law.nyu.edu/library/foreign_intl/canada.html)

QuicklawAmerica (Canadian Legal Materials) (http://www.quicklawAmerica.com/) Fee-based database. For access, ask the Reference Librarian for Foreign and International Law.
Lexis (http://www.lexis.com/research) Canadian laws and jurisprudence.

COSTA RICA
Legal Net (http://www.costaricalaw.com/legalnet/) Law and regulations (http://www.costaricalaw.com/legalnet/lawindx.html)
Primary and Secondary Legal Materials from the National Law Center for Inter-American Free Trade (http://www.natlaw.com/cr/cr.htm)

FRANCE (http://www.law.nyu.edu/library/foreign_intl/france.html)
Jurifrance (http://www.jurifrance.com/wjuridiq/index.ow)—Journaux Officiels, Fichier national de Jurisprudence. Fee-based database. Contains all existing French databases. Passwords available.
Lexis (http://www.lexis.com/research)— French laws and jurisprudence in the vernacular.

GERMANY (http://www.law.nyu.edu/library/foreign_intl/germany.html)
Refact (http://www.refact.de/rda_inh.htm) Fee-based. Passwords available. Tax laws and tax jurisprudence.
Steuerrecht im Internet (http://www.pinkernell.de/) by Reimar Pinkernell. A directory of German tax sites and international tax sites; information on the taxation of electronic commerce and U.S.-German tax materials (U.S. tax glossary, U.S.-Germany tax treaties).

JAPAN (http://www.law.nyu.edu/library/foreign_intl/japan.html)
Japanese Legal Databases (http://law.leh.kagoshima-u.ac.jp/staff/ibusuki/best50.html) by Makoto Ibusuki.
Links to Japanese Laws (http://www.ibjs.co.jp/e/res_links/res_15.html) and financial topics (http://www.ibjs.co.jp/e/res_links/index.html).

LUXEMBOURG
Chambre des Deputes (http://www.chd.lu/chd/fr/menu/main.htm).
Finance Ministry (http://www.etat.lu/EC/).

MEXICO (http://www.law.nyu.edu/library/foreign_intl/mexico.html)
Infojus (http://www.juridicas.unam.mx/legislac/). Codes and laws. See also commentaries (http://www.juridicas.unam.mx/mtexto/) on jurisprudence (http://www.juridicas.unam.mx/mtexto/).
Legislación Federal de México (http://www.cddhcu.gob.mx/leyinfo/). Codes and laws.
Lexis (http://www.lexis.com/research)—Mexican laws and jurisprudence.

NEW ZEALAND (http://www.law.nyu.edu/library/foreign_intl/newzealand.html)
Lexis (http://www.lexis.com/research) Case Law (NZCAS) from 1970-; Law Reports; Legal Encyclopedia; Legislation and Commentaries.
Status (http://www.status.co.nz/) — Free session legislation and regulations, a number a fee-based databases on Folio Views, business and newspaper databases.

ROMANIA (http://www.law.nyu.edu/library/foreign_intl/romania.html)
Romanian Parliament (http://diasan.vsat.ro/). Index to the legislation published in the Official Journal (Monitorul Oficial).

SWITZERLAND (http://www.law.nyu.edu/library/foreign_intl/switzerland.html)
Systematische Sammlung des Bundesrechts—Recueil Systematique du Droit Federal). Systematic compendium of Swiss federal law)(http://www.admin.ch/ch/f/rs/rs.html).
Swiss Federal Supreme Court (http://www.eurospider.com/BUGE/). Decisions from 1975 to the present in German, French and Italian. Official citation and pagination as well as full-text search.

VENEZUELA (http://www.law.nyu.edu/library/foreign_intl/venezuela.html)
The National Law Center for Inter-American Free Trade Database (NATLAW)—Venezuela (http://natlaw.com/venez/venez.htm). Fee-based database. Password available.

USA (http://www.law.nyu.edu/library/foreign_intl/us.html)
Internal Revenue Service (http://www.irs.ustreas.gov).
Lexis (http://www.lexis.com/research)and Westlaw (http://www.westlaw.com) (FTX-ALL).
US Tax Code online (not an official page) (http://www.fourmilab.to/uscode/26usc/ustax.html).
U.S. Code at the U.S. House of Representatives Internet Law Library (http://uscode.house.gov/usc.htm).
Bills and legislative history from THOMAS: Legislative Information on the Internet (http://thomas.loc.gov/).
Code of Federal Regulations from the U.S. House of Representatives Internet Law Library. (http://www.access.gpo.gov/nara/cfr/cfr-table-search.html).
GPO Access. Connect to GPO Access online databases through a federal depository library gateway (Federal Register, Code of Federal Regulations, etc.) (http://www.access.gpo.gov/su_docs/aces/aaces004.html).
Tax Analysts Home Page (http://www.tax.org/default.htm).

Teaching in the School of Library and Information Science

There is a growing demand in schools of library and information science, and in legal associations and legal institutions around the world, for foreign, comparative, and international law research skills. In spite of this, however, courses in this field are not too many. In the US, the FCIL summer institutes provided for a few years by the American Association of Law Libraries have become a *rara avis*, a "rare bird". In recent years, however, the Palmer School of Library and Information Science Summer Institutes, a program sponsored jointly with the New York University Law Library, have been gaining in popularity.

The Introduction to Foreign, Comparative, and International Law Research Course at the Palmer School of Library and Information Science of Long Island University has been a continuously inspiring teaching experience. The course is always filled, and has become very influential. The first summer institute, "Foreign and International Law Research: A Basic Introduction for the Non-Specialist", was compiled in a book edited by Jeanne Rehberg and Radu D. Popa,[94] with contributors including Professor M. Kathleen Price, Jolande Goldberg, Thomas H. Reynolds, Radu D. Popa, Jeanne Rehberg, Mirela Roznovschi, Marylin J. Raisch, and Victor Essien. The 1996 course was conducted at the New York University School of Law Library from June 28 to July 3, 1996. The1998 Summer Institute, "Introduction to International Organizations and Their Documentation", developed into an interactive course, a combination of presentations and hands-on sessions.

The 2000 "Introduction to Foreign, Comparative, and International Law Research" was a five-week intensive course taught one day each week. Lectures, online presentations, hands-on sessions, examples, and homework, with an increased number of exercises comparing traditional and online resources, created a complex e-learning environment. Lectures were offered by three NYU Law Library professionals—Radu Popa, Director of Research and Online Services; Jeanne

[94] Rehberg, Jeanne and Radu D. Popa, *Accidental Tourist on the New Frontier: An Introductory Guide to Global Legal Research.* Littleton, Colo.: Fred B. Rothman & Co., 1998.

Rehberg, Special Assistant to the Director and Reference Librarian for International and Foreign Law; and Mirela Roznovschi, Reference Librarian for International and Foreign Law—and by Jean Davis, Reference Librarian and Adjunct Assistant Professor of Law, Brooklyn Law School.

Many attendees had no legal background, and surprisingly the best performances /grades/ final papers belonged to these students. The 2000 Summer Institute was generally structured to address secondary resources, search engines, databases, and listservs for FCIL; general introduction to foreign, comparative and international law (private and public); treaties and international jurisprudence; international organizations; foreign law (introduction to Civil Law systems, compared to Common Law; typical vernacular sources in Civil Law systems, finding foreign law in English, vernacular collections in U.S. libraries, online sources of foreign law, generally); collection development, acquisitions, bibliographic control/access to print and electronic collections; management of international and foreign documents collections.

The Institute taught the fundamentals of foreign, comparative, and international law research in both traditional and electronic formats. The objectives were proficiency in using the major resources for research in foreign, comparative, and international law; proficiency in using the major tools for identifying other resources for FCIL law research; and the acquisition of skills and demonstrated knowledge in both theory and practice of law librarianship related to foreign, comparative, and international law. Required texts and readings were sent in advance, along with homework assignments due at the start of class.

The class took place in the computer room from 9 AM to 5 PM, with a one-hour break for lunch and two other 15-minute breaks. Evenings were dedicated to homework in the library under the instructor's supervision. Lectures on substantive law research were combined throughout the course with online presentations, hands-on sessions and hands-on exercises. Homework included questions relating to both traditional and electronic documents. A special course reserve was set up for the class, and passwords for fee-based databases were provided for students. At the very end of the course, the classmates played a game in teams, reviewing the entire course.

Teaching Abroad

More and more lecturers from the US, the UK, The Netherlands, or Australia teach modern legal research in different legal institutions around the world. The cyberlegal environment has dramatically changed not only the field of legal research, but also the teaching structure. It has made possible the creation of modern and up-to-date collections, as well as the fast integration into the cyberlegal community of legal centers which had been without resources before. It has also occasioned a giant step forward against the discrimination that favors libraries with big resources over smaller but deserving institutions. The primary issue in this context is the emergence of legal professionals able to use modern technology and resources and to pass this knowledge on to others.

Programs developed by the US government under the Rule of Law Project are in the process of building legal research competencies and modern legal centers in China, the former Soviet Union countries, South Africa, and elsewhere. Changing the ways learners from other jurisdictions and legal cultures think and learn in a teaching environment without traditional collections and modern reference tools, yet with an Internet connection and a computer lab, is one of the most challenging educational undertakings of our time. It is accomplished by adding new styles of learning, by creating new skills, and relying on the Web as almost the only learning environment. The nonlinear thinking of the cyberlegal domain arises from the activities and experience of creating a virtual collection of resources, learning new concepts and a new vocabulary, and learning to evaluate and build the information age collections.

Certain issues must be dealt with at the outset. A computer lab with a connection to the Internet has no meaning if one cannot enter it because it is locked up, or if nobody knows how to use a computer, or what electronic sources are available and how to use them efficiently. In addition, even if a legal professional knows how to perform modern legal research and has passwords to the best databases in the world, censorship of the Internet may be a problem in some countries. It is also true that some legal professionals having all of the above refuse to share passwords to electronic resources with their peers, and do not pass their knowledge on to others. Knowledge is power. In some countries passwords are kept secret and are traded as a favor.

The only effective way to prevent this is to discourage singular competencies, i.e., a single well-trained information specialist, in favor of groups of experts. The practice demonstrates that, in order to assure the knowledge dissemination process, a "critical mass" of expertise should be created.

Planning teaching abroad is a critical activity. Lecturers must foresee and be prepared for potential changes in programs and other inconveniences, from the content and technical level to anything that might interfere with the teaching process. To prevent possible mishaps, it is wise to upload the syllabus, handouts, exercises, model pages, and tutorials on to the Internet. The interactive sessions should be duplicated as printed handouts. Classroom examples must also be carefully chosen, and attendees should be made aware of how critical it is to expand traditional law research with Internet-based sources.

Comments are also crucial. It should be mandatory for each student to fill out the evaluation forms handed out at the end of the course. Students should become evaluators of every step of the course through critiques and daily tests. Evaluation is "a constructive, ongoing process within the course through which students learn how to efficiently and effectively articulate the strengths and weakness of their work as a basis of improvement."[95]

The students' continuing professional development should also be on their professors' agenda. Assisting them with their future projects is a must. They must be encouraged to become contributors to legal information publications, build new libraries and new collections, attend important professional conventions, and become trainers in their own workplaces.

The basic level

The first step in teaching abroad foreign students requires a careful evaluation of the layers of the learning environment and the attendees' skills, the content to be taught, the computer interface, and the Internet access infrastructure. This process entails evaluation of:

- the library collection;

[95] See *Internet Based Learning, supra* n. 87, p. 174.

- the legal systems and international organizations to be emphasized;
- the performance of the computers in the lab and the connection to the Internet;
- the group's knowledge of the WWW environment;
- the group's skills in computer and legal research;
- languages;
- religions;
- political sensitivities; and
- analysis of skill discrepancies

In March and April of 1999 I spent ten days in Yerevan, where I had been invited to teach for the Rule of Law project funded by USAID. The project involved both the Armenian State University Law School and the New York University Law Library. My assignment was to train faculty and law students in online legal research and to build the School of Law Home Page. A computer lab with an Internet connection was provided to facilitate lectures, presentations, and hands-on sessions. The syllabus covered topics from HTML editing and designing the Law School Home Page to the creation of a virtual electronic library, building research skills, and using foreign and international databases.

I taught an average of 5 hours per day. In the afternoons and evenings I assisted the sixteen students with their homework, and prepared lectures in accordance with the reality I encountered at the Yerevan Law School. Despite Internet connection problems, language obstacles (in the beginning, not all my students were able to follow English, even though they were able to read English quite well), and software complications, the program covered all proposed objectives.

At the time, I did not know that troubles related to the Internet connection were due to censorship exerted through the proxy server. Finally, after several painful days, and with the assistance of the USAID representative in Armenia, the computer lab was allowed a direct connection to the Internet.

Students did not have email. They had little knowledge of

word processing. Only the director of the law library, the vice dean, and the person in charge of the computer lab had knowledge about the electronic environment. The former two were previously trained at New York University Law Library. The latter held a computer science degree.

During the teaching proper, individual research and independent work were encouraged, while tests checked the level of acquired knowledge every day. The concrete reality I came across at the YSU forced me to stress basic computer and Internet skills, basic search strategies on the Internet, Lexis, Westlaw, and other fee-based and access-free subject-oriented databases. The collection holdings of the law library amounted to around one thousand books in Russian, as well as gifts from different foundations which were mostly old textbooks and out-of-date serials. Legal research priorities were based on European Union and Russian primary sources. European Union legal literature was required because it provides guidance for the implementation process of the European Convention on Human Rights in Armenia. As far as Russia is concerned, it is the closest jurisdiction for Armenian scholars, the model jurisdiction that has influenced the Armenian legal system in the past century. Politically speaking, Armenian ties with Russia are still very strong. In this context, the Russian collection offered by Lexis is critical, as are Russian legal databases such as Kodeks and Garant. During the training, students were provided with passwords to all fee-based databases discussed in class.

The SYLLABUS

First Day

Class evaluation.
Introduction to the Internet.
Introduction to Microsoft FrontPage Editor.
HTML basics.
Document conversion into HTML (from Word or Word Perfect).
Search engine structure and basic search strategies.
Basic elements for database evaluation and acquisition of electronic resources.

Class exercises: HTML.

Second Day
Microsoft FrontPage Editor (continuation).
Servers and server privileges.
Writing your own HTML documents and uploading them to the Internet via FTP.
Advanced features for HTML documents and home pages: WebBot; Stamptime; Insert; Columns; Fonts; Colors; Images (gif, jpg files).

Class exercises: Use FrontPage Editor to create an HTML document and upload it to the Law School server.

Third Day
WESTLAW, LEXIS, LOIS. Content and basic search strategies.
Indexes and Catalogs: Presentation of fee-based and free-of-charge databases—Readex (UN), Index to Legal Periodicals, Index to Foreign Legal Periodicals, Legal Trac, SCAD, ECCLAS, a.s.o.

Class exercises: Westlaw, Lexis, LOIS.

Choose a topic for a project: designing a Home Page and an index of links on a law topic.

Fourth Day
Introduction to the European Union, the Council of Europe (CELEX, LEXIS etc), the United Nations databases; GLIN (Global Legal Information Network of the Library of Congress), international trade databases (WTO, CISG, LEXIS), international environment databases (CIESIN, PACE, LEXIS).

Class exercises: UN, GLIN, WTO, PACE/CIESIN, LEXIS.

Fifth Day
Introduction to electronic collections on Human Rights, International Organizations (WTO, OAS, etc), International Courts (ICJ, ECHR, etc.), Treaties (multilateral, bilateral—UN Treaty Collection, European Union treaties), etc.

Class exercises: ICJ, ECHR, subject-oriented databases, Lexis and Westlaw.

Sixth Day
Foreign law databases : collections; by jurisdiction. Civil law and common law collections on the Internet, Lexis, and Westlaw.

Class exercises.

Seventh Day
Reference and Collection Development.
Listserv Archives and Online Guides.
School of Law Virtual Library. Uploading the School of Law and the Law Library Home Pages in Armenian, English, and Russian (http://www.law.ysu.am/).
Locating Web resources and online databases; basic concepts for planning, setting up, maintaining the virtual collection; principles for electronic collection development.

At YSU I encountered surprises related to cultural background and Armenian traditions. For legal background, I discovered I had to focus on Russian law. For the Armenian point of view of Armenian tradition, I did not know that I myself was in error as in Armenia a married woman does not work. The fact that I was divorced gave me some credibility, even though divorce is not fully acceptable. The class, mostly men, looked at me in wonder. My jokes in the class were not welcomed. Because I spoke about women's rights and said that equality among the partners of a couple should be encouraged in Armenia, I was reported to the Dean for "using anti-Armenian propaganda in the classroom". In order to adjust to the local culture and earn my students' confidence, I had to tell about the country were I was born, my religion, my family status, actual and former profession, my job, how much money I earn, etc. The great thing was that, after days of intensive work, the students were able to take the leap to a higher level of legal research skills.

The intermediate level

This level is decided by the students' basic proficiency in the field of law research and computer skills. Teaching modules must take into consideration such elements as:

- Online versus printed sources in an environment with a scarcity of traditional legal resources. This requires the presence of a computer lab with an Internet connection as a complementary resource of the library's collection. Instruction should focus on:
  - Building more advanced research skills;
  - Teaching advanced Internet complexities; and

- Teaching software specifics related to the legal research performance in the WWW environment.

- Designing the training sequences and modules from creating state-of-the art HTML interfaces to online specialized legal research in the field of international and foreign law.

- Customized teaching tailored to the needs of particular groups, focusing on the most needed jurisdictions and the most influential jurisdictions and international organizations.

- Different approaches to the legal research process, depending on the goals to be attained.

- The most wanted or needed legal resources, e.g., legal literature versus primary sources in civil law jurisdictions.

I had an opportunity to test this teaching pilot in October 1999 at the Constitutional and Legal Policy Institute (COLPI) in Budapest. In cooperation with the Open Society Institute, COLPI organized "Training for Law Librarians", an intensive course for legal professionals from developing countries. The selection of participants was done according to criteria sent in advance. Basic computer skills and basic legal research skills were required. Participants had to be affiliated with legal institutions with access to a computer lab and connections to the Internet. Knowledge of English or another Western language was also required. Homework (due at the beginning of the training) and required readings were sent in advance by email to participants.

The training took place at the Central European University Residence and Conference Center. Central European University (CEU), with teaching sites in Budapest and Warsaw, is an international institution for postgraduate study and research with students from more than forty countries. The computer lab provided untroubled access to the Internet. The network functioned beautifully; access to legal databases was not a problem for either professors or students. Computer assistance was provided full-time during the hands-on sessions.

The group convened twenty-two professors of law, law librarians, and directors of law libraries or legal centers from seventeen countries (Albania, Armenia, Azerbaijan, Belarus, Estonia, Georgia, Kazakhstan, Kyrgyzstan, Latvia, Lithuania, Moldova, Mongolia, Russia, Tajikistan, the Ukraine, Uzbekistan, and Yugoslavia). The course was designed to help attendees build electronic law collections and conduct modern substantive law research. I was invited not only to teach, but also to design the training. My partner, Anne P. Pries-Heijke from the Institute of East European Law and Russian Studies in The Netherlands, focused on building traditional collections (selection, acquisition, etc.).

The advantage of being conversant in French, Italian, and Romanian (spoken in Moldova) was immediately evident. My working knowledge of Russian was vital for building a bridge with the Russian group. My knowledge of Italian and Albanian (I studied Albanian for one year at college) helped the librarian from Albania (who addressed me at the beginning in Italian) to switch soon to English. The librarian from Belgrade was fluent in French, but after a while she too moved to English. The same occurred with librarians from the Ukraine, Belarus, and other countries. My knowledge of "Moldavian", which is actually Romanian, gave more confidence to the librarians from Moldova to use English. Something similar occurred during my lecture in Brasilia in May 2001, where my knowledge of Portuguese—the closest romance language to Romanian—allowed me to read the descriptions of projects and databases and other preparatory material provided for me, as well as to understand the attendees.

The fact that I was born in an Eastern European country and was familiar with Communist-style bureaucracy, the post-Communist era, the political issues, and factors related to European educational styles (teaching strategies, the learning environment, student's expectations) was also valuable as I discussed techniques with my students for improving libraries in their homelands and for developing training courses of their own.

The training was conducted in English. Explaining that English is the fundamental language of computers, international legal databases, international organizations, and modern legal research, as well as the language of the Westlaw,

Lexis, Celex, and European Union legal databases (along with, to some extent, French and Spanish), and not merely an imperialist language, took a lot of energy. In the beginning, several participants rejected English for Russian, even though they had some knowledge of English. For them, Russian was the universal language. On the first day I did not allow translators in the class. I matched attendees with good English with others less proficient. The next day I was forced to use translators, but twelve participants (out of twenty-two) did not use their services. By the last teaching day, only four or five used translators' services. Unfortunately, the two Mongolians spoke only Mongolian, and the training was lost on them.

While teaching foreign law research, I used online and traditional legal dictionaries to look up legal equivalents, right there in the classroom. This was the case when searching Dutch, French, and German legal databases. These exercises, as well as the exercises on the European Union and the Council of Europe databases, imparted to my students the flavor of what it is like to do real foreign and international law research.

Attendees belonged to civil law countries with such wide-ranging interests as common law jurisdictions (the UK) and the civil law of an Islamic country (Tajikistan). Participants' religions were Catholic, Orthodox Christian, Islamic, and Buddhist. I was very careful with human rights examples in order to avoid religious conflicts or delicate issues related to religious beliefs. However, life is very unpredictable, and I was unable to keep my commitment. It so happened that on September 30, 1999, while I was teaching about the European Court of Human Rights, the CNN database revealed that the court of Strasbourg had decided the case of *Moore and Gordon v. The United Kingdom* and the case of *Smith and Ford v. The United Kingdom*, related to homosexuality in the UK army. There arose a high murmur in the class among students, most of whom came from very conservative countries where homosexuality is punished by law influenced by religion. I explained to them that this new information should be regarded as an exercise about how fast jurisprudence can be uploaded by the international courts' databases. The class put the moral issue aside and took the entire issue as an exercise.

Regional groups visible in the class included the Baltic group, the Russian/ CIS group, the Central Asian group, and the Central European group. There were unspoken tensions in the class between representatives from Azerbaijan and Armenia, between the Baltic group and the Russian group, and between Yugoslavian and Albanian attendees. It is important to remember in situations like this that political sensitivities are never far from the surface. The librarian from Yugoslavia, for example, viewed me as an imperialist representative of USA and NATO when the Kosovo Tribunal appeared on the screen. To avoid political animosity, human rights examples in the classroom were related to faraway regions like Rwanda, South Africa, or Chile (the Pinochet case).

The idea of a regional cooperative group dedicated to obtaining grants for library needs (to develop home pages, online catalogs, and electronic collections) and sharing resources became stronger and stronger, especially for the Russian Group on the last teaching day.

I taught an average of four hours a day, and spent about additional two or three hours assisting the class with homework in the computer lab. The homework was prepared in accordance with the syllabus distributed in advance. Students ran searches in parallel databases, compared results, and learned to understand the strong points and the weak points of databases. This effort helped them to realize which databases might fit their actual or future needs. The homework was in English, another strong incentive for students to switch to English.

During classes, differences in the participants' levels of achievement were noticeable. The Baltic group was the most advanced, and the Russian group was a close second. Others countries were far behind Russian expertise. Moving eastward, knowledge and technical know-how about a modern library appeared less and less. The Armenian librarians were an exception because they benefitted from New York University and USAID training programs.

Access needs to legal materials were different in the Yerevan and the Budapest training. While the European Union and Russian documents and primary sources were prominent in both cases, in Budapest there was also a need for French, German, and UK primary and secondary sources. Lexis and Westlaw were crucial in both situations. There was no interest in US case law, other than some interest in US primary sources that originated with a law professor and director of a law library who was writing a book on civil and Islamic law. The situation was quite the opposite in Brasilia during a presentation for librarians of the Senado Federal and other government agencies, where the most needed jurisdictions were the US and the UK. Such considerable interest in secondary legal resources and legal literature of common law jurisdictions is typical for participants with a background in civil law.

The advanced level

Prerequisites for advanced training include the basic and intermediate instruction of the above levels, as well as a working environment on the job allowing one to develop and create a strong legal research team. Students must know computer technicalities, and possess software and Internet skills. Advanced training prepares students to be WWW developers, database designers, information analysts, organizers and managers of information, and partners in the cyberlegal culture. They have to learn to use digital multimedia, and information technologies in instruction, research, and in the production of scholarly materials.

The focus is on substantive law research. An interactive learning environment and familiarity with both traditional and electronic collections allow self-sufficient legal information professionals to develop collections, legal information centers, and legal research courses, and also to write articles, compile annotated bibliographies on topics of interest, and become members of the cyberlegal community through participation in listserv discussions.

Presentations of online software for catalogs designed for libraries of different sizes need special attention. Attention must also concentrate on the analysis of catalogs of online libraries from all over the world such as The British Library (http://portico.bl.uk), Bibliothèque Nationale de France (http://www.bnf.fr), and others found at Libraries Online (http://libraryspot.com/librariesonline.htm), Library WWW Servers from all Continents (http://sunsite.berkeley.edu/Libweb), and the Canadian Library Gateway (http://www.nlc-bnc.ca/gatepasse/index_e.htm). The Home Page course must contain all materials of subjects related to the course and notes of class discussions, linked by interactive class syllabi. The electronic classroom has to be equiped with state-of-the-art technology. Feedback via email, sharing ideas and resources through electronic documents, the creation of a students' home page, and debates related to evaluation of traditional and electronic resources must all contribute to an advanced e-learning environment. Concepts and behaviors of cyberlegal culture must be reviewed and practiced. The generic steps are the following:

- General introduction to substantive law research in both traditional and electronic formats:
  - Public International Law
  - Private International Law
  - Comparative Law
- Management and acquisition in the modern law library
- Participants as potential trainers in their legal institutions
- Creating and developing the virtual collection
  - Online catalogs and home pages
  - Partnership with other libraries

I drew up and successfully employed this advanced interactive teaching model for an international audience in Moscow. In October 2000, the Constitutional and Legal Policy Institute (COLPI) in Budapest, the Open Society Institute, the National Soros Foundation, and the Library of Foreign Literature in Moscow organized "Training the Law Librarian", an intensive course in international, comparative, and foreign law research. Attendees were directors of law libraries and legal centers, law librarians, and law pro-fessors from the Baltic, the Caucasus and Central Asia. Half of them had attended the Budapest training. The training was conducted in English. More than half of the class did not need translators. Groups of advanced and less advanced participants were created. Daily tests and contests checked the progress of learning.

Topics addressed focused on introductions to foreign, comparative and international law (public and private), treaties and international jurisprudence, international organizations, civil law systems compared to common law, collection development, management of international collections, management of electronic resources, the newest library information technology, and state-of-the-art operation of electronic legal resources. It was interesting to discover that most of the lawyers participating had little knowledge of foreign and international law, not unlike most of their US counterparts! Special attention was given to online legal research in Lexis/Nexis, Westlaw, Celex, the European Union databases, the United Nations indexes and databases, and full-text databases for international law, foreign law, legal literature, etc. Libraries and home pages of legal centers and law schools, electronic collections, and electronic catalogs were introduced and compared. Issues related to the digitization of domestic law texts and the criteria of the reliability of online legal documents were on the agenda. Regional initiatives were closely evaluated.

One case study was related to the project of the Open Library for Legal Information (http://www.lawlib.uz) in Tashkent (Uzbekistan). Criteria for reliability and accuracy of online documents were closely debated. This library had started and is now expanding its database of domestic laws of Uzbekistan in Russian. The director of the legal center wanted to know if this database meets the required WWW international standards. As of 2001, the database contains the Constitution and the codifications of air (07.05.93), criminal (01.04.95), criminal procedure (01.04.95), administrative (01.04.95), labor (01.04.96), civil (01.03.97), criminal executive (01.10.97), economic procedure (01.01.98), tax (01.01.98), civil procedure (01.01.98), land (30.04.98), custom (01.05.98), family (01.09.98), and housing (24.12.98) law. The database also offers full-text materials on the Constitutions of Uzbekistan, Kazakhstan, Kyrgyzstan, Turkmenistan and Tajikistan, and all codes of Kazakhstan and Kyrgyzstan. There are also laws of the Republic Uzbekistan on political parties and religious organizations, and lists of legal documents on constitutional rights and social support (family, pension, insurance, enterprise legislation and so on). English abstracts provide citations to original documents through displayed and searchable fields such as the law title, number, date of enactment, amendment date, section number and section title, and so on.

Isolated rejections of Western languages and values occured in the classroom. In one case, I was told that "there is no need for Russian librarians to know what is available elsewhere as long as there are Russian indices and books good enough for Russian library needs." One student refused to read the name of the *Journal Officiel* because it was in French and in the Latin alphabet.

I found a way to partially beat the difficulties encountered with the Internet connection due to the proxy server with a very restricted configuration access rejected by many legal servers outside Russia. From my experience I know that in any Communist or post-Communist system there is always a way to get around obstacles. I discovered that bureaucrats were censoring the Internet between 9 AM and 6 PM. A less restrictive access was in place at other times, so I moved the bulk of online demonstrations on databases that reject proxy servers from 7 AM to 9 AM and 6 PM to 8 PM Moscow time. This tactic was not one hundred percent successful, as some very smart servers with powerful firewalls such as Lexis still evaded the Russian server configuration, so some rejection still occurred.

The electronic learning environment was enhanced by the presentation of attendees' legal institution home pages, such as the Yerevan State University School of Law (Armenia) (http://www.law.ysu.am/), the Open Library for Legal Information Development (http://www.lawlib.uz) in Tashkent (Uzbekistan), the Sverdlosk Library named Belinsky (http://library.uraic.ru) in Ekaterinburg (Russia), the Riga Graduate School of Law (http://www.rgsl.edu.lv) in Latvia, the Legal Information Center (http://www.litlex.lt) in Vilnius (Lithuania), the Tartu University Library (http://www.utlib.ee) of Estonia, the Legal Information Center (http://www.pl.spb.ru/) in Saint Petersburg City Public Library (Russia), the Legal Center from the M.I. Rudomino All-Russia State Library for Foreign Literature (http://www.libfl.ru/) of Moscow, and others. Recently, they have all been linked together.

In-depth comparisons of legal developments (such as the comparison between the Dutch and the Russian Civil Codes, and the Dutch Civil Code's influence on the recent drafting of the Russian Civil Code) addressed the process of cross-jurisdictional influences. Bibliographies on building international law and foreign law collections were examined.

We reviewed legal databases with more or less the same content but offered in different formats (CD-ROM and online), such as the Russian databases Kodeks, Garant, and Kon stantPlius. Students were exposed to all the real problems encountered by a legal information professional who is building a collection of foreign, comparative, international, and domestic laws from scratch. The students' Home Page was drafted and uploaded by the Tashkent attendee (http://www.lawlib.uz/conference/conferences.html) with the help of the participants.

How to Build an Electronic Law Library in a Foreign Country

One of the major weaknesses of the world's library resources is the scarcity of foreign and international law collections. In desperate need for reliable and up-to-date materials, libraries often try to fill the gap with ad hoc solutions. My experience in offering assistance to some of the third world libraries clearly showed that obtaining out-of-date books from "generous donations", importing short-term visiting "brains" or even buying computers (which are sometimes used as furniture covered with elegant red velvet, or are carefully locked) does not solve the problem. On the contrary, these stop-gaps feed frustration.

The real solution is to build online capability and access and to learn how to use the resources available online. The Internet is more flexible than printed sources and makes foreign and international substantive law research more effective. Although difficulties may be experienced in accessing certain databases, these are just minor inconveniences compared to the riches the cyberlegal world provides.

In the WWW legal environment, a good foreign law collection is no longer a privilege of the prestigious "star libraries". If a library does not own foreign law books of primary sources, it can acquire the same legal information in electronic format, complementing it in time with printed commentaries, monographs, and dissertations. Today, in fact, it does not matter how remote or unknown a library is; any library in the world can have access to online resources once it creates a bridge to the WWW world of legal resources. For that purpose the library needs a trained staff (which may require foreign internships or

MLS study abroad),[96] a computer network, and a system for sharing law resources.

There is also a philosophical dilemma that should be discussed whenever a library decides to build an electronic bridge to the world, namely, that not only will the library have access to the world, but that it will also expose itself to the world. If the library and legal information specialists are not ready for this exposure, they may be overwhelmed by the amount and variety of information available to them, and by the sudden increase in their responsibility to the international legal community. Building an electronic bridge is an enormous responsibility and a challenge. Legal information specialists may want to maintain a bridge "under construction" until they are ready for the invasion of the outside world.

As a member of a legal research team dealing with foreign and international law, the information professional should not only be knowledgeable about legal systems but also well-informed about information technology. The information professional evaluates and implements new technologies and keeps his team (attorneys, researchers, students) informed about new sources in electronic format. The uniqueness of his or her position in the legal team is that he or she is "emerging as the quality leader in an information environment. By applying standards to information, the librarian will be able to advise researchers on the validity of resources."[97]

The levels and the process of helping legal information professionals to build electronic law collections in the cyberlegal

[96] In the United States, law librarians are generally experts in content (law, social sciences, languages) as well as in organization, acquisition, and service of information. They are expected to be able to analyze inquiries to determine appropriate sources, and to maintain peer networks in order to facilitate acquisitions even of unpublished materials. Frequently they have faculty status, which recognizes the importance of their contributions to the research enterprise, and empowers them to negotiate for information on behalf of the institution. In addition to finding information directly, they also train end users and other information professionals to be self-sufficient. In Europe these roles may be performed by junior professors or postgraduates in specialized research centers.

[97] Ruth A. Fraley, "Renaissance in Law Librarianship—Another Perspective," in *Toward a Renaissance in Law Librarianship*. American Association of Law Libraries: West Information Publishing Group (1997), 103.

culture milieu can be tailored to meet particular goals anywhere in the world. Beyond content, software platform, and Internet access, issues are further divided among communication options, research patterns, and acquisition policies.

A potential law library or legal information center that wishes to become a member of the cyberlegal community should take the following steps:

1. Set up a server, a network of PCs with up-to-date hardware configuration, and email for librarians so they can communicate with professionals over the Internet. E-mail enables the librarian to be in touch with his or her peers from all over the world, and to contact governments, agencies, international organizations, international courts, law schools, and well- known experts in order to obtain legal information or legal support when needed.

2. Subscribe to listservs (discussion groups) related to law, and learn to search the archives of listservs. Listservs gather people of like competencies from any country in the world, debate hot legal issues, offer research assistance, and help beginners in the legal research domain. Discussion lists could be compared, in a way, with an "electronic academy" of subject specialists. Their role will grow in the years to come.

3. Tap into current awareness legal groups that provide summaries of current legal topics and information on legal seminars, spotlight legal news and hot legal issues, and offer counsel.

4. Build a library home page with links to specific databases on the World Wide Web, legal portals and vortals, including the best-known guides and virtual libraries. Implement an online catalog; integrate the resources available through the Internet into reference services and the online catalog; promote the strengths of the collection of the library through the home page; verify that it is listed in Internet directories under the correct keywords; get the site mentioned as a valuable link to other related Web sites; and generally turn a passive visitor to the library's home page into an interactive one.

5. Develop an electronic information acquisition policy for the Internet in order to ensure that patrons get authoritative, up-to-date, reliable and useful primary and secondary re-

sources. The acquisition policy must be consistent and structured. The following principles should at least be respected: a) create links to original sources, especially those provided by governments and IGOs; b) implement reliable mirrors to avoid congestion (a mirror site is a copy of the original site on a separate server with a separate URL); c) identify value-added features; and d) continually maintain indexing, update URLs, delete entries that are no longer reliable, etc.

6. Develop training courses for your team and patrons in order to endow users with advanced levels of self-sufficiency—a process that will allow you to grow in your profession.

Conclusion

The proliferation of international and foreign law materials on the Internet in so many formats presents one major disparity. International materials (documents, conventions, treaties, cases) are very well represented; with few exceptions they can be accessed free of charge. Foreign materials (domestic laws), however, are more difficult to find, and access is usually mostly fee-based.

There is no settled trend in the development of foreign law collections in the cyberlegal world. We see many governments or national universities offering free access to their country's legislation, while others are charging fees or leaving the issue in the hands of private vendors. The dilemma of public versus private ownership may well determine the future of access to legal information on a global basis, and the viability of those that serve the international legal community.

Today, more and more institutions around the world are engaged in digitization projects of old collections. Historical Newspapers Online (http://historynews.chadwyck.com) provides full-text reference material of eighteenth, nineteenth, and twentieth century history. Digital initiatives in the US may be found in universities and libraries such as Oklahoma State University Library Digitization Center (http://digital.library.okstate.edu/mission.htm), University of Minnesota Libraries Digital Initiatives (http://digital.lib.umn.edu), Colorado Digitization Project (http://coloradodigital.coalliance.org), Cornell University Library Department of Preservation and Conservation (http://www.library.cornell.edu/preservation), The Library of

Congress—the American Memory Project (http://lcweb2.loc.gov), New York Public Library Digital Library Collections (http://digital.nypl.org), and so on.

In Europe, projects funded by the European Commission[98] speak about the anatomy and the configuration of libraries of the future. I would mention Biblioteca Universalis Project (http://www.konbib.nl/gabriel/bibliotheca-universalis/index.htm), British Library Digital Library Programme (http://www.bl.uk/diglib/dlp/overview.html), Telematics for Libraries Projects Candle Project (http://www.cordis.lu/libraries/en/projects/candle.html), Denmark Electronic Research Library Project (http://www.deflink.dk/english), Decomate Project—Developing the European Digital Library for Economics (http://www.bib.uab.es/decomate2), Dieper Project (http://www.SUB.UNI-goettingen.de/gdz/dieper) (designed to build a virtual network and a central access point for access to periodicals that have been retrospectively digitized in Europe or elsewhere in the world), Gallica Project at the Bibliothèque Nationale de France (http://gallica.bnf.fr), Memoria Hispanica Project (the generic name of the Biblioteca Nacional of Spain Digitization Project, http://www.bne.es/ingles/europ4.htm), the National Library of Scotland Digitization Projects (http://www.nls.ac.uk/digframe.htm), and so on. Moreover, in the absence of older materials, libraries rely on partnerships with libraries of other jurisdictions that can provide older documents on demand.

Crucial to any information system is the well-trained librarian/legal information specialist. Cyberlegal culture highlights the necessity for skilled professionals who can search, organize, and deliver authentic, reliable information to the user in a timely manner. Cyberlegal culture professionals have to be trained in using also paper sources in order to perform. Sometimes, there is a need to return to basics. Generally speaking, there is a perceived link between quality law research and living online searching. To quote Robert C. Bering, substantive law research "is going to bring back the books but some people seem to want to draw a line in the sound." [99]

[98] Raitt, David, "Projects Funded by the European Commission," 20 *Computers in Libraries* Number 10, November/December 2000, p. 27.

[99] Robert C. Bering, *Computer v. book research*. Message posted to lawlibdir-l@lablib.wuacc.edu (April 24,2001).

I should like to add that the members of the cyberlegal culture are, historically speaking, engaged in a quest. It is a quest for the highest quality of research, learning, and teaching in a diverse, cosmopolitan, and innovative community. The psychological scaffolding of resources and skill discrimination are diminishing. The reflexive preferences for similarities instead of dissimilarities are also decreasing. An environment where many people from many nations communicate effectively has been created, step by step.

The integrating of the Internet into teaching and learning is both an exciting and disturbing event. The enrichment of teaching with Internet-based learning technology, and the ongoing process of introducing Internet-based technology into education, are inevitably changing the ways learners think. Definitely, this is an occasion for both celebration and concern. Anomalies in cyberlegal culture have arisen in the context of discrimination and censorship; between what has been created and access to this treasure. While what has been created is tangible and often praiseworthy, we must be concerned about the brutal trend of replacing the teacher/professor/trainer with a tutorial, as well as about the possibility of destroying the value of the traditional classroom in an Internet-based learning environment unable to sustain such a remote learning process. Serious difficulties also arise from the copyright and intellectual property protection of teaching materials in the WWW environment. And in many countries restriction of access to information—i.e., censorship—is still powerful.

In this connection I would also mention the dilemma of private versus public ownership of materials (if a library cancels a subscription to a printed reporter or serial, it still owns whatever was bought before, while conceling a subscription in the WWW environment means no access to any kind of resources whatsoever); the lack of financial resources at so many legal institutions for acquiring electronic legal collections; and the absence of technical equipment to access the cyberlegal culture products in so many universities around the world.

The presence of a computer and a free Internet connection through a server is still a luxury instead of a commodity. On the large scale, we live in an age similar to the early Gutenberg Era, when books were the privilege of lords, aristocrats, and monasteries. Books had in the beginning an occult significance, very much as cyberlegal culture does today. This new occult significance has both a positive and a negative impact. Its negative component is manifest in the multiple layers of technology and instruction interposed between the virtual world and the end user. It also appears in the widespread feeling that the Internet is yet another tool for the destruction of traditional cultural values, and a milieu of strange behaviors and nonhuman practices.

History shows that any new discovery has always had creative and destructive aspects, derived, I believe, from the binary structure of the physical matter of the universe. The latter is in its turn reflected in humanity's perpetual ambivalence: mortals must continuously decide their place in the eternal conflict between good and evil. But in the fuzzy logic of the cyberlegal world, which allows for no crisp borders, which side of this conflict you choose is decided by the degrees of your positive and negative attitudes. For my part, I have always striven to be on the side of the angels.

Appendix

International and Foreign Law Databases

This is a selective annotated listing of the most reliable, accurate, and comprehensive full-text/ bibliographic databases and online guides available at this moment. It might be considered the backbone of any legal specialist's virtual collection on international, comparative, and foreign law. Almost all these databases have been analyzed and discussed in previous chapters. The online version of this book reflects the current reality (URLs, content, and so on) of all mentioned databases, contributions, and articles, with margins of error due only to the speed of the updating protocols.

I will indicate whenever necessary the fact that the databases are fee-based, without further remark. These databases have an "about us" or a "publications" file disclosing (without charge) the source of data, content, coverage, formats, publisher, platform to be used, search strategies, copyright policy, and so on. For in-depth evaluations, Chapter Three (above) provides guidelines to assess particular cases for acquisition purposes (i.e., the archiving commitment, access, pricing, and so on.)

Readers might encounter URL errors due to the migration of some WWW databases to more secure servers and/or more accurate domain names. In such situations it would be wise to visit the root databases of the legal institutions originally hosting and publishing those particular collections of legal materials (governments, international organizations, institutes, universities, law schools, law libraries, private publishers), or to visit the Guide to Foreign and International Legal Databases, http://www.law.nyu.edu/library/foreign_intl.

General Sources for Public and Private International Law

1. Treaties

UN Treaty Collection Database (http://untreaty.un.org) contains the United Nations Treaty Series (over 40,000 treaties and international agreements registered or filed and recorded with and published by the Secretariat since 1946, in English and French), and Multilateral Treaties Deposited with the Secretary-General (providing information on the status of major multilateral instruments deposited with the Secretary-General of the United Nations). The database also contains Texts of Recently Deposited Multilateral Treaties that have not yet been published in the United Nations Treaty Series. Fee-based. IP access. For sample access, see http://untreaty.un.org/English/sample.asp.

The Avalon Project (http://www.yale.edu/lawweb/avalon/avalon.htm) at Yale University provides old treaties (pre-18th century, 18th century, 19th century, and 20th century selected documents), as well as a review of European Diplomacy from 870 to the Present: Bilateral Treaties and Agreements, European History: A Chronology 802-1992, and other historical materials.

The Australian Treaties Library (http://www.austlii.edu.au/au/other/dfat/) contains multilateral and bilateral treaties, in full text, both in force and not yet in force. The database make available the following information: the Australian Treaty List (as at 31 December 1997 plus monthly updates), the Australian Treaty Series (treaty texts, 1930-1997), Australian Treaties (not yet in force), Multilateral Treaties and Conventions in the "Select Documents" series (originally published prior to entry into force for Australia, 1966-1997), National Interest Analyses for treaties tabled in Parliament (1996–present), List of Multilateral Treaty Actions under Negotiation or Consideration (provided to Parliament), and other regional treaties.

The Council of Europe (http://conventions.coe.int) treaty database has helpful features such as Recent Changes, Draft Treaties, Introduction to Treaties, and Partial Agreements. See also European Union Selected Instruments taken from Treaties (http://europa.eu.int/abc/obj/treaties/en/entoc.htm), for the full text of the updated European Union Treaties.

Geneva Conventions of 12 August 1949 and Additional Protocols of 8 June 1977: ratifications, accessions and successions (http://www.icrc.org/eng/party_gc). At The Swiss Federal Department of Foreign Affairs in Bern (http://www.eda.admin.ch/eda/f/home/foreign/intagr/train/iprotection.html) you can find the 1929 Geneva International Humanitarian Conventions and the 1949 Geneva Conventions for the Protection of War Victims as well as the additional protocols in French, provided by the Red Cross Organization (http://www.icrc.org/dih) database.

The Hague Conference on Private International Law established in 1893 (http://www.hcch.net/e/conventions/), contains in its database the full texts of conventions drafted over the years. The database is under the supervision of the Dutch Minister of Foreign Affairs. It is the best source for determining the status of private international law conventions, signatories, reservations, and other related information. For each convention, an explanatory report, a status report, a bibliography and a list of citations to various translations is provided. The database contains multilateral treaties (conventions) in the different fields of private international law (e.g., international judicial and administrative cooperation; conflict of laws for contracts, torts, maintenance obligations, status and protection of children, relations between spouses, wills and estates or trusts; and jurisdiction and enforcement of foreign judgments).

Human Rights Treaties at the University of Minnesota (http://www1.umn.edu/humanrts/treaties.htm) provides human rights treaties and related instruments organized by subject matter, with a complete list of treaties and other instruments in five languages. A complex search engine allows searches by keyword on multiple databases. The results depend upon the selected databases.

LEXIS (http://www.lexis.com/), International Law Library, contains Agreements and Treaties in various categories such as ASIL, BDIEL, IBFD, GTT/WTO, ILMTY, NAFTA, USTRY, and TNY. Fee-based.

Multilateral Project of the Fletcher School of Law and Diplomacy (http://www.tufts.edu/fletcher/multilaterals.html) makes available the texts of international multilateral conventions and other instruments contained in its own server or other reputable databases. Multilateral treaties are organized both chronologically and according to subject. Multilateral Conventions by Subject links to Treaty secretariats with known Internet servers and other collections of international law. The collection includes historical texts, from the 1648 Treaty of Westphalia to the Covenant of the League of Nations.

The International Institute for the Unification of Private Law (UNIDROIT) (http://www.unidroit.org/) provides the texts of conventions since 1964 adopted by member states, as well as a status section with signatures, ratifications, declarations and reservations, the implementation of UNIDROIT conventions, the UNIDROIT News (newsletter), Principles of International Commercial Contracts, *Uniform Law Review*, and the Principles and Rules of Transnational Civil Procedure. See also under Business Laws—Treaties and Country Legislation.

The Organization of American States provides the organization's treaties (http://www.oas.org/treaties/treaties.htm) since 1949 in Spanish and English. The status of the treaties, signatories, ratification and other related issues are supplied. The database is under development. The French and Portuguese interfaces are not complete at this time.

The South African Cyber Treaty Series (http://home.earthlink.net/~apronto/treaties/trindex.htm) by Arnold Pronto provides a comprehensive, up-to-date list of multilateral treaties entered into by South Africa, with, where possible, links to full text versions placed on the Internet, as well as to ratification information. It makes no attempt to cover bilateral agreements. The treaty series is based primarily on the United Nations Multilateral Treaties Deposited with the Secretary-General, and is arranged according to the categories found in the United Nations Treaty Series.

TIARA (http://www.oceanalaw.com) by Oceana Online is a fee-based database containing U.S. Treaties and International Agreements in force from 1783 to the present in full text. The database offers two products: U.S. Treaties and International Agreements, and The U.S. Treaties Index (free of charge). Searches for treaties can use a combination of fields including country, location signed, treaty name, date in force, subject, and so on. A Country Thesaurus gives information related to the newly created or lesser-known countries. Parallel citations to

BEVANS, LNTS, TIAS, and UST are provided. The status of an agreement is easily found by the CTIA (Consolidated Treaties and International Agreements) number. See the evaluation/description at the Boston University Law Library Electronic Resources Product Status: TIARA Researcher (http://www.bu.edu/lawlibrary/tech/etitles/tiara.htm). Free trial passwords available. TIARA has recently been offering the Oceana publication *International Tax Treaties of All Nations* containing annotated income tax treaties for about 200 countries.

The United States Treaties in Force (http://www.state.gov/www/global/legal_affairs/tifindex.html) is a list of treaties and other international agreements in force as of the first of each year, in pdf format, made available by the Office of the Legal Adviser. TIF contains no treaty texts. Most of the citations in TIF point to United States treaties and other international agreements. Part 1 of TIF is a bilateral treaty index. Part 2 is a multilateral treaty index by topic. To find the full text of the treaties, go to the United States.Senate Treaties (http://www.senate.gov/activities/treaties.html) for treaties and conventions submitted recently by the President to the Senate (before they are announced in Congressional Index or in International Legal Materials) or to United States. Senate, House and Treaty Documents (http://www.access.gpo.gov/congress/cong006.html) for U.S. Bilateral Treaties since 1995, via GPO as "treaty documents". At the database of the Senate, House, and Executive Reports (http://www.access.gpo.gov/congress/cong005.html) are all related Treaty Documents.

WESTLAW (http://www.westlaw.com/) contains Multinational Treaties and Agreements in different files such as the CCH Tax Treaties Reporter, International Environmental Law Documents, International Legal Materials, U.S. Treaties and Other International Agreements, and Tax Analysts—Worldwide Tax Treaties. Fee-based.

Guides:

Conducting Research in Public International Law. An Introduction to Information Sources (http://www.jb.law.uu.nl/jb-vol/cover.html) by George Middeldorp.

Guide to Electronic Resources for Private International Law (http://www.asil.org/resource/pil1.htm) by David A. Levy.

International Family Law: A Selective Resource Guide (http://www.llrx.com/features/int_fam.htm) by Marylin J. Raisch.

International Treaties Guide (http://www.law.nyu.edu/library/treatiesguide.html) by Radu Popa.

Legal Research on International Law Issues Using the Internet (http://www.lib.uchicago.edu/~llou/forintlaw.html) by Lyonette Louis-Jacques.

Researching U.S. Treaties and Agreements (http://www.llrx.com/features/ustreaty.htm) by Marci Hoffman.

Researching Non-U.S. Treaties (http://www.llrx.com/features/non_ustreaty.htm) by Stefanie Weigman.

Treaties (http://www.asil.org/resource/treaty1.htm) by Jill Watson.

2. Judicial Decisions

a. International Courts and Tribunals

The International Court of Justice (http://www.icj-cij.org/icjwww/icj002.htm) database has three mirror sites —in Ithaca, New York (http://www.lawschool.cornell.edu/library/cijwww/), Paris (http://www.u-paris2.fr/cij/), and Glasgow (http://www.icj.law.ac.gla.uk). The official site is maintained by the Registry of the ICJ. It contains basic documents, decisions of the ICJ, current Docket of the Court, and Publications. It does not replace at this time *Recueil des arrêts, avis consultatifs et ordonnances—Reports of Judgments, Advisory Opinions, and Orders* (Leiden: Société d'éditions A.W. Sijthoff (1947–), because not all old cases are in the database. An e-mail notification system for Press Communiqués provides up-to-date notice of new information. Subscribers to the service, which is free, will receive an e-mail each time a new Press Communiqué is issued by the Court. The e-mail will indicate the title, the date and the Internet address of the Press Communiqué.

The European Court of Human Rights (http://www.echr.coe.int) contains pending and old cases, judgments, and basic texts. The full text of cases is searchable with HUDOC (http://hudoc.echr.coe.int/hudoc/). Although old cases are continuously loaded, it cannot yet replace the *European Commission of Human*

Rights Decisions and Reports (Strasbourg : The Commission, 1975–) or other similar reports.

The Court of Justice of the European Communities called the European Court of Justice—CURIA (http://europe.eu.int/cj/en/index.htm), the database of the judicial institution of the Community, contains recent judgments of the Court of Justice (http://www.curia.eu.int) and the Court of First Instance and the Advocate General's Opinions, in the language of the Advocate General as well as in the language of the case. The Proceedings of the Court of Justice and of the Court of First Instance of the European Communities are published every week on the Court database. Most of these documents are available in the eleven official languages. Judgments are available from 3 P.M. on the day of delivery. The definitive version of cases is published in the *Reports of Cases before the Court of Justice and the Court of First Instance* (Luxembourg: Court of Justice of the European Communities), and *the Reports of European Community Staff Cases*. The database is loading pre–1995 jurisprudence, so one day it may become comprehensive. So far, however, the database cannot replace the *Digest of Case-Law Relating to the Community Law* and other research and documentation tools published by the Court.

Inter-American Court of Human Rights (http://www1.umn.edu/humanrts/iachr/iachr.html) provides basic documents relevant to the Inter-American Court of Human Rights, case law, and press releases. Contentious cases are published selectively. The database cannot yet replace the *International Human Rights Reports* (Nottingham, United Kingdom: Human Rights Law Centre, Department of Law, University of Nottingham, 1994–), and the *Inter-American Court of Human Rights Serie A, Fallos y opiniones* (1982–); *Serie B, Memorias, argumentos orales y documentos* (1983); *Serie C, resoluciones y sentencias* (1987); *Serie D, Memorias, argumentos orales y documentos* (1994–); *Series E, Provisional measures* (1999–) (San José, Costa Rica : Secretaría de la Corte).

Guides:

Introduction to International Law Research (http://brkl.brooklaw.edu/screens/rgintl.html) by Jean Davis and Victoria Szymczak.

International Criminal Law (http://www.asil.org/resource/crim1.htm) by Gail Partin.

International Criminal Law: A Selective Resource Guide (http://www.llrx.com/features/int_crim.htm) by Marylin J. Raisch and Gail Partin.

b. National courts

There are numerous recognized WWW guides and annotated indices directing the researcher to national jurisdictions and domestic courts. I would mention here the guides prepared by the Global Legal Information Network (GLIN) of The Library of Congress ((http://lcweb2.loc.gov/law/GLINv1/GLIN.html), the New York University Law Library Guide to Foreign and International Legal Databases—Foreign Databases by Jurisdiction (http://www.law.nyu.edu/library/foreign_intl/country.html), Foreign and International Law at the Washburn University (http://www.washlaw.edu/forint/forintmain.html), the Political Database of the Americas at Georgetown University (http://www.georgetown.edu/LatAmerPolitical/), the Guide to European Legal Databases (http://www.llrx.com/features/europenew.htm), the East Asian Law Guide at the Marian Gould Gallagher Law Library of the University of Washington School of Law (http://lib.law.washington.edu/eald/eald.html), Foreign and International Law Resources from Cornell University Law Library (http://www.lawschool.cornell.edu/lawlibrary/International_Resources/foreign.htm), Legal Information by Country/Continent at Bayreuth University (Jurweb) (http://www.uni-bayreuth.de/students/jurweb), LLRX.Com (http://www.llrx.com/resources4.htm) guides to foreign jurisdictions, ElSweb (http://www2.unimaas.nl/~elsweb/) at the European Law School in Maastricht, the Netherlands, the Foreign and International Law Resources at Harvard (http://www.law.harvard.edu/library/ref/ils_ref/ils_web_sites.htm), and The World Law Index at AUSTLII (http://www.austlii.edu.au/links/World).

c. Arbitral tribunals

These tribunals are found under the headings of arbitration, international trade, and international business, or are recorded within the guides related to these topics of international law. I will mention here databases such as the WTO Dispute Resolution (http://www.wto.org/english/tratop_e/

dispu_e/dispu_e.htm); the New York Convention on the Recognition and Enforcement of Foreign Arbitral Awards (http://www.epms.nl/arbit/nycmain.htm) and its case law (http://www.epms.nl/arbit/casesear.htm); the International Center for Settlement of Investment Disputes—ICSID cases (http://www. epms.nl/arbit/casesear.htm); Case Laws on UNCITRAL Texts—CLOUT—(fee-based) (http://www.uncitral.org/english/clout/index.htm); and the CISG Online Project (http://www.jura.uni-freiburg.de/ipr1/cisg/title.htm) maintained by the Institute of Foreign and International Private Law at the University of Freiburg, Germany (providing the status of convention, text, articles, cases, bibliographic references and German case law on the U N Convention on Contracts for the International Sale of Goods), and its mirror site, the Pace Database on the CISG and International Commercial Law (http://cisgw3.law.pace.edu).

The Hague Permanent Court of Arbitration (PCA) (http://www.pca-cpa.org/) is "an international organization offering a broad range of services for resolving disputes between States, as well as disputes between States and private parties and those involving inter-governmental organizations". This database and its mirror site at the Cornell School of Law (http://www.lawschool.cornell.edu/library/pca/) contain settlement of international disputes, optional rules for arbitration, and conciliation rules. The basic documents of the Permanent Court of Arbitration are the Procedural Guidelines for Requesting Designation of an Appointing Authority by the Secretary-General of the Permanent Court of Arbitration under the UNCITRAL (United Nations Commission on International Trade Law) Arbitration Rules, Permanent Court of Arbitration Procedures for Cases under the UNCITRAL Arbitration Rules, Model Clauses for Permanent Court of Arbitration Services under the UNCITRAL Arbitration Rules, and the UNCITRAL Arbitration Rules (1976) themselves.

3. Scholarly Writings

The Institute of Foreign and International Private Law (Freiburg) (http://www.jura.uni-freiburg.de/ipr1us) has a Newsletter on European Private Law and links to Law Reform Projects, courses, seminars, and so on. A list of the Institute's publications is provided.

The Institute for Swiss and International Civil Procedure and Private International Law (http://www.cx.unibe.ch/civpro/index.html) contains links to the Brussels Convention and the Lugano Convention, and contributions such as the book of Moloney and Robinson on *The Brussels Convention on Jurisdiction and the Enforcement of Foreign Judgments*, linked also by many other databases (http://www.cyberia.ie/~twinkle/cover.html).

Jean Monnet Working Paper Series (Harvard) (http://www.jeanmonnetprogram.org/papers/index.html) (1995-) publishes contributions on international, comparative, and foreign law. A searchable Table of Contents and World Wide European Integration Events Calendar are among the best features.

Lauterpacht Research Centre for International Law at the University of Cambridge (http://www.law.cam.ac.uk/RCIL/HOME.HTM) contains the State Responsibility Project of the International Law Commission. The texts of the Draft Articles provisionally adopted by the Commission are available and linked to detailed commentary as well as government comments on draft articles, and the draft articles adopted by the Drafting Committee (1998–).

Max Planck Institute for Comparative Public Law and International Law (http://www.mpiv-hd.mpg.de/) has German and English interfaces. The Virtual Institute contains the electronic collections of the Max Planck Institute, as well as documents and information of other contributors within the fields of foreign, comparative, and public international law. The *Max Planck Public International Law Bibliography* is linked to the Virtual Institute, the *World Court Digest*, and the Comparative Public Law documents.

RAVE—Articles and Decisions in Public International Law and European Law (http://www.jura.uni-duesseldorf.de/rave/e/englhome.htm) (1995–) is a bibliographic database listing and providing citations to articles and decisions in public international law and European. There are links to materials published on the WWW such as judicial decisions, national statutes, documents of international organizations, and full-text articles.

Subject-Oriented Databases (Collections of International and Domestic Laws)

Arbitration

International Alternative Dispute Resolution (http://www.internationaladr.com) is the achievement of an international group of experts working on a database located on a USA server. The database provides information on international mediation and arbitration, such as full texts of treaties (the United Nations Convention on the Recognition and Enforcement of Foreign Arbitral Awards of 1958 called the "New York Convention"; the Convention on the Settlement of Investment Disputes Between States and Nationals of Other States which established the International Centre for the Settlement of Investment Disputes, called "ICSID Convention" or "Washington Convention"; the Inter-American Convention on International Commercial Arbitration called the "Inter-American Convention"; etc.), national arbitration laws, judicial decisions and arbitral awards, institutions and rules, model clauses, arbitrators, recent articles and books, and upcoming conferences, events and seminars. Domestic laws are provided in English and the vernacular. The English version is usually provided by a foreign government body.

Guides:

International Commercial Arbitration: Locating the Resources (http://www.llrx.com/features/arbitration.htm) by Jean M. Wenger is an up-to-date index to full-text primary and secondary sources such as Treaties, Arbitral Institutions, Compilations of Arbitral Institutions, Cooperative Agreements between Arbitral Institutions, Arbitration Rules, National Law Compilations, Drafting Arbitration Clauses—Model Clauses, and Decisions/Awards .

Constitutional Law

International Constitutional Law Project (Wuerzburg University), coordinated by Axel Tschentscher (http://www.law.nyu.edu/library/foreign_intl/constitutions.html), provides English translations of current constitutions of many countries of the world and other textual material related to constitutional documents. It cross-references documents for comparison of constitutional provisions and country information. Each constitution has an Editor's Note disclosing the legal background, the translator's name, and the source of the original text in the vernacular. Each text contains the adoption date, the official title, etc. A Key System Index (http://www.uni-wuerzburg.de/law/xr__indx.html) permits the comparison of constitutional provisions. The Model Constitutional Code (MCC) is a sample constitution with typical provisions and references to the ICL Key System (http://www.uni-wuerzburg.de/law/xx00t___.html). An index to Constitutional Courts (http://www.uni-wuerzburg.de/law/courts.html) is linked to judicial institutions with the function of constitutional review.

Constitutions, Treaties, and Official Declarations (http://www.psr.keele.ac.uk/const.htm) at Keele University, UK, contains a collection of in-force constitutions (many links refer to the Wuerzburg ICL Project, but many others point to country databases or other valid sources) and historical documents related to them. Also listed are links to various documents including the UN Charter, GATT, the Treaty of Rome, the Maastricht Treaty, Human Rights documents, etc.

Commonwealth Constitutions (http://www.echr.net/) contains 43 constitutions via the Human Rights Directory (EchrNet), an organization based in England. Microsoft Internet Explorer version 4 or later must be used in order to see the content. This site aims to provide a comprehensive source of information on human rights for British lawyers. Links give access to the latest case law, both European and British.

European Commission for Democracy through Law (Venice) (http://venice.coe.int), known as the Venice Commission of the Council of Europe, is the work of a body of independent experts in constitutional law. The database has both English and French interfaces. The Commission collaborates with about forty constitutional courts in Europe and elsewhere, publishing summaries of their most important decisions in the Bulletin on Constitutional Case-Law. The dissemination process is realized also by comparative seminars. Full-text documents since1990 are provided. Documents are free, but publications (such as the bulletin) must be purchased. Links to constitutional courts and equivalent bodies (http://venice.coe.int/site/main/court_links_e.htm) provide the decisions of 34 constitutional courts all over the world, many of them in full text in the vernacular.

Decisions:

International Court Network—Constitutional Courts (http://www.uni-wuerzburg.de/law/courts.html) at the International Constitutional Law Project (Wuerzburg University). The database offers selected decisions from selected courts.

Guides:

An Online Encyclopedia for Legal Researchers (http://www.llrx.com/guide/index.htm) by Andrew Zimmerman.

Foreign and International Law (http://www.lib.uchicago.edu/e/law/intl.html) at D'Angelo Law Library.

Researching Constitutional Law on the Internet (http://www.lib.uchicago.edu/~llou/conlaw.html) by Lyonette Louis-Jacques.

Copyright

Questel-Orbit (http://www.questelorbit.com) is a fee-based private service dedicated to intellectual property information (patents, scientific and technical information, trademarks and Internet domain names), in French and English. The database combines the European Union (http://www.european-patent-office.org), US (http://www.uspto.gov/), and Japanese (http://www.jpo-miti.go.jp/) Patent Office information databases. It allows access to over 25 patent databases containing information from the major patent-issuing organizations and information providers, including the World Intellectual Property Organization, the US Patent and Trademark Office, the Japanese Patent Office, the European Patent Office, the French Patent Office (INPI), the Japan Patent Information Organization, Derwent Information, and IFI/Plenum.

The United States Copyright Office (http://lcweb.loc.gov/copyright) contains informational circulars, US copyright law, new pending legislation, WIPO documents, application forms for copyright registration, and links to the copyright law and to copyright-related organizations. Congressional testimony and press releases, regulations, and online copyright records cataloged since1978 are also provided.

Guides:

Researching Intellectual Property Law in an International Context (http://www.llrx.com/features/iplaw2.htm) by Stefanie Weigmann examines the current international intellectual property regimes and the accessibility of foreign laws and bilateral treaties, both in English and the vernacular. The article lists up-to-date primary and secondary sources as well as databases of foreign jurisdictions.

Environmental Law

Treaties:

Asia-Pacific Centre for Environmental Law (http://sunsite.nus.edu.sg/apcel/) at the Faculty of Law at the University of Singapore contains ASEAN Regional Agreements, Action Plans, Declarations and Resolutions, as well as full texts of the domestic legislation of the countries in the region. This database has not been regularly updated, but the process will resume soon, according to Professor Koh Kheng Lian, Faculty of Law, the National University of Singapore, and the Director of APCEL. For more current information go to the Australasian Legal Information Institute(AUSTLII) Home Page (http://www.austlii.edu.au/).

CIESIN /ENTRI—Environment Information Resources (http://sedac.ciesin.org/entri/) is a joint project between the Center for International Earth Science Information Network at Columbia University and NASA. It is a searchable database containing international environmental treaties, treaty summaries, treaty status files and natural resource indicators. It includes its own search engine, (ENTRI) Broker (http://www.ciesin.org/harvest/brokers/entri2/query.html), as well as a thematic guide, a text index of the complete treaty texts, and a searchable index of the treaty summary files to help navigate within the database. There are also listings of treaty titles (both alphabetical and chronological). You can also look up treaties by subject area.

ECOLEX (http://www.ecolex.org/TR/index.htm) contains more than 480 multilateral treaties relating to environmental conservation. "Recognizing the necessity for a single gateway to this information, the UNEP Governing Council (Decision 18/9) called upon United Nations Environmental Program (UNEP) (http://www.unep.org) and IUCN (http://www.iucn.org/themes/law)—The World Conservation Union (http://iucn.org/)—to join forces in providing access to international and national environmental law information primarily to assist developing countries." ECOLEX is therefore designed to use IUCN's Environmental Law Information System (ELIS) as its core archival system, linked to full-text information available with UNEP's Computerised Environmental Law Information Base (CELIB) and other authoritative sources. In this database, the term "multilateral treaty" refers to treaties that are open to three or more States. Go to "State", and browse for treaties of relevance to a given State in order to locate the desired source.

The European Environmental Law Homepage (http://www.asser.nl/EEL/index.htm) contains full texts of European Union treaties and European Communities legislation, provided by the official servers of the European Union, as well as case law and domestic laws in the vernacular from government servers. Treaties are in all official languages of the EU. The T.M.C. Asser Instituut, Maastricht University and Groningen University are responsible for maintaining this project.

Pace Virtual Environmental Law Library (http://www.law.pace.edu/env/vell6.html) at Pace University has English and French interfaces. It contains both full-text documents and links to International Laws, Comparative Laws (domestic laws or legal documents related to them), United States Laws, General Agreements, and so on. *Pace Virtual Environmental Law Library: Reliability of Internet Data* by Robert J. Goldstein, Director of Environmental Programs at the Pace Law School, addresses the issue of the sources and accuracy of the database content.

The Penelope Project (http://www.penelope.gr/penelope/about.htm) is designed to inform and educate users about the development and application of environmental law in Europe. It represents the work of experts in information technology and leading European environmental law institutes. It has English and French interfaces. Microsoft Explorer is required in order to view the database. It should be seen primarily as a new European educational resource, but the information can also be of value to legal practitioners. There are overviews of the most important relevant topics in France, Germany, Greece, Spain and the United Kingdom. Full-text laws, regulations, and court decisions are provided in the vernacular.

The United Nations Environment Program (UNEP) at the Geneva Executive Center in Switzerland (http://www.unep.ch) maintains links to The Basel Convention on Transboundary Movements of Hazardous Wastes, the Convention on International Trade in Endangered Species (CITES), the Intergovernmental Panel on Climate Change (IPCC), the Rotterdam Convention on Trade in Hazardous Chemicals, and other instruments and institutions. Its mirror database (http://www.unep.org) provides environmental legal instruments such as environmental conventions, non-binding environmental instruments, and legal instruments under preparation.

Decisions:

The International Court of Justice (http://www.icj-cij.org/icjwww/icj002.htm) CURIA—The Court of Justice of the European Communities (http://curia.eu.int/)

The European Court of Human Rights (ECHR) (http://stars.coe.fr)

The Organization of American States (OAS) (http://www.oas.org/)

The World Health Organization (http://www.who.org)

NAFTA—the *North American Commission for Environmental Cooperation* (http://www.cec.org/)

Guides:

International Environmental Law (http://www.asil.org/resource/Home.htm) by Anne Burnett. This article reviews online resources of international environmental law (general search strategies, primary and secondary sources), and also covers CD-ROMs and library catalogs.

Human Rights

Treaties:

United Nations Human Rights Database (http://www.un.org/rights/)

United Nations Treaty Collection (http://untreaty.un.org/ENGLISH/series/simpleunts.asp) (fee-based).

United Nations High Commissioner for Human Rights Treaty Database (http://www.unhchr.ch/huridocda/huridoca.nsf) and the *Human Rights Treaty Bodies Database* (http://www.unhchr.ch/tbs/doc.nsf)

Project DIANA at Yale (http://diana.law.yale.edu/) and the mirror site at the Bora Laskin Law Library University of Toronto (http://www.law-lib.utoronto.ca/Diana/) important for secondary sources.

University of Minnesota Human Rights Library (http://www1.umn.edu/humanrts/)

Decisions:

Human Rights courts are linked at the University of Minnesota Human Rights Library (http://www1.umn.edu/humanrts). They are also listed in the annotated guides described below, and can be found as well in this appendix under General Sources for Public and Private International Law—Judicial Decisions—International Courts and Tribunals.

Guides:

Guide to Country Research for Refugee Status Determination (http://www.llrx.com/features/rsd.htm) and *Annex: Human Rights, Country and Legal Information Resources on the Internet* (http://www.llrx.com/features/rsd_bib.htm) by Elisa Mason directs readers to the key texts and resources available on the web.

Human Rights by Marci Hoffman (http://www.asil.org/resource/humrts1.htm) focuses on electronic sources available on this topic such as bibliographic databases, catalogs, research guides and bibliographies, periodical indexes, primary sources, compilations of Human Rights Instruments, Status of Human Rights Instruments, Reservations/Declarations, jurisprudence, caselaw, decisions, reports, secondary sources, country reports, periodical literature, and so on.

Human and Constitutional Rights (http://www.hrcr.org/) at Columbia University divides information resources into Country Reports, International Links, Regional Links, National Links, Documents, and Other Web Resources. "Bills of Rights Comparative Law Materials" is a database for human rights cases. New cases are added daily.

Also of value are *The Rights International Research Guide for International Human Rights Lawyers* (http://www.rightsinternational.org/links.html) by Stephen J. Schnably of the Center for International Human Rights Law, and the *Directory of Human Rights Resources* (http://shr.aaas.org/dhr.htm) by the American Association for the Advancement of Science.

International organizations

The Council of Europe

The Council of Europe (http://www.coe.int/portal.asp?strScreenType=100&L=E&M=$t/1-1-1-1/EMB1.asp) is the official portal of the organization. It provides the European Treaties, the Statute of the Council of Europe, Signature and Ratifications of treaties for each member State, as well as Human Rights documents and many other related materials.

The Council of Europe Human Rights Web Site (http://www.humanrights.coe.int/) is maintained by the Directorate of Human Rights of the Council of Europe. It provides French and English documents and links to the European Court of Human Rights, the Directorate General of Human Rights, Human Rights activities, the European Convention on Human Rights, the European Social Charter, the European Convention for the Prevention of Torture, the Framework Convention for the Protection of National Minorities, and related legal materials.

Guides:

Guide to Researching the Council of Europe (http://www.llrx.com/features/coe.htm) by Anne Burnett.

European Union

The Court of Justice of the European Communities—CURIA (http://curia.eu.int) is the judicial institution of the Community. Its judges must ensure that Community law is not interpreted and applied differently in each Member State, that as a shared legal system it remains a Community system and that it is always identical for all in all circumstances. See more under General Sources for Public and Private International Law—Judicial decisions—International Courts and Tribunals, above.

Celex Web Service (http://europa.eu.int/celex). Fee-based Celex (*Comunitatis Europae Lex*) is managed by the Office for Official Publications of the European Communities. It covers legislation, caselaw, preparatory acts, Parliament questions, and national measures for implementing directives. It provides all judgments and orders of the Court of Justice and the Court of First Instance with summaries, and the opinions of the Advocate General, in all official languages of the Union. It also includes the full texts of legislation published in the Official Journal of the European Communities in the L Series and the citations to information in the C Series. The *Celex* database can be also found in *Westlaw*. CELEX access presents problems, but this will be alleviated by July 2001 when a new law portal is scheduled for release.

EUROPA (http://europa.eu.int/) is the umbrella platform for the home pages of all EU institutions, their individual components and specialized agencies. It contains links to the jurisprudence and recent caselaw of the Court of Justice and the Court of First Instance. EUR-Lex (http://europa.eu.int/eur-lex/) offers the complete L and C series of the Official Journal, the full texts of legislation in force, treaties, judgments of the European Court of Justice, and COM documents in eleven languages, all for a period of 45 days after the date of publication. PreLex (http://europa.eu.int/prelex/apcnet.cfm?CL=en) follows the major stages of the decision-making process between the Commission and other EU institutions, including all Commission proposals (legislative and budgetary files, conclusions of the international agreements) and communications to the Council or to the European Parliament, until their adoption or their rejection by the Council, their adoption by the Parliament, or their withdrawal by the Commission. Links allow users to reach available electronic texts directly (COM documents, Official Journal, *Bulletin of the European Union*, documents of the European Parliament, press releases). RAPID (http://europa.eu.int/rapid/start/welcome.htm), the Spokesman's Service of the European Commission, contains press releases and the French version of the Proceedings of the Court of Justice and the Court of First Instance. SCAD (http://europa.eu.int/scadplus/) is the bibliographical database, with references to Community legislation, official publications, articles, and recent documents on the activities of the EU; the full texts of updated versions of the major European

Union Treaties (http://europa.eu.int/abc/obj/treaties/en/en toc.htm) are also available here. However, pursuant to a reorganization of European Commission services, SCAD is no longer being updated as of March 1, 2001. The Commission's Central Library has taken over responsibility for articles from periodicals, which are now indexed in the ECLAS database. This transfer will probably take some months. In the meantime, sources, subjects, and language cover will remain unchanged, so that all articles can be found in the same database. Links are being created from the Central Library's homepage to SCAD and vice versa, and SCAD will remain available at least until the end of the transfer. Responsibility for the other sectors of SCAD, including SCADPlus, has been assigned to the Commission's Press and Communication Service.

Guides:

Accessing European Union Information (http://www.eur union.org/infores/resguide.htm) by the European Union Delegation of the European Commission to the United States.

Best European Union Law Websites (http://www.eurun ion.org/infores/BestLawSites.HTM) by Ann R. Sweeney.

The European Union—A Guide for Americans (http://www. eurunion.org/infores/euguide/euguide.htm), from the Delegation of the European Commission to the United States.

European Union Internet Resources (http://lib.berkeley.edu/ GSSI/eu.html) at the University of California at Berkeley.

The European Union—A Brief Guide to the Basic Print and Electronic Sources for Legislation, Case Law, and Secondary Material (http://www.law-lib.utoronto.ca/resguide/eubrief.htm) by Marylin J. Raisch.

Western Europe and the European Union Information Sources (http://www.columbia.edu/cu/libraries/indiv/lehman/gui des/westoid.html) at Columbia University.

International Labor Organization

International Labor Organization ILO (http://www.ilo.org/ public/english/index.htm) has English, French, and Spanish interfaces. NATLEX (http://natlex.ilo.org/) is the ILO's national labor law database. It contains full texts of basic legislation, as well as abstracts with citations to original laws. ILOLEX (http://ilolex.ilo.ch:1567/public/english/50normes/infleg/iloeng/index.htm) contains all ILO conventions as well as related international conventions containing ILO Conventions and Recommendations. Cornell's mirror site (http://www.lawschool.cornell.edu/library/International_Resources/ilo.htm) may provide faster access. TRIBLEX (http://ilis.ilo.org/ilis/trib/ilintrtr.html) is a thematic database in French and English on the case law of the Administrative Tribunal of the International Labor Organization. A thesaurus (http://ilis.ilo.org/ilis/trib/ilthestr.html) helps find relevant thematic analysis of the case law of the ILO Administrative Tribunal.

Guides:

ILO Research Guide (http://www.lawschool.cornell.edu/library/International_Resources/iloguide.htm) by Charlotte Bynum.

North American Free Trade Agreement

NAFTA Secretariat (http://www.nafta-sec-alena.org) contains the text of the Agreement as well as official documents such as the Dispute Settlement Rules and Provisions, NAFTA and FTA Decisions and Reports, and Extraordinary Challenge Committee decisions reviewing Chapter 19 binational panel decisions emanating from the US. NAFTA Trade Negotiations and Agreements: Dispute Settlement Chapter 11 (http://www.dfait-maeci.gc.ca/tna-nac/NAFTA-e.asp) can be found at the Canadian Department of Foreign Affairs and International Trade (http://www.dfait-maeci.gc.ca/tna-nac/menu-e.asp). See also the U.S. Department of Commerce (http://www.doc.gov/)—International Trade Administration (http://www.ita.doc.gov/) and Market Access and Compliance (http://www.mac.doc.gov/); the NAFTA Home Page from the U.S. Department of Commerce—International Trade Administration (http://www.mac.doc.gov/nafta/nafta2.htm); The U.S. Department of Agriculture Home Page (http://www.usda.gov/); the National Law Center for Inter-American Free Trade (http://www.natlaw.com/index.htm), which contains full texts of Mexico's related materials in English and Spanish; and the Organization of American States—Trade Unit (http://www.sice.oas.org/) for Chapter 19 Decisions, FTAA documents, NAFTA Dispute Settlement, and Investment Treaties. To check the current status of NAFTA, search the Congressional Record and the Federal Register (http://www.gpo.ucop.edu) for proclamations, regulations, and admini-strative actions.

Guides:

North American Free Trade Agreement (NAFTA) (http://lcweb2.loc.gov/glin/x-nafta.html) at the Library of Congress.

NAFTA (http://www.law.duke.edu/lib/libser/publicat/researchGuides/nafta/naftaframe.html) by Katherine Topulos.

Research Guide on the North American Free Trade Agreement (NAFTA) (http://www.vanderbilt.edu/Law/library/research research_guide_on_the_north_american_free_trade_agreement.html) at Vanderbilt University.

Organization of American States

Organization of American States OAS (http://www.oas.org) is the main portal of the organization. It contains Juridical Information, Treaties and Conventions, Resolutions and Declarations, Legal Documents and Services, Speeches of the Secretary General (1994-1999), Annual Reports, General Assembly Documents, and OAS Official Documents 1889-2000. The database has English, Spanish, French, and Portuguese interfaces.

Organization of American States—Trade Unit—SICE (http://www.sice.oas.org/) provides information on the Free Trade Area of the Americas (FTAA), FTAA documents, NAFTA Dispute Settlement, Investment Treaties, full texts of trade agreements between countries of the Western Hemisphere (Spanish and English), information on dispute settlement, full texts of bilateral investment treaties between countries of the Western Hemisphere (mostly in Spanish), and links to intellectual property official databases.

Guides:

SICE Multi-National Sources of Information Trade-Related Links (http://www.sice.oas.org/trl_e.asp).

United Nations

United Nations (http://www.un.org/) is the official portal to the UN documentation system. It contains General Assembly Resolutions and Decisions since 1981; Security Council Resolutions since1946; and Economic and Social Council (ECOSOS) Documents and Resolutions since 1982 under Archives (http://www.un.org/esa/coordination/ecosoc/archives.htm). For orientation on the structure and goals of the organization, look at the United Nations Charter (http://www.un.org/aboutun/charter/), UN organs and document symbols (http://www.un.org/Depts/dhl/resguide/symbol.htm), and main bodies (http://www.un.org/aboutun/mainbodies. htm).

UN Tribunals related to violations of humanitarian law developed under the UN Charter include the International Criminal Tribunal for the Former Yugoslavia (http://www.un.org/icty/); the International Criminal Tribunal for Rwanda (http://www.ictr.org/); the Rome Statute of the International Criminal Court (http://www.un.org/law/icc/index.html); and the Preparatory Commission for the International Criminal Court (1999–) (http://www.un.org/law/icc/prepcomm/prepfra.htm). Another important body, The International Law Commission (http://www.un.org/law/ilc/index.htm), was established by the General Assembly in 1947 to promote the progressive development of international law and its codification.

United Nations ODS (Optical Disk System) (http://www.ods.un.org/) (updated daily; fee-based) contains searchable, full-text UN documents since 1993 and resolutions back to 1946 in all official languages. It can also be accessed with the same password at the mirror database *Geneva* Optical Disk System Web Server (http://www.undocs.unog.ch/) .

UN Treaty Collection (http://untreaty.un.org/) (fee-based and available IP access) displays the imaged version of the *United Nations Treaty Series.* The database contains the texts of over 34,000 bilateral and multilateral treaties in their authentic language(s), along with translations into English and/or French as appropriate. It is more current than its printed counterpart. All information related to the ratification, status, signatories, and protocols are provided as of the current day.

United Nations Dag Hammarskjöld Library UNBISnet (http://unbisnet.un.org/) is the UN Bibliographic Information System. It contains a catalogue of UN publications and documentation indexed by the United Nations Dag Hammarskjöld Library and the Library of the UN Office at Geneva, as well as non-UN publications held in the collection of the Dag Hammarskjöld Library. It is also the best place to look for United Nations Voting Records and the Index to Speeches.

Guides:

UN Documentation Research Guide (http://www.un.org/Depts/dhl/resguide/) at the United Nations Dag Hammarskjöld Library.

United Nations (http://www.asil.org/resource/un1.htm) by Marci Hoffman and Paul Zarins.

World Health Organization

World Health Organization (http://www.who.org), the official portal of the organization, contains a selection of national and international health legislation primary sources, in the vernacular, with texts summarized in English. Citations to official gazettes are available, as are direct links , when possible, to full-text legislation. The main source of the International Digest of Health Legislation comes from the member states.

The World Intellectual Property Organization

The World Intellectual Property Organization (WIPO) administers 21 international treaties dealing with different aspects of intellectual property protection. Database categories include Industrial Property, Inventions (Patents), Trademarks, Industrial Designs, Copyright, Rights Related to Copyright, and Collective Management of Copyright. The Organization has 175 member states. The Collection of Laws for Electronic Access (CLEA) (http://clea.wipo.int/lpbin/lpext.dll?f=file[ibrowse-j.htm]) is an international electronic archive of intellectual property legislation, providing easy access to intellectual property laws in English, French and Spanish. Updated on an ongoing basis, it contains the full texts of intellectual property legislation of a large number of countries and the European Communities, as well as the full texts of all treaties administered by WIPO.

Each of the legislative texts and treaties is preceded by a detailed bibliographic data entry which includes details such as publication date, entry into force, related texts and language availability. Texts are linked. The Bibliographic Description gives an index of specific countries' laws and amendments.

Guides:

Legal Research Guide:Intellectual Property Law (http:/www.virtualchase.com/resources/ip.shtml) by Ballard Spahr Andrews & Ingersoll, LLP.

Intellectual Property Research Guide (http://www.law-lib.utoronto.ca/resguide/intprop.htm) by Nicholas Pengelley.

SICE Dispute Settlement: Commercial Arbitration, World Intellectual Property Organization, Complete Guide to WIPO Mediation (http://www.sice.oas.org/DISPUTE/comarb/wipo/wip mgde.asp).

WIPO Guide to the Uniform Domain Name Dispute Resolution Policy (http://www.arbiter.wipo.int/domains/guide/) by WIPO Arbitration and Mediation Center.

World Trade Organization

World Trade Organization (http://www.wto.org/) is the major source of the organization's documentation. It contains dispute settlements, legal texts, official documents, statistics, analysis, and over 60,000 official documents produced by or for the WTO's councils, committees, working groups, etc.

Guides:

WTO/GATT Research (http://www.llrx.com/resources4.htm) by Jeanne Rehberg.

General guides to international organizations:

Learning About International Law and International Organizations (http://www.oceanalaw.com/default.asp?contentpage=/freestuff/learning.htm) by Jean Davis.

Directory of International Organizations (http://www.uia.org/website.htm) compiled by the Union of International Associations. Fee-based. It provides links to over 5,000 IGOs and NGOs.

Index to International Organizations at Northwestern University Library (http://www.library.nwu.edu/govpub/resource/internat/igo.html).

Patents and trademarks

Patents Information Services—The British Library of Science Technology and Business (STB) (http://www.bl.uk/services/stb/patents.html) contains the United Kingdom's national patent library. Fee-based. Patents Online, Current scan Patent Watch Service, Patent Express—Document Delivery Service (http://www.bl.uk/services/bsds/pxp/overview.html), File Histories and Transcripts are all available on request.

US Patent and Trademark Office (USPTO) (http://www.uspto.gov/) contains relevant US and international laws. The full-text Patent Database offers all US patents issued since 1790 in the form of searchable patent numbers and current US classifications hyperlinked to full-page images of each page of each patent. From Search Databases go to Patent Full-Text Database with Full-Page Images (http://www.uspto.gov/patft/index.html), and then to Manual search or Boolean and so on. For Trademarks, go to the Trademark Electronic Search System (TESS) (http://tess.uspto.gov/bin/gate.exe?f=tess&state= hrceaf.1.1), which contains more than 2.9 million pending, registered and "dead" federal trademarks. The site has an excellent search engine. USPTO is a free searchable patent database.

United Kingdom Patent Office (http://www.patent.gov.uk) contains trade mark laws since 1996 and decisions since 1998, copyright and related rights legislation, Patent Legal Decisions since 1998, and the Manual of Patent Practice. It also provides information on European patent law.

The World Intellectual Property Organization (WIPO (http://www.wipo.org), the major source of international and national legislation, contains Conventions, Treaties, Contracting Parties, Annual Reports, and so on. *CLEA—WIPO* (http://clea.wipo.int) is a collection of country laws in English, French, and Spanish. For a fuller description, see above under International Organizations.

Guides:

Researching Intellectual Property Law in an International Context (http://www.llrx.com/features/iplaw2.htm) by Stefanie Weigmann.

Transnational business and international trade

The Economist Intelligence Unit (EIU) (http://store.eiu.com/) provides information for companies establishing and managing operations across national borders anywhere in the world. Fee-based and available IP access. The EIU offers analysis and forecasts of the political, economic and business environment in more than 180 countries, with reports on certain strategic industries. It includes full-text commercial laws, tax laws, and business regulations of 60 countries worldwide, as well as information on investment opportunities and banking and other financial services for 47 countries.

OECD (http://www.sourceoecd.org/content/html/index.htm) is the online publications portal of the Organization for Economic Cooperation and Development (http://www. oecd.org/). It provides full-text access to subscribers and authorised users at subscribing institutions. It offers studies by themes, containing monographs and reports; 19 periodicals; some reference titles; and the OECD statistical databases. Delivery is in pdf format. Access by either password or IP address.

a. Tax laws

Treaties and country legislation:

Foreign Tax Laws (http://foreignlaw.com) by Foreign Tax Law Inc. (fee-based) provides full consolidated legal texts of the tax laws of over 100 countries, in English. A news service keeps users informed of daily developments around the world. The database is under development.

International Bureau of Fiscal Documentation (http://www.ibfd.nl). Fee-based. Contains tax and social security treaties, conventions, protocols, etc. IBFD also conducts tailor-made research.

Lexis (http://www.lexis.com/) contains Worldwide Tax Daily (TNI); International Bureau of Fiscal Documentation

(IBFD)—Tax Treaties & News; Tax Analysts Publication Library (TAXANA); and Federal Tax Library (FEDTAX). Fee-based.

TaxBase (http://taxbase.tax.org/) by Tax Analysts. Fee-based. Covers federal, state, foreign, and international levels. Its Worldwide Tax Treaties Collection contains over 5,500 tax treaties, amending protocols, and other documents from over 180 jurisdictions, including estate and gift tax treaties, limited agreements, and model tax treaties. Worldwide Tax Daily is a very useful extra feature.

Westlaw (http://www.westlaw.com) Fee-based. Contains Tax Analysts Worldwide Tax Treaties, Worldwide Tax Daily, international tax treaties and agreements, summaries and full-text articles about new developments in the field, and foreign and international administrative judicial rulings, in addition to secondary sources.

Guides:

International Taxation (http://www.law.nyu.edu/library/foreign_intl/taxint.html) by Mirela Roznovschi.

Steuerrecht im Internet (http://www.pinkernell.de) by Reimar Pinkernell. A directory of German and international tax databases, with information on the taxation of electronic commerce and US-German tax materials (US tax glossary, US-Germany tax treaties).

b. Business laws

Treaties and country legislation:

UN Convention on Contracts for the International Sale of Goods (CISG) (http://cisgw3.law.pace.edu/). The United Nations Convention on Contracts for the International Sale of Goods is the uniform international sales law of countries that account for two-thirds of all world trade. See also the CISG Online Project (http://www.jura.uni-freiburg.de/ipr1/cisg/title.htm) maintained by the Institute of Foreign and International Private Law at the University of Freiburg, Germany, which provides the status of the convention, text, articles, cases, bibliographic references and German case law on the CISG.

United Nations Commission on International Trade Law (http://www.uncitral.org/en-index.htm) (UNCITRAL) contains conventions, ratifications, preparatory documents, and case-law.

International Institute for the Unification of Private Law (UNIDROIT) (http://www.unidroit.org/) has English and French interfaces. UNIDROIT examines ways of harmonizing and co-ordinating the private law of States and groups of States; its mission is to prepare gradually for the adoption by States of uniform rules of private law. The database contains international instruments, including Conventions (in force unless otherwise indicated), drawn up by UNIDROIT and adopted at diplomatic Conferences convened by member States. It contains the texts of the UNIDROIT Principles of International Commercial Contracts, Principles and Rules of Transnational Civil Procedure, Franchising, and International Interests in Mobile Equipment (see also above under General Sources for Public and Private International Law —Treaties).

Conventions on International Trade and International Intellectual Property at the Eye on International Business Law (http://www.uni-muenster.de/Jura.iwr/english/berger/linkse/linkse.html) by Professor Dr. Klaus Peter Berger at the Institute for International Business Law, University of Muenster, Germany. This database provides a useful starting point for legal research in the areas cited above.

The National Law Center for Inter-American Free Trade The Inter-American Database (http://www.natlaw.com/index.htm) is fee-based, but offers a free searchable index with citations to national official gazettes. The Center's various projects serve to identify and eliminate the structural legal obstacles to free trade through the harmonization of commercial laws and practices and the standardization of legal documentation. The Center's database offers the following substantive areas: Banking, Environment, Intellectual Property, Labor, Secured Financing, Securities, and Transportation. English translations are included for selected Mexican laws. It also offers Latin American commercial codes in the vernacular, with some English translation.

Guides:

Guide to International Trade Law Sources on the Internet (http://www.llrx.com/features/trade2.htm) by Marci Hoffman.

International Economic Law (http://www.asil.org/resource/iel1.htm) by Jean M. Wenger is an overview of electronic resources in international trade law, international financial law, private international law, international business regulation, and intellectual property law. The article provides access to legal literature, guides, primary and secondary sources, and reference materials.

Regions of the World and Individual Jurisdictions

1. Comparative law databases

Consolidating European Public Law (http://www.iue.it/LAW/conseulaw) at the European University Institute, Law Department. The Comparative Database contains a collection of those national constitutional provisions that relate to the European Union integration and international law. Searchable by fields and assigned topics of constitutional law.

European, International and Comparative Materials (http://civil.udg.es/epclp/default.htm) at the University of Girona. Projecte Norma Civil (http://civil.udg.es/normacivil) provides access to The European Group on Tort Law (Tilburg Group) (http://civil.udg.es/tort/), whose aim is to draft a collection of Principles of European Tort Law (http://civil.udg.es/tort/principles.htm) similar to the Principles of European Contract Law that are now being drafted by the European Contract Law Commission ("Lando Commission"). The Group also cooperates with the European Center of Tort and Insurance Law in Vienna (http://civil.udg.es/EUROCENTRE/). There is also a Research Group for the Draft of a Project of an EC Directive on personal injury damages (http://civil.udg.es/epclp/default.htm).

Guides:

Research in Foreign & Comparative Law (http://lib.law.washington.edu/ref/forcomp.htm) by Mary Whisner.

2. Collections of foreign materials

Bibliography of Asian Studies (BAS) (http://ets.umdl.umich.edu/b/bas/). Fee-based. Contains more than 410,000 records on all subjects pertaining to East, Southeast, and South Asia published worldwide from 1971 to the present.

Center for Research Libraries CRL (http://wwwcrl.uchicago.edu/) is a fee-based international not-for-profit consortium that makes available scholarly research resources to users everywhere. CRL is governed by the major research libraries of North America. Area Studies Programs describes cross-regional projects and projects supporting resources for international preservation and foreign microfilming efforts for all regions of the world .

Central and East European Legal, Political, Business and Economic Resources at Gonzaga University Law Library (http://law.gonzaga.edu/library/ceeurope.htm) focuses on English-language materials from government, academic, NGO, and news agency sources. It points to primary sources of countries such as Albania, Belarus, Bosnia and Herzegovina, Bulgaria, Croatia, the Czech Republic, Estonia, Hungary, Latvia, Lithuania, Macedonia, Moldova, Poland, Romania, Russia, Serbia and Montenegro, the Slovak Republic, Slovenia, Ukraine, and the former USSR.

Compilation des lois sur la nationalité des pays et territoires européens contenant les versions vernaculaires des lois sur la nationalité de 46 juridictions européennes (http://www.geocities.com/nationalite/) by Andy Grossman is a compilation of European Nationality Laws from forty-six jurisdictions in the vernacular.

Foreign (International) Supreme Court Decisions (http://www.mossbyrett.of.no/info/links.html) is an index to the decisions of forty-two foreign courts prepared at the Moss City Court (Norway).

The GLIN Home Page—The Library of Congress Global Legal Information Network (http://lcweb2.loc.gov/law/GLINv1/GLIN.html) is a restricted-access database of full-text primary sources in the vernacular of fifty countries from all continents. The Latin American collection of laws is very well represented. Free only to contributing state governments. A free searchable index for guests gives citations to national official gazettes as well as a summary of each law in English. No information is provided regarding data coverage by jurisdiction as of the year 2001. The search form is not yet fully operational, and accepts only legal terms from a required database thesaurus.

International Constitutional Law Project (http://www. un i- wuerzburg.de/law/index.html) at Wuerzburg University provides unofficial translations of foreign constitutions in English. It would be wise to verify the data regarding the status of a particular constitution by comparing it with the vernacular version provided by the foreign government database.

Latin American Government Documents Project at Cornell University (http://lib1.library.cornell.edu/colldev/ladocshome.html) organizes and describes Latin American official documents on the Internet under such headings as Executive and Ministerial documents, National Legislative Documents, National Judicial Documents, and so on.

LANIC—Latin American Network Information Center (http://lanic.utexas.edu/) and Law & Justice Country Resources (http://www.lanic.utexas.edu/la/region/law/) point to specific subject information in the vernacular related to Government in Latin America, Government and Political Science, State and Municipal Resources, Political Parties and Elections, Human Rights, Regional Resources, etc.

Law in Transition States LexInfoSys (http://lex.gtz.de/lexinfosys/) at the University of Bremen is a collection of legal materials prepared and maintained by the German Technical Assistance Agency (GTZ) in cooperation with the University of Bremen, Faculty of Law. It contains primary sources in Russian and English (selective) for such "transition states" as Armenia, Azerbaijan, Georgia, Kazakhstan, Moldova, Mongolia, Tajikistan, Turkmenistan, and Uzbekistan.

Lexis (http://www.lexis.com) by LEXIS-NEXIS is a fee-based database with materials arranged in libraries and individual files by area of law and by jurisdiction. It is a comprehensive source for US legal research. A very sophisticated search engine, using Boolean connectors and free natural language, is able to search multiple libraries at once. The connection is by Telnet and hypertext. Documents may be delivered through assigned printers in various formats, by downloading, or by email. Shepard's citation service is a useful feature for US caselaw and for checking the history of cases. The legal literature database (LAWREV) includes a a large number of international and domestic journals. The Nexis database, specializing in news, is a unique source for legal news from all over the world. The Political Universe, the Academic Universe, and the CIS Congressional Universe (a Federal Legislative History finding tool with full texts of Congressional documents) are subject databases for US legal research. LEXIS-NEXIS Academic Universe provides access to a wide range of news, business, legal, and reference information. The International Law Library INTLAW contains legislation and cases from many jurisdictions, including Australia, Canada, China, Israel, Italy, England, Hong Kong, Ireland, Mexico, New Zealand, Singapore, Malaysia, Russia, South Africa, and others. Matthew Bender International Doing Business in . . . (numerous jurisdictions of the world) is also provided. The International Tax Library ITN contains international and domestic tax treaties and laws. However, the high price make this database virtually prohibitive in most countries outside the USA. Academic flat rates are available, but they are still very high for most institutions around the world. Moreover, the database is very sensitive, and its highly effective security system rejects many proxy servers used by governments for censoring and filtering information.

Political Database of the Americas at Georgetown University (http://www.georgetown.edu/LatAmerPolitical/) has English, French, Spanish, and Portuguese interfaces. It contains primary and secondary materials organized by such subject areas as Constitutions and Constitutional Studies , Civil Society, Political Parties, etc.

Penal Codes/Penal Procedure (http://wings.buffalo.edu/law/bclc/resource.htm)at SUNY Buffalo Law School's Criminal Law Center is an index to vernacular sources. Countries covered: Argentina, Austria, Bosnia and Herzegovina, Canada, Finland, France, Germany, Israel, South Korea, Spain, Switzerland, United States (federal and state), Venezuela, Yugoslavia. There are links to Model Criminal Codes (including a Standard Penal Code for Latin America), International Criminal Law (Nuremberg War Crimes Trials/International Military Tribunal via Court TV); European Penal Law Treaties via the Council of Europe; United Nations Crime and Justice International Network UNCJIN; the Office of International Criminal Justice; etc., and other criminology resources.

The Slavic Research Center (SRC) (http://www.slavweb.com/index-e.html) at Hokkaido University, Japan. Look under Resources for Russian and East European Studies—Updated

Russia, Newly Independent States, Central and Eastern Europe, Databases and Statistical Resources where a unique collection of laws in the vernacular can be found with selected primary sources and legal commentaries in English.

Westlaw (http://www.westlaw.com), a major database for US legal research, has recently expanded to the international arena. Key Cite is the counterpart of Lexis Shepard's, providing the history of cases. Laws and caselaw of Australia, the European Union, the United Kingdom, and Canada, as well as business literature from almost any jurisdiction, are represented. A gate to Dialog, another excellent but expensive database, offers access to trademark, patent, copyright, and other business primary materials from all over the world. Index to Foreign Legal Periodicals is one of the most useful indexes to foreign legal literature available. The uniqueness of Westlaw lies in its law reviews, international law journals, international texts, and treaties collection (TP-ALL). It is much needed by scholars all over the world interested in comparative, foreign, and international legal literature and scholarly commentaries. However, it is very expensive, and unlike Lexis does not offer modules for sale. Westlaw would be very valuable and popular outside the common law area if it offered reasonable subscriptions to legal literature alone. The recent addition of United Kingdom and European Union legal databases makes it even more appealing to European practitioners, universities, scholars, and legal institutions.

World News Connection. A Foreign News Service from the U.S. Government (http://wnc.fedworld.gov/) is a fee-based database furnishing laws and landmark case law from all jurisdictions, in unofficial English translations. WNC is a full-text database covering news from the entire world, providing immediate notice if a new law is enacted or a supreme court decision is issued in any jurisdiction of the world. If the official newspaper(s) of a particular country publish it, an unofficial translation appears in full text on WNC. Free trial passwords are supplied. Search forms are provided with broad criteria selection, so it is possible to narrow queries to the finest levels. Searches can be focused by region of the world, country, date of publication, etc. Both Boolean and natural language searches are available.

Guides:

Towards Cooperation in Access to Foreign Primary Law by Andrew Grossman (http://www.llrx.com/resources4.htm).

3. Individual jurisdictions

This selection is not intended to duplicate bibliographic resources already recognized and reviewed elsewhere in this book. Its purpose is to introduce selected databases most likely to be sought in the general conduct of foreign law research. For more information, see the guides listed above under General Sources for Public and Private International Law—National Courts and *passim* throughout this book.

Argentina

Sistema Argentino de Informatica Juridica - SAIJ (http://www.saij.jus.gov.ar/) is a fee-based database in Spanish developed by the Ministry of Justice. It contains laws since 1894, decrees since 1975, and all codes, jurisprudence, and legal literature at the federal and provincial levels. The database offers free legal news and similar services. Fee-based research services are available on demand. The database has an excellent search engine, and provides remarkable online assistance. Subscriptions, available per user or group of users, are for unlimited use.

Guides:

Argentina (http://lcweb2.loc.gov/glin/argentin.html) at the Library of Congress.

Outline of the Judicial Argentine System for a Citizen in the Globalized World (http://www.llrx.com/resources4.htm) by Ernesto Nicolas Kozameh, Julio O. Trajtenberg, C.P. Nicolas Kozameh, Jr. and Ezequiel Trajtenberg.

Australia

LexisLegal Butterworths Information Center (http://www.lexislegal.com/aus/butterworths/butterworths.asp) is a fee-based database offering a wide range of legal databases such as Casebase, Halsbury's Laws of Australia, and unreported and reported judgments. Documents are displayed in html and pdf formats. Administrative Law Decisions, Australian Capital Territory Reports, Australian Corporations and Securities

Reports, Australian Family Law Reports, Australian Law Reports, Butterworths Property Reports, Intellectual Property Reports, Motor Vehicle Reports, Northern Territory Reports, Victorian Reports are provided. There are full-text journals such as the *Australian Bar Review, Australian Journal of Corporate Law, Australian Journal of Family Law, Australian Journal of Labour Law, Australian Property Law Journal, Competition and Consumer Law Journal, Insurance Law Journal, Journal of Contract Law,* and *Torts Law Journal.* More than fifty legal bulletins are available. An email service, Content Notifier, sends Tables of Contents to subscribers by email each time the publications listed above are updated. An online users' guide, legal research guides, a list of trainers and consultants, and other help features offer online assistance to users. Free trial passwords are available.

SCALEplus (http://law.agps.gov.au/) is the legal information retrieval system owned and operated by the Australian Attorney General's Department. SCALEplus is an integral part of the Window On The Law initiative to bring low or no-cost access to the law for the community. The database is an updating tool for The Australasian Legal Information Institute(AUSTLII) (http://www.austlii.edu.au/), which contains full texts of primary and secondary legal resources; however, AUSTLII is current only for jurisprudence, and for legislation is updated only once a year, so SCALEplus must be used to check the currency of legislation. AUSTLII and SCALEplus contain Commonwealth Legislation, Commonwealth Caselaw, State and Territory Legislation, State and Territory Caselaw, and Historical Databases, but the coverage is quite irregular: Administrative Orders (current), Tables of Commonwealth Acts since1993, Popular Acts Table (current), Repealed Acts Table since 1995, Consolidated Acts Table since 1901, Statutory Rules Table since 1901, and Commonwealth Regulations since 1992.

Guides:

Researching Australian Law (http://www.llrx.com/features/australian.htm) by Nicholas Pengelley.

Legal Research (http://www.butterworths.com.au/shopfront/legres/default.htm) by Colin Fong.

Legal Research in Australia and New Zealand—LRANZ (http://www.butterworths.com.au/cfm/legresearch/lranz.htm) at LexisLegal Butterworths Information Center.

Austria

Republic Oesterreich Bundeskanzleramt—Rechts-informationssystem—RIS (http://www.ris.bka.gv.at/) (Republic of Austria: Office of the Federal Chancellor—Legal Information System) is the official site of the Austrian Government. It provides full texts of laws and decisions in the vernacular, such as federal law, law of the individual states, Parliamentary materials, and Constitutional and Administrative Court decisions. RIS offers former versions of laws.

RDB Die Rechtsdatenbank (http://www.rdb.at/frame set_g.htm) is a fee-based database providing full texts of laws, codes, decisions of all supreme courts and appellate courts, and legal literature. This unique feature makes RDB essential for legal research in any domain of Austrian law.

Belgium

E-Justice (http://www.cass.be/e-justice/menu_flash.htm) at the Ministry of Justice is the main entry point for primary and secondary resources in Belgian Law. The database has French and Dutch interfaces. In addition to the laws, the jurisprudence of all courts and tribunals, including the Supreme Court *(Cour de Cassation)* are represented, and are full-text searchable. Legislation contains all texts published in the Official Gazette, *Moniteur belge*. There are more than 40,000 legal materials, all updated on a current basis. Earlier versions of laws are also available.

Guides:

Research Guide to Belgian Law (http://www.llrx.com/features/belgian.htm) by Christoph Malliet.

Canada

eCarswell's (http://ww1.ecarswell.com) law.pro (http://ww1.ecarswell.com/law.pro) is a fee-based database containing all judgments printed in Carswell Law Reports, including headnotes, articles, annotations and case comments; judgments reported in other commercial or official print law reports since 1986; unreported judgments provided by the courts from January 1996 forward; Carswell's Abridgment Case Digests; Canadian Case Citations; and Canadian Statute Citations. Free trial passwords are offered. Carswell Law Reports were formerly available electronically at Quicklaw Systems.

QuicklawAmerica (http://www.quicklawamerica.com) is a fee-based private database containing all Canadian laws and caselaw (federal collections, provincial collections, and topical collections), as well as legal literature. It is an outstanding collection for tax and labor issues at the federal and provincial level. Its coverage has recently been extended to US caselaw and legislation as well. The database also provides decisions from South Africa and Uganda courts; Australian legislation, caselaw, and secondary sources; court decisions of Caribbean courts; and United Kingdom case law and digests. Free trial passwords are available.

Guides:

Doing Legal Research in Canada (http://www.llrx.com/features/ca.htm) by Ted Tjaden.

Overview of Sources of Canadian Law on the Web (http://www.llrx.com/features/canadian2.htm) by Louise Tsang.

China

Isinolaw.com (http://www.isinolaw.com/home.html) by Isinolaw Limited is a fee-based authoritative reference source covering Chinese laws and regulations, judicial interpretations, court judgements, contracts, arbitration, intellectual property, etc., all in both English and the vernacular. Free-of-charge abstracts are available, and some laws are free. The database contains information on Chinese legal systems, statutes, arbitration, trademarks and patents, import/export, and intellectual property laws. The main sources of primary materials include the Supreme People's Court of China, China International Economic and Trade Arbitration Commission, China Maritime Arbitration Commission, the Department of International Economic Affairs, the Ministry of Foreign Trade and Economic Commission (MOFTEC), the Shanghai WTO Research Institute, and the Intellectual Property Research Institute of Peking University. The database has rights to provide the following materials both in Chinese and in English translation: China Law Reports Series and judicial interpretations provided by the Supreme People's Court; Selected Works of China International Economic and Trade Arbitration Commission Awards; Maritime Arbitral Awards; and PRC Laws provided by The Publishing House of Law (China).

Sinolaw (http://www.sinolaw.com.cn/) by SinoLaw Information Co., Ltd. is a fee-based database. It consists of SinoLaw Online, a Chinese online legal database in English, and CGG, the Chinese Government Guide. SinoLaw Online includes the major business laws and regulations, and CGG has the most complete database of information on the National People's Congress, the Communist Party of China, and the State Council. The database allows users to search the indexes for free and inspect the English abstracts. Every abstract provides the following fields: the Promulgate Date, Promulgated By, Effective Date, Amended Date, and Brief Intro.

Guides:

Beyond the Border: The Construction of the Chinese Legal Information System in Cyberspace (http://www.llrx.com/features/china2.htm) by Joan Liu.

Chinese Legal Research (http://lib.law.washington.edu/eald/cres.html) by Bill McCloy.

France

Jurifrance—Le droit francais en ligne (http://www.jurifrance.com/) by ORT /Reuters is a fee-based database in French containing laws and decrees, codes, jurisprudence, and legal literature as follows: laws and decrees published in the Official Gazette *(Journal Officiel)* since 1990; conventions; consolidated laws and decrees in force or obsolete; Supreme Court decisions; Constitutional Council decisions; Council of State and Administrative Court caselaw; Appeal Court abstract of cases; European Union legal materials; and so on. Documents are linked. The database is equipped with excellent search forms and a good document delivery system in many formats, including html and rtf. Charges are by the amount of information (you pay to see the documents and also for downloading or printing). A bill is issued each time the database is accessed. Many types of subscription are available, but the main procedure is charge per byte for viewing and downloading.

Jurifrance is the only added-feature source for French law now available, as the French collection was removed from Lexis.

Guides:

Guide to French Law (http://www.llrx.com/features/french.htm) by Jerome Rabenou and Stephane Cottin.

France (http://www.lawschool.cornell.edu/library/encyclopedia/countries/france/) by Claire M. Germain.

Germany

JURIS (http://www.juris.de/) Das Juristische Informationssystem fur die Bundesrepublik Deutschland by Juris GmbH is a comprehensive fee-based database in German. The German government is the source of all materials. The coverage is explained in detail in the Juris Suche (http://www.juris.de/search) file. The charge is per byte ($1 for 1,000 bytes), but a flat rate is also available.

REFACT Online Plus (http://www.refact.de/rda_inh.htm)—REFACT Online Rechtsdatenbank by ATM REFACT Software GmbH is a fee-based database in German. It contains virtually all important German laws (constitutional, environmental, civil, administrative, commercial, corporate, labor, cases, decrees, etc.), as well as tax codes, tax regulations, and decisions of the tax courts dating back to the 1970s. This compilation of statutes, tax case law, and commentaries (all in German) includes the Civil Code (BGB, *Burgerliches Gesetzbuch)* searchable by sections; the Code of Civil Procedure (*Zivilprozessordnung)*; the Commercial Code (HGB); the Reorganization Tax Act; the Corporate Income Tax Act; and other major laws. Some of the laws have a search option by code, and provide cross-references to other laws citing that particular code section. Laws come with a clickable index (Register), which is sometimes very detailed. Subscriptions are per year/per password/per user, with unlimited access.

Guides:

German Business and Commercial Laws: Guide to Translations into English and Select Auxiliary Sources (http://www.llrx.com/features/german.htm) by Martina Kammer.

Legal Research in Germany: At the Crossroads of Print and Electronic Sources (http://www.llrx.com/resources4.htm) by Rita Exter and Martina Kammer.

India

JUDIS Judgements Information System (http://www.judis.nic.in/) under the authority of the Supreme Court of India, the National Informatics Center, the Planning Commission, and the Government of India, is a fee-based caselaw library that contains all reportable judgments of the Supreme Court of India since 1950. From 1950 to 1998 they are on CD-ROM; since 1998 they can be obtained online. The subscription provides access to the CD-ROM and a password to the online database. JUDIS provides relevant precedents to a case on virtually any subject that has arisen in the Supreme Court of India. It contains Acts and Headnotes for the judgments up to 1993 only. A security system makes it impossible to install the CD-ROM more than once. A "locker" is needed in order to see the CD-ROM. A JUDIS counterpart, INCODIS India Code Act Retrieval System (http://164.100.10.12/), is a free legislative full-text database.

Guides:

India Law & Business (http://www.singhania.com/newssep.htm) and *India Business Law Guide* (http://www.singhania.com/lawguide/content.htm) from Singhania & Co. Solicitors & Advocates.

Guide to Indian Law (http://www.llrc.com/resources4.htm) by V. Ramakrishnan.

Israel

Haim Ravia, Law Offices Legal Links (http://www.law.co.il) has become the main portal to Israeli laws in both Hebrew and English, with some Arabic also. The database provides links to legislation, case law, and legal literature. There are also links to Canadian Legal databases, due to the influence of the Canadian Constitution on the latest Basic Laws of Israel.

Guides:

Guide to Israeli Legal Research (http://www.llrx.com/features/israel.htm) by Ruth Levush.

Italy

Istituto per la Documentazione Giuridica del Consiglio Nazionale delle Ricerche (http://www.idg.fi.cnr.it) is one of the main portals to Italian law resources. Databases, catalogs, and legal institutions are linked by subjects. The database has an explanatory English interface (http://www.idg.fi.cnr.it/homeeng.htm). There are guides (http://www.idg.fi.cnr.it/guide/guide.htm) to different subjects of law, but the most important is Diritto Italia—Banca dati dei riferimenti ai materiali d'interesse giuridico e amministrativo in rete (http://www.idg.fi.cnr.it/guide/dirittoitalia/dirittoitalia.htm), which is generally excellent for Italian laws and jurisprudence.

Italgiure—Servizio di informatica Giuridica Elettronico di Documentazione (http://www.cilea.it/ari/italgiur1.htm) of the Ministry of Justice has as its main database the fee-based Corte Suprema di Cassazione (http://www.giustizia.it/cassa zione/bancadati.htmm). However, special software, EasyFind, must be installed in order to access it. Corte Suprema di Cassazione and Corte Costituzionale (http://www.giustizia.it/cassazione/giurisprudenza/giuris.html) offer some free jurisprudence (cases) since1999.

Guides:

Overview of the Sources of Italian Law (http://www.llrx.com/features/ladu2.htm) by Raffaele Ladu.

The Netherlands

SDU Wettenbank (http://wettenbank.sdu.nl/) is a private, fee-based, full-text database of laws, statutes, and jurisprudence in Dutch. Laws and jurisprudence are sold separately. Jurisprudence is searchable by subjects. Charges are per password per year, with unlimited access. Texts are linked. They are provided in html or as Word documents that can be easily downloaded. Citations to the *Staatsblad,* the Official Gazette, are supplied.

Guides:

Researching Dutch Law (http://www.llrx.com/features/dutch.htm) by Oswald Jansen and George Middeldorp.

New Zealand

The Knowledge Basket (http://www.knowledge-basket.co.nz/) is a fee-based database containing all Acts of New Zealand. BRIEFCASE indexes contain New Zealand case law since 1986. This index provides full reports on cases. Legislation and cases are searchable by name, subject, and other criteria (for example, judges' names). Charges are by subscription or by usage. The Acts database may be browsed for free.

Case law of the new Zealand Court of Appeal, High Court, and District Court can be found free-of-charge at the Australasian Legal Information Institute AUSTLII (http://www.austlii.edu.au/).

Guides:

An Overview of New Zealand Law (http://www.llrx.com/features/nz.htm) by Margaret Greville.

Pacific Basin Jurisdictions

The Australasian Legal Information Institute AUSTLII (http://www.austlii.edu.au/) is the main source for case law and laws of many island countries of the region.

Guides:

Law of the Pacific Islands: A Guide to Web Based Resources (http://www.llrx.com/features/pacific.htm) by Ruth Bird.

Romania

Romanian Parliament Database (http://diasan.vsat.ro/) has English and French explanatory interfaces, but is searchable only in Romanian. Only very selected documents are provided in full text, while most display the citation to the Official Gazette (*Monitorul Oficial*). There is an index to the legislation (http://www.cdep.ro/legis/owa/legis_pck.frame) and an index of legislation published by the Romanian Official Gazette since 1990.

Superlex (http://domino2.kappa.ro/mj/superlex.nsf) is the Ministry of Justice database in the vernacular. It covers acts since 1863, codes, laws, and jurisprudence searchable by subject or court.

Guides:

Doing Legal Research in Romania (http://www.llrx.com/features/romania.htm*)* by Dana Neacsu.

Russia

Kodeks (http://www2.kodeks.net/) is a fee-based private database in Russian, but offers some business laws in English (http://www2.kodeks.net/english.html). It provides laws, decrees, and cases at the federal, regional, and Saint Petersburg levels, as well as free legislative news. Full-text legal commentaries are also available. Passwords are available for one user or multiple users for unlimited access.

KonsultantPlius (http://www.consultant.ru/)Online Systems (http://www.consultant.ru/go.phtml?Mode=Section &Section=Online&Page=/Online/Systems/) is a private database in Russian with excellent search form (http://www.consultant.ru/dbs/nbu.phtml?B0CKQ) able to narrow the query when the user knows Russian legal terms. It is a fee-based affordable database containing not only primary materials, but also commentaries on any subject of law. The database allows free-of-charge search and abstracts, and even free access to full-text documents from 8 PM to 12 AM Monday through Friday, and from 12 AM Saturday to 12 AM Monday, Moscow time.

Garant (http://garant.park.ru/eng/default.asp?page =internet) is a fee-based private database providing an explanatory English interface (content, coverage, pricing, and so on). It comprises 80 databases containing all federal and regional laws and normative acts, with commentaries. Legis-lation of Russia in English covers the Constitution, the federal level, the Presidency, arbitration, and business. Garant also covers selected cases and Moscow's legislation. Controlled vocabulary from a Thesaurus must be used in order to search the database. Charges are only by bytes ($1/1Kb). You can see the indexes, search the database, and see the records with number of bytes for free.

The Universal Database of Russian Publications (http://www.eastview.com/) by EastView is a fee-based database providing newspapers, government and parliamentary publications, regional publications, social sciences and humanities journals—all in Russian—as well as English- language Russian publications. An excellent search engine allows searching in Russian (an online Russian keyboard is provided) and English transliteration using the Library of Congress transcription (lcweb.loc.gov/rr/european/lccyr.html). The coverage is variable, from 1996 in some cases, sometimes only from 1999. Eastview (http://online.eastview.com/) offers also *Social Sciences and Humanities*, *CIS and Baltic Publications*, *Regional Russian Newspapers* and other similar products.

Guides:

Guide to Russian Law Research (http://www.llrx.com/resources4.htm) by Marina Konjukhova.

Law of the Russian Federation in English: Selective Listing of Translations and Other Sources (http://www.llrx.com/resources4.htm) by Lucy Cox.

South Africa

JUTASTAT (http://jutastat.com) by JUTA LAW is a fee-based database in Dutch and English covering legislation, caselaw, and legal literature of South Africa and other countries as well. Jutastat provides the Statutes of Zimbabwe; Case Law of Zimbabwe; Tanzania Law Reports; Zambia Law Reports; Laws of Jamaica; Jamaica Law Reports; English Reports; Laws of Malaysia; and the Statutes of the Isle of Man. The Index to the South African Law Reports is free and searchable. The database is sold by subject modules or libraries, at various prices. Subscriptions per single user with unlimited access are offered for different periods of time, such one month, three months, one year, etc.

Guides:

South Africa (http://lcweb2.loc.gov/glin/s-africa.html) at the Library of Congress.

Switzerland

Confederatio Helvetica (http://www.admin.ch/ch/index.fr.html) is the main portal of the Swiss Confederation. It provides primary and secondary sources in French, Italian, and German, the official languages of the Confederation. Texts are available in pdf and html format with pagination. Recueil systématique du droit fédéral (http://www.admin.ch/ch/f/rs/rs.html), the Constitution, jurisprudence, federal decisions, and other related documents are available, as well as commentaries.

Guides:

Introduction to the Swiss Legal System: A Guide for Foreign Researchers (http://www.llrx.com/features/swiss.htm) by Fridolin M.R. Walther.

United Kingdom

Butterworths Lexis Direct (http://www.butterworths.com/) is a fee-based database providing English and Scots laws by topic—banking laws, civil procedure, Halsbury's laws, financial laws, and so on—as well as links to online legal services. The database is composed of libraries of subjects offered separately or as a whole. Case law, for example, has a separate library. All England Direct contains the All England Law Reports since 1936 and the All England Reporter. Links to different online legal services, such as Law Direct (http://macdonald.butterworths.co.uk/), are also available. Subscriptions are offered for the entire database or for individual modules.

Lawtel (http://www.lawtel.com), a subsidiary of Centaur Communications Limited (http://www.centaur.co.uk/), provides daily updates, case law (a fully searchable archive of decisions including unreported cases, all cases reported in the major law reports since 1980, and cases decided before 1980), and legislation (statutory law, statutory instruments, parliamentary bills, and command papers). An index to articles is included. Free trial passwords are available.

Guides:

A Guide to the UK Legal System (http://www.llrx.com/features/uk.htm) by Sarah Carter.

United States

GPO Access (http://www.access.gpo.gov/su_docs/index.html) is a service of the U.S.Government Printing Office that provides free electronic access to information products produced by the Federal Government. Any information furnished is the official, published version. GPO Access databases include regulatory materials such as the Federal Register since 1995 (http://www.access.gpo.gov/su_docs/aces/aces140.html), the

Code of Federal Regulations since 1995 (http://www.access.gpo.gov/nara/cfr/index.html), the Congressional Record since 1995 (http://www.access.gpo.gov/su_docs/aces/aces150.html), Congressional Bills since 1993 (http://www.access.gpo.gov/congress/cong009.html), business materials such as Commerce Business Daily (CBDNet) (http://cbdnet.access.gpo.gov/index.html), and the United States Code (http://www.access.gpo.gov/uscode/uscmain.html).

Lexis (http://www.lexis.com) by Lexis-Nexis Group is a fee-based database comprising the legal holdings of 210 libraries. It contains federal and state laws and regulations, caselaw, and legal literature. Coverage depends on the particular library chosen. The Shepard's service included is an important tool for US caselaw research. All Lexis features are very advanced, from search forms to downloading procedures. Subscriptions are available at different levels and profiles; their descriptions can be seen at the database home page. Recently, Lexis has begun to offer modules or customized interfaces such as The Academic Universe and The Political Universe.

LoisLaw.com (http://www.pita.com/) is a fee-based private service providing state and federal materials, GlobalCite (a citation research service) and LOIS LawWatch (an electronic searching service). LOIS publishes case law, statutory law, constitutions, administrative law, court rules, and other materials for all 50 states and the District of Columbia, plus the 18 federal law libraries database. Free trial passwords are available. Prices are more affordable than Westlaw or Lexis. LOIS is a good and reasonable choice for foreign practitioners and scholars interested in US law and caselaw. The database is offered as a whole, but also by state and subject databases.

Westlaw (http://www.westlaw.com), by West Group, presents databases and services in categories of jurisdictional materials (federal, combined databases, individual states), international, practice-area materials, legal texts and periodicals, news, etc. Starting dates of coverage are listed. KeyCite, the citation research service, covers all cases on Westlaw, the US Code Annotated, the Code of Federal Regulations, and statutes from all fifty states. Charges are by hour, by transaction, or by flat fee. The hypertext version is feasible and reliable and can be accessed worldwide.

Lexis and Westlaw are among the finest databases in the world, unique for their services, collection of laws, and legal literature.

Guides:

A Guide to the U.S. Federal Legal System: Web-Based Publicly Accessible Sources (http://www.llrx.com/features/us_fed.htm) by Gretchen Feltes.

The Virtual Chase: Legal Research on the Internet—Internet Research Guides (http://www.virtualchase.com/resources/index.shtml) by Genie Tyburski (editor).

Bibliography

I. Books

A. General:

American Bar Association. *Web-Linking Agreements: Contracting Strategies and Model Provisions.* Book Publishing ABA: Chicago, 1997.

Guide to International Legal Research, 2nd ed. Charlottesville, VA: LEXIS Law Publishing, 1998. Compiled by the editors and staff of the *George Washington Journal of International Law and Economics.* Previous edition published: Salem, NH: Butterworth Legal Publishers, c.1993.

Banks, Cate, and Heather Douglas. *Law on the Internet.* Leichhardt, NSW, Australia: Federation Press, 2000.

Barton, John. *Law in Radically Different Cultures.* Saint Paul, MN: West Publishing Co., 1983.

Botluk, Diana. *The Legal List: Research on the Internet.* Saint Paul, MN: West Publishing Co, 2000.

Bowman, M.J., and D.J. Harris. *Multilateral Treaties: Index and Current Status.* London: Butterworths, 1984. Kept up to date by supplements through 1995.

Brownlie, Ian. *Principles of Public International Law.* Oxford: Clarendon Press; New York: Oxford University Press, 1998.

Cohen, L. Morris and Kent C. Olson. *Legal Research in a Nutshell.* Saint Paul, MN: West Publishing Co., 2000.

Cohen, Morris, Robert O. Berring, and Kent Olson. *How to Find the Law*, 9th ed. Saint Paul, MN: West Publishing Co., 1989.

Danner, Richard A., and Marie Louise Bernal. *Introduction to Foreign Legal Systems.* New York: Oceana Publications, c. 1994.

Danner, Richard A., ed. *Toward a Renaissance in Law Librarianship : The Report, Recommendations, and Materials of the American Association of Law Libraries Special Committee on the Renaissance of Law Librarianship in the Information Age.* Chicago, Ill.: American Association of Law Libraries / West Information Publishing Group, 1997.

David, René. *International Encyclopedia of Comparative Law.* Tübingen: Mohr ; New York: Oceana Publications, 1971-.

David, René, and John Brierley, eds. *Major Legal Systems in the World Today: An Introduction to the Comparative Study of Law.* London: Steven & Sons, 1985.

Dixit, K. Avinash, and Barry J. Nalebuff. *Thinking Strategically: The Competitive Edge in Business, Politics, and Everyday Life.* New York: W.W. Norton & Company, 1991.

Evans, James. *Law on the Net: Easy Access to Over 2000 Law-Related Sites,* 2nd Edition. Berkeley, CA: Nolo Press, 1997.

Fielden, Ned L., and Garrido, Maria. *Internet Research: Theory and Practice.* Jefferson, N.C.: McFarland & Company, Inc., 1998.

Fox, James R. *Dictionary of International and Comparative Law.* Dobbs Ferry, NY: Oceana Publications, 1997.

French, Deanie, Charles Hale, Charles Johnson, and Gerald Farr, eds. *Internet Based Learning: An Introduction and Framework for Higher Education and Business.* Sterling, VA: Stylus, 1999.

Garner, Diane L., and Diane H. Smith. *The Complete Guide to Citing Government Information Resources: A Manual for Writers and Librarians,* Revised Edition. Bethesda, MD: Congressional Information Service, 1993.

Germain, Claire. *Germain's Transnational Law Research: A Guide for Attorneys.* Ardsley-on-Hudson, NY: Transnational Publications, Inc., c. 1991.

Glendon, Mary Ann. *Comparative Legal Traditions.* Saint Paul, MN: West Publishing, 1994.

Glendon, Mary Ann. *Comparative Legal Traditions in a Nutshell.* Saint Paul, MN: West Group, 1999.

Halvorson, T.R., ed. *Law of the Super Searchers: The Online Secrets of Top Legal Researchers.* Medford, NJ: Cyber Age Books, 2000. Available WWW: www.infotoday.com/supersearchers.

Harris, Myra A. *Legal Research: FUN-damentals and Principles.* Upper Saddle River, NJ: Prentice Hall Paralegal Series, 2000.

Hoffer, Steven. *World Cyberspace Law.* New York: Juris Publishing, Inc., 2000.

Jacobstein, Myron, Mersky, and Dunn. *Legal Research Illustrated.* Westbury, NY: Foundation Press, 1990.

Katz, William A. *Introduction to Reference Work.* Vol. 1: *Basic Information Sources,* 6th Edition. New York: McGraw Hill, Inc., 1992.

Kavass, Igor. *World Dictionary of Legal Abbreviations.* Buffalo, NY: 1991-.

Kurz, Raymond A. *Assignment and Licensing: Internet and the Law. Legal Fundamentals for the Internet User.* Rockville, MD: Government Institutes, 1996.

Libutti, Patricia, ed. *Librarians as Learners, Librarians as Teachers: The Diffusion of the Internet in the Academic Library.* Chicago: Association of College and Research Libraries, A Division of the American Library Association, 1999.

Merryman, Henry. *The Civil Law Tradition: An Introduction to the Legal Systems of Western Europe and Latin America.* Stanford, CA: Stanford University Press, c. 1985.

Negoita, Constantin Virgil. *Fuzzy Sets.* Tempe, AZ: New Falcon Publications, 2000.

Oppenheim, L. *Oppenheim's International Law,* 9th ed. Harlow, Essex, England: Longmans, 1992-.

Redden, Kenneth R., and William Brock. *Modern Legal Systems Cyclopedia*. Buffalo, NY: W.S. Hein, 1984.

Rehberg, Jeanne. *An Accidental Tourist on the New Frontier: An Introductory Guide to Global Legal Research*. Littleton, CO: Fred B. Rothman & Co., 1998.

Reynolds, Thomas, and Arturo Flores. *Foreign Law: Current Sources of Codes and Basic Legislation in Jurisdictions of the World*. Littleton, CO: F.B. Rothman & Co., 1989-.

Rohn, Peter H. *World Treaty Index*. Santa Barbara, CA: ABC-Clio Information Services, c.1983.

Rosenoer, Jonathan. *Cyber Law: The Law of the Internet*. New York: Springer, 1997 (See the Chapter on Copyright, pp. 1-93).

Shaffer, Ellen. *Dictionary of Foreign Law Collections in Selected Law Libraries*. Littleton, CO: F.R. Rothman & Co. (Publication Series No. 41), 1991.

Sloan, Amy E. *Basic Legal Research: Tools and Strategies*. New York: Aspen Law and Business, 2000.

Street, F. Lawrence, and Mark P. Grant. *Law of the Internet*. Charlottesville, VA: LEXIS Law Publishing, 2000.

Watt, Robert. *Concise Legal Research*. Sydney: The Federation Press, 1997.

Zweigert, Konrad. *Introduction to Comparative Law*. Oxford: Clarendon Press, 1998.

Xia, Li, and Nancy B. Crane. *Electronic Styles: A Handbook for Citing Electronic Information*, Third Edition. Medford, NJ: Information Today, 2000.

B. Guides to specific jurisdictions and legal systems:

Belgium, Luxembourg, The Netherlands:

Graulich, Paul. *Guide to Foreign Legal Materials: Belgium, Luxembourg, Netherlands*. Dobbs Ferry, NY: Published for the

Parker School of Foreign and Comparative Law, Columbia University in the City of New York, by Oceana Publications, 1968.

Canon Law:

Coriden, James. *An Introduction to Canon Law.* New York: Paulist Press, 1991.

France:

Pollard, David. *Sourcebook on French Law.* London: Cavendish Publishers, c. 1998.

Szladits, Charles, and Claire Germain. *Guide to Foreign Legal Materials: French.* New York: Oceana Publications, 1985.

Germany:

Foster, Nigel. *German Law & Legal System.* London: Blackstone, 1993.

Kearley, Timothy. *Charles Szladits Guide to Foreign Legal Materials: German.* Dobbs Ferry, NY: Published for the Parker School of Foreign and Comparative Law, Columbia University in the City of New York, by Oceana Publications, Inc., c. 1990.

Islam:

Herr, Nicholas. *Islamic Law and Jurisprudence.* Seattle: University of Washington Press, c. 1990.

Japan:

Wang, Dominique. *Les Sources du Droit Japonais.* Genève: Droz, 1978.

United Kingdom:

Cohen, Morris L., Robert Berring, and Kent Olson, eds. *English and Commonwealth Legal Materials: How to Find the Law.* Saint Paul, MN: West Publishing Co., 1989.

Jeffries, John and C. Miskin. *Legal Research in England and Wales.* Rodmer Clough, Blackshawhead, Yorkshire, England: Legal Information Resources Limited, 1990.

II. Articles

Raitt, David. "Projects Funded by the European Commission." *Computers in Libraries* 10 (November/December 2000), p.27.

Alexander, Jan, and Marsha Ann Tate. "Evaluating Web Resources." Available WWW: http://www2.widener.edu/Wolfgram-Memorial-Library/webevalution/webeval.htm [September 20, 2000].

Bloxham, Sefton. "Common Law I: WWW-Based Negotiation Exercises." Available WWW: http://www.warwick.ac.uk/seminars/98-2-sb.html [October 2000].

Botluk, Diana. "Update to Search Engines Compared." Published online July 15, 2000. Available WWW: http://www.llrx.com/features/engine3.htm [October 20, 2000].

Brandt, Scott D. "Evaluating Information on the Internet." Available WWW: http://thorplus.lib.purdue.edu/~techman/evaluate.htm [May 1, 1998].

Cartwright, Martin J. "The Wolverhampton Experience." Seminar: *Using the Internet to Teach Law.* Available WWW: http://www.law.warwick.ac.uk/seminars/98-2-mc.html [November 2000].

Charlesworth, Andrew. "Primary Legal Information on the Internet: Vision and Reality." *New Directions in Legal Information Systems: A one-day seminar for academics, librarians, and legal practitioners*, Friday 20 February 1998, Scarman House Conference Centre, University of Warwick, Coventry. Available WWW: http://www.law.warwick.ac.uk/seminars/sem98„1b.html [September 25, 2000].

Ciolek, T. Matthew. "Information Quality WWW Virtual Library." The Internet Guide to Construction of Quality Online Resources. Available WWW: http://www.ciolek.com.InfoQuality.html [August 22, 2000].

Clarke, Sarah J. "Search Engines for the World Wide Web: An Evaluation of Recent Developments." *Journal of Internet Cataloging* 81 (No. 3/4), 2000.

Collins, Hugh. "The Place of Computers in Legal Education." Available WWW: http://www.law.warwick.ac.uk/ltj/3-3b.html.

Danner, Richard A. "Redefining a Profession." Available WWW: http://www.law.duke.edu/danner/paper1.html [1998].

DeMulder, R.V. and M.J. vand den Hoven. "The Concept in Conceptual Legal Information Retrieval." *Law Technology Journal* 1 [Online]. Available WWW: http://www.law.warwick.ac.uk/ltj/3-1c.html [November 10, 2000].

Dewey, Barbara. "In search of services: analyzing the findability of links on university libraries' Webpages." *Information Technology and Libraries* 210 (December 1999).

Diaz, Karen R. "The best of the best: ranking and rating digital reference sources." *Reference and Users Services Quarterly* 17 (Fall 1999).

Fenton, Serena Jardine. "Information Quality: Is the Truth Out There?" Available WWW: http://ils.unc.edu [April 23, 1998].

Glassel, Aimee. "Finding Quality Resources on the Internet: Filtering and Selecting for the Internet Scout Project." http://scout.cs.wisc.edu [August 20, 2000.] Available WWW: http://www.ifla.org/IV/ifla64/glassel.pdf.

Gordon Murnane, Laura. "Evaluating Net Evaluators." *Searcher* 57 (February 1999).

Grassing, Esther. "Thinking Critically about World Wide Web Resources." Available WWW:http://www.library.ucla.edu/libraries/college/instruct/web/critical.htm [September 22, 2000].

Harris, Dave. "Creating a Complete Learning Environment," in *Internet Based Learning: An Introduction and Framework for Higher Education and Business,* edited by Deanie French, Charles Hale, Charles Johnson, and Gerald Farr. Sterling, VA: Stylus, 1999.

Harris, Robert. "Evaluating Internet Research Resources." [Online 17 November 1997.] Available WWW: http://www.sccu.edu/faculty/R_Harris/evalu8it.htm [August 28, 2000].

He, Wei Peter. "What Are They Doing on the Internet? Study of Information Seeking Behaviors." *Internet Reference Services Quarterly* 1 (1996), 31-51.

Herberger, Maximilian. "Collaborative Learning via WWW in Legal Education." Available WWW: http://elj.warwick.ac.uk/jilt/cal/98-2kauf/kauffman.htm [October 2000].

Introna, Lucas, and Helen Nissenbaum. "Defining the Web: The Politics of Search Engines." *Computer*, Vol. 33, No. 1, January 2000 [Online]. Available HTML and PDF: http://computer.org/computer/co2000/r1054abs.htm [October 24, 2000].

Jones, Richard and John Scully. "Effective Teaching and Learning of the Law on the Web." Available WWW: http://webjcli.ncl.ac.uk/1998/issue2/jones2.html [November 2000].

Ikda, Katsuyoshi, Kenji Kawahara and Yuji Oie. "Performance Evaluation of the Architecture for End-to-End Quality-of-Service Provisioning." *IEEE Communications Magazine* 76 (No. 4, April 1, 2000).

Kibirige, Harry N., and Lisa De Palo, "The Internet as a Source of Academic Research Information: Findings of Two Pilot Studies." *Information Technology and Libraries* 1 (March 2000), 11-16.

Kirk, Elisabeth E. "Evaluating Information Found on the Internet." Available WWW: http://milton.mse.jhu.edu:8001/research/education/net.html [August 28, 2000].

Litman, Jessica. "War Stories." Early Draft, February 19, 2001. Lecture delivered at New York University School of Law, 2001 Innovation Policy Colloquium.

McLachlan, Karen. "Cyber Guide Ratings for Content Evaluation." Available WWW: http://www.cyberbee.com/guide1.html [September 22, 2000].

Merrill, Jeanne. "The Internet and Classical Civilization." 23 *Acquisitions Librarian* 97 (2000).

Newman, Stefanini Marie. "Evaluation Criteria and Quality Control for Legal Knowledge Systems on the Internet: A Case Study." *Law Library Journal* 1, 9 (Winter 1999).

Notess, Greg R. "Tips for Evaluating Web Databases." *Database* 69 (April/May 1998).

Paliwala, Abdul. "Preserving Educational Values." Available WWW: http://www.warwick.ac.uk/ltj/4-2a.html [November 2000].

Quinton, Brian. "Roadmaps to Content: Akamai debuts service to route users to distributed Websites." *Telephony* 23 (June 2000).

Smith, Alan, and Michael Walpole. "An Australasian Experience of the Use of Selected Technologies in the Delivery of a Legal Education Program." Available WWW: http://elj.warwick.ac.uk/jilt/98-3/smith.html [October 2000].

Smith, Alastair. "Criteria for Evaluation of Internet Information Resources." Available WWW: http://www.vuw.ac.nz/~agsmith/evaln/index.htm [August 29, 2000].

Smith, Alastair G. "Testing the Surf: Criteria for Evaluating Internet Information Resources." *The Public-Access Computer Systems Review* 8 (1997). Available WWW: http://info.lib.uh.edu/pr/v8/n3/smit8n3.html [August 28,2000].

Sweeney, Terry. "Content delivery needs improved management tools." *Information Week* 166 (March 6, 2000).

Tillman, Hope N. "Quality Librarian Web Sites." *Information Outlook* 1 (March 1997), 25-26, 46. Available WWW: http://www.sla.org/pubs/serial/io/1997/mar97/marnet.html [September 22, 2000].

Weiler, Robert M., and Lisa N. Pealer. "The Site Legend: Twelve Components of a New Strategy for Providing Website Documentation." 70 *The Journal of School Health* 148 (April 2000).

Wilkinson, Gene L. "Evaluating the Quality of Internet Information Resources." Available WWW: http://itech18.coe.uga.edu/faculty/gwilkinson/webeval.html [August 23, 2000].

Williamson, Robin. "Free Access to Electronic Law?" *New Directions in Legal Information Systems: A one-day seminar for academics, librarians, and legal practitioners*, Friday 20 February 1998, Scarman House Conference Centre, University of Warwick, Coventry. Available WWW: http://www.law.warwick.ac.uk/

seminars/sem98-1b.html [September 25, 2000].

Worsfold, Emma. "Questioning the Quality of Internet Information." General Conference, August 1998 [Online]. Available WWW: http://www.ifla.org/IV/ifla64/worsfold.pdf.

Index